Foundation Flash Cartoon Animation

Tim Jones
Barry J. Kelly
Allan S. Rosson
David Wolfe

D1445395

friendsof

DESIGNER TO DESIGNER™

an Apress® company

Foundation Flash Cartoon Animation

ISBN-13 (pbk): 978-1-59059-912-9

ISBN-10 (pbk): 159059-912-8

Printed and bound in the United States of America 9 8 7 6 5 4 3 2 1

Distributed to the book trade worldwide by Springer-Verlag New York, Inc., 233 Spring Street, 6th Floor, New York, NY 10013. Phone 1-800-SPRINGER, fax 201-348-4505, e-mail orders-ny@springer-sbm.com, or visit www.springeronline.com.

For information on translations, please contact Apress directly at 2855 Telegraph Avenue, Suite 600, Berkeley, CA 94705. Phone 510-549-5930, fax 510-549-5939, e-mail info@apress.com, or visit www.apress.com.

The source code for this book is freely available to readers at www.friendsofed.com in the Downloads section.

Credits

Lead Editors
Chris Mills, Ben Renow-Clarke

Senior Production Editor
Laura Cheu

Technical Reviewer
Tiago Dias

Compositor
Dina Quan

Editorial Board
Steve Anglin, Ewan Buckingham,
Tony Campbell, Gary Cornell,
Jonathan Gennick, Jason Gilmore,
Kevin Goff, Jonathan Hassell,
Matthew Moodie, Joseph Ottinger,
Jeffrey Pepper, Ben Renow-Clarke,
Dominic Shakeshaft, Matt Wade,
Tom Welsh

Artist
April Milne

Proofreader
Elizabeth Berry

Indexer
John Collin

Cover Illustrator
Jerry Richardson

Project Manager
Kylie Johnston

Cover Image Designers
Tim Jones, Barry J. Kelly,
Allan S. Rosson, David Wolfe

Copy Editor
Heather Lang

Interior and Cover Designer
Kurt Krames

Associate Production Director
Kari Brooks-Copony

Manufacturing Director
Tom Debolski

*To my wife, Julie, for picking up all the slack while I worked
on this book. And for my daughter, Bea, who makes
all sacrifices seem worthwhile.
—Tim*

*To my parents, Richard and Denis Kelly, for their never-ending support, love,
and care. And for letting me stay up late
to watch more cartoons and scary movies.
—Barry*

*My portion of this book is dedicated to my Father, William Daniel Rosson
M.D., for being my first and best art teacher, for his ever-present
encouragement and support, and for setting me
on the path to success with an artistic career.
—Al*

CONTENTS AT A GLANCE

CONTENTS

ABOUT THE AUTHORS

Tim Jones is an Emmy Award–winning producer and writer who currently serves as Head of Production at ANIMAX Entertainment (www. animaxent.com), a leading Flash animation and interactive company in Los Angeles, CA. With over seventeen years of entertainment industry experience, including stints at Warner Bros., Disney, and Klasky Csupo, Jones is a seasoned pro at leading creative and technical teams on a wide range of projects. Jones began his career in Flash at the Internet pioneering company Icebox in 2000 and has worked on hundreds of Flash animation projects for Internet, television, and 35mm film.

Barry J. Kelly is an Emmy Award–winning editor and artist, currently working at Animax Entertainment. Developing skills in filmmaking and traditional illustration merged with digital media tools, he's had many positions such as a storyboard artist, writer, director, and editor, working in all stages of the production pipeline, from development all the way to post production and effects. With a background of experience in film, video, and animation, Barry brings a cinematic eye to various media projects and has done so for many clients such as Warner Bros., Disney, ESPN, NBC, ABC, and Kodak.

Allan S. Rosson has over 20 years of professional and international experience as an animator in a variety of media including Internet, television, motion picture production, and laser light shows for several prominent planetariums across the United States. He has worked for and with several major animation studios including, Warner Bros., Disney, Dic, and Klasky Csupo. His credits and awards include *Animaniacs, Histeria, Sabrina the Teenage Witch, The Animated Adventures of Bob and Doug McKenzie, Tom and Jerry's Martian Mission, Catching Kringle,* and the ESPN Internet animated series *Off Mikes,* the very first broadband animated series to earn an Emmy Award. Allan is currently the animation director for ANIMAX in Culver City, CA.

Dave Wolfe joined Cartoon Network Studios in 2007 as an animator on *Foster's Home for Imaginary Friends.* Prior to working for Cartoon Network, Dave worked at ANIMAX Entertainment as an animator on the Emmy Award–winning Flash series *Off-Mikes* for ESPN, as well as projects for Disney and AOL. During the course of the production, David taught himself JavaScript Flash and quickly started building various plug-ins to automate routine tasks and make Flash more animation friendly.

ABOUT THE TECHNICAL REVIEWER

 **Tiago Dias** started to get into Flash around the time of Flash 3, after seeing his first Flash site. He started off by doing freelance work on the side from his day job as a network/systems engineer. On the motion graphics side of things, he accumulated a lot of After Effects and Premiere experience at multimedia school in Zurich. From those humble beginnings, he now works as a VFX Artist and Flash developer at World Television, a video production company based in Zurich, Switzerland. This is Tiago's ideal job, as it combines two of his favorite technologies! Tiago coauthored *From After Effects to Flash: Poetry in Motion Graphics* (friends of ED, 2006, ISBN: 1-59059-748-6); he's an Adobe Community Expert, writes tutorials for a variety of communities, and is active on a variety of forums.

In his free time he tries to go snowboarding every time the sun is shining in the Swiss Alps, or he hops on a plane to visit new countries.

ACKNOWLEDGMENTS

The authors would like to acknowledge and thank ANIMAX Entertainment (www.animaxent.com) for generously allowing us to share much of the artwork, sample files, and information contained in this book. ANIMAX is an Emmy Award–winning digital production studio based in Los Angeles, California that produces character-driven experiences for all screens. Best known for creating animated content and interactive applications, ANIMAX has produced character animation for ABC Family, AOL, BET, Disney, Film Roman, Fox, WWE, and Warner Bros.; interactive web sites, virtual worlds, and games for ABC Family, Qantas, Sesame Workshop, Starlight Starbright Children's Foundation, and Ty; and educational applications for PeopleSoft, University of Southern California, University of Texas Medical Branch, Starlight Starbright Children's Foundation, and StudyDog. Animax has won a number of awards for client work including the first ever broadband Emmy Award for ESPN.com's *Off-Mikes*.

Oh, and the authors would like to thank Animax for their jobs, too!

Thanks to Dave Thomas and Rick Moranis for images of *The Animated Adventures of Bob & Doug Mckenzie* and a special thanks to Dave (a founding member of ANIMAX) for sharing his enormous talents as a writer, comedian, and mentor. We are eternally grateful.

Thanks to Warren Fuller for building the Generic Man for us.

Images and sample files of *Off-Mikes* are courtesy of ESPN.com. Thanks for the Emmies!

Images of "Slammo & Sloshie's Super Sexy Interstellar TV Jamboree" are courtesy of AOL.com.

INTRODUCTION

The term "Flash animation" has changed radically over the last seven years. Back in 2000, many professional animators turned up their noses at Flash, considering it to be worthy only of poorly-drawn internet animation about hamsters and poop. But blaming Flash for bad animation is like blaming 35mm film for a bad movie, and slowly but surely, professional animators began to warm to Flash as a serious tool capable of some amazing things.

Today, Flash is becoming the tool of choice for animators, studios, and networks alike, and you'd be hard-pressed to flip through the TV channels or surf the Internet and not see an example of this within a very short time. The authors of this book have been working with Flash for quite some time, so when the opportunity to write a book about Flash animation presented itself, we jumped at the chance. This is not a book that is trying to sell you a software program. This is a book by a group of people who are passionate about 2-D animation. We try to speak frankly about what Flash is good at and what is best left for other programs (such as Photoshop and After Effects). But mostly, this book is about the *how* of Flash animation. Having worked on literally hundreds of Flash animation productions, we distill our collective experience into a manual that we hope will be constructive, informative, and fun. Because after all—if you can't have fun making cartoons, what's the point?!

Who this book is for

This book is for anyone who is making—or thinking about making—a cartoon in Flash. Whether you are a rank amateur or seasoned professional animator, this book has something for you.

Prerequisites

We have assumed some basic knowledge of Flash, so if you have *never* used Flash before, you will need to become familiar with the interface and tools before doing many of the tutorials included in the text. Likewise, in the chapters covering After Effects, we assume some knowledge of the program, and therefore do not cover basic information that would be included in a beginner's guide to After Effects.

As for animation, this book does not purport to be a manual about how to animate. Again, we assume some basic knowledge about the principles of animation. This *is*, however, a manual about how to animate in Flash. If you are a traditional animator interested in learning how to animate in Flash, this book is for you. If you are a truck driver who likes to watch cartoons but has never used a computer before . . . well, keep on truckin'!

Layout conventions

To keep this book as clear and easy to follow as possible, the following text conventions are used throughout.

Important words or concepts are normally highlighted on the first appearance in **bold type**.

Code is presented in `fixed-width font`.

New or changed code is normally presented in **`bold fixed-width font`**.

Pseudo-code and variable input are written in *`italic fixed-width font`*.

Menu commands are written in the form Menu ➤ Submenu ➤ Submenu.

Where we want to draw your attention to something, we've highlighted it like this:

> *Ahem, don't say I didn't warn you.*

Sometimes code won't fit on a single line in a book. Where this happens, we use an arrow like this: ➥.

```
This is a very, very long section of code that should be written all on ➥
the same line without a break.
```

Downloading the code

The source code for this book is available to readers at `www.friendsofED.com` in the Downloads section of this book's home page. Please feel free to visit the friends of ED web site and download all the code there. You can also check for errata and find related titles from friends of ED.

Contacting the authors

You can contact the authors at the following e-mail addresses:

- **Tim Jones**: `friend_of_tim@animaxent.com`
- **Al Rosson**: `al@animaxent.com`
- **Barry J. Kelly**: `bjkner@gmail.com`
- **Dave Wolfe**: `dave@ironwagon.com`

Chapter 1

THE PROJECT PLAN

By Tim Jones

Flash is quickly becoming one of the most popular tools for character animation. Originally a web-based creation and delivery solution, Flash has extended its reach and is now being used by amateur and professional animators alike in practically every medium. From major Hollywood TV productions (*Foster's Home for Imaginary Friends*, *El Tigre*, and *Slacker Cats* to name just a few) to one-man bands (Jennifer Shiman's *30-Second Bunnie*s series at http://www.angryalien.com/ or Adam Phillips's *Brackenwood* movies http://www.brackenwood.net/), Flash is becoming the tool of choice for 2-D animators and producers.

This chapter is so important precisely *because* Flash is so versatile. Whether you're creating animated sprites for an interactive mobile game or producing a feature film, Flash may be your tool of choice. Like any tool, it must be used properly to achieve the desired result. The purpose of this book is to help you use Flash for character animation in the most efficient manner, and this chapter gives you an overview of the most important parameters you should consider at the outset of your project to help you achieve your goals.

Outline your goals

Very simply put, you cannot achieve your goals if you don't know what they are. A good project plan helps you outline your goals and plan your project to meet them. This is valuable for amateurs and professionals alike. If you are animating for your own pleasure, you may be tempted to open Flash and dive right in when you have a good idea, but you may find yourself losing momentum if things take longer than you anticipated or if you have to undo or redo work because you didn't foresee some of the issues you are confronted with as you are animating. If you are a professional, you have time, budget, artistic, and technical constraints to consider, and a good plan can mean the difference between profitability and disaster.

What are you trying to accomplish?

To make your project plan, you must determine what you are trying to accomplish. In other words, what are you going to create? Are you making a feature film? A TV show? An Internet cartoon? An interactive avatar? Even though you can use Flash for any of these projects, the approach that you take will be very different, and all the choices that you make will flow from this one basic question. Because Flash is so versatile it is impossible to outline every possible scenario and give precise instructions for your particular project, but in general, the answer to this basic question will impact your use of Flash in two important ways: creation and delivery.

By "delivery," I mean this: do you intend your animation to be seen as a SWF or in some other form? By "creation," I mean this: will you use *only* Flash to create your project, or will you incorporate other software? The answers to these questions are fundamental to your production and will affect almost everything you do. Let's explore each topic in more depth, beginning with delivery.

Using Flash for delivery

Whether you intend to deliver animation to your audience via .swf files (to run in the Flash Player) or not is perhaps the most basic question from which all other choices will flow. If the answer is "yes," you will be relying on your audience's hardware (e.g., PC or mobile device) for playback and will most likely need to consider file size and playback constraints. If the answer is "no," and you intend to deliver your animation in some other way (e.g., film, broadcast, DVD, or QuickTime movie), you will most likely not need to consider file size and playback constraints, at least not as they pertain to your use of Flash as an animation tool. Let's explore each scenario.

Delivery as a SWF

Using Flash (and Flash alone) is arguably the fastest, cheapest, and easiest way in the world to a make a cartoon and get it in front of a worldwide audience. Flash gives you everything you need to create a cartoon from beginning to end (assuming any sounds you want to incorporate have already been recorded and are ready to be imported into Flash) and provides an excellent way for you to deliver it to practically anyone, anywhere in the world with the click of a button. When you work in Flash, the source file you create is called an FLA (say "F-L-A" or "fla") and the resulting output file you create when you publish that .fla file is known as a SWF (pronounced "swiff"). The Flash Player is used to view these .swf files, and according to the Adobe site (http://www.adobe.com/products/player_census/flashplayer/), it is "the world's most pervasive software platform, reaching 98 percent of Internet-enabled desktops in mature markets (which includes U.S., Canada, U.K., France, Germany and Japan) as well as a wide range of devices," as demonstrated in Figure 1-1.

Because Flash is such an animator-friendly program that natively publishes .swf files and because the Flash Player is so widely used, making the decision not only to animate in Flash but to publish your animation as a .swf file is logical and reasonable in many instances. There are, however, some instances where a .swf is *not* the best choice. The following sections will help you understand what factors you should consider before making this very important decision.

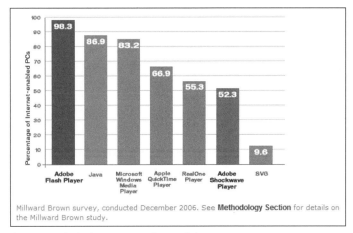

Figure 1-1. Flash Player penetration statistics

How a SWF works

In the early days of the Internet, when connection speeds were very slow, `.swf` files gained tremendous popularity because of their small file size. They were so much smaller than other types of image files being used on the Internet, because SWFs utilized *vector* graphics whereas most of the other formats (such as `.jpg`, `.png`, and `.gif` files) used *raster* images. Vector graphics use mathematics to describe the image; raster images use pixels to do the same thing. Take the example of a red circle shown in Figure 1-2.

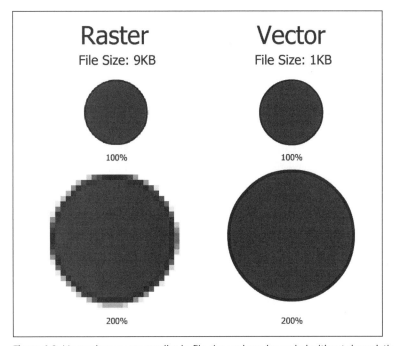

Figure 1-2. Vector images are smaller in file size and can be scaled without degredation.

3

The vector image uses a mathematical formula to describe the line, basically saying "draw a black circle and fill it with red." When the Flash Player loads a `.swf` with these instructions, the Flash Player renders the image on your computer screen. In this example, the size of the `.swf` was 1KB.

The raster image, on the other hand, uses pixels to describe the image. A pixel is simply a very small square shape that holds some color information. If the red circle were, say, 100 pixels wide by 100 pixels tall, the image would be comprised of 10,000 pixels in a square grid pattern. Each pixel would either be white, black, or red. Therefore, a `.jpg` image of the same red circle would be comprised of 10,000 pixels, and the resulting file's size would be 9KB—or nine times the size of the vector file.

Aside from the file size difference between these two formats, vector files have another major advantage over raster images. Vector images are *resolution independent*, meaning that you can enlarge the image without a loss in the quality of the image. In the example in Figure 1-2, the red circle is displayed at both 100 percent and 200 percent. You will notice that vector images look identical; this is because the mathematical formula used to describe the image can easily tell the Flash Player to draw the image larger. On the other hand, if you enlarge a raster image from 100 percent to 200 percent, the same 10,000 pixels are now occupying 4 times as many grid spaces, which degrades the image. Most people think that doubling the size of an image will create twice as many pixels, but look at it this way:

$100 \times 100 = 10,000$

$200 \times 200 = 40,000$

When using raster images, doubling the image size means that one pixel must occupy four grid spaces. This causes the aliasing, or stair-stepped line, that is typical of highly compressed or over-enlarged raster images. In practical terms, this means working with vector images in Flash is much easier, because you can resize them at any time without compromising the image quality of your work, and (generally speaking) vector images will have a smaller file size than raster images.

In a larger sense, SWF files operate on this same principal. A `.swf` file contains mathematical instructions that describe the movie contained inside. The Flash Player takes those mathematical instructions and renders them in real time on the end user's computer. This keeps the file size of a `.swf` much lower than other similar formats.

Smaller file size and better image quality do not, however, come without a price. As mentioned previously, a vector image is merely a mathematical formula describing an image, not the image itself. Therefore, when you create an animation in Flash and deliver it to your audience via `.swf`, you are reliant on your audience's hardware and software to view the animation properly. For now, we'll assume that your audience has the Flash Player version you've published your animation in (or there is an easy way for them to download it) and concentrate instead on the audience's computer hardware.

Let's assume you've created a 30-second cartoon and posted it to your web site as a `.swf`. Let's further assume that you've added a Flash-detection scheme so that anyone trying to watch the cartoon is assured to have the proper Flash Player. Finally, assume that you've added a preloader to the cartoon that forces your audience to download the `.swf` in its entirety before viewing. This will ensure that the viewing experience is not interrupted by unwanted buffering.

Two different viewers, X and Y, come to your web site and click the link to view your cartoon. Viewer X has a brand new computer with a fast CPU and a good graphics card, and the cartoon plays wonderfully on her system. Viewer Y, however, has a 5-year-old computer with a very slow CPU and a poor graphics card, and the cartoon plays very poorly on his machine. This is because, as described previously, a .swf is a mathematical instruction that describes the movie it contains, but it relies on the Flash Player to decode the information and render the movie on the end user's computer. Because viewer Y has a very slow computer, your cartoon cannot be rendered properly, in real time, on his machine. Therefore, the cartoon will either play slower than it should (if your sounds are set to Event) or skip frames to keep up with the sound (if your sounds are set to Stream). In either case, your audience is not seeing your cartoon as you intended.

How SWFs affect your animation

In real-world terms, when you have decided to deliver your animation as a .swf, you must constantly weigh file size (and image quality) against playback issues and find a balance that is right for you. Sometimes, especially if you are working for a client, you may have clear-cut directives regarding file size (e.g., all files must be smaller than 1MB) and minimum system requirements (e.g., Windows 2000, 366 Mhz CPU). At other times, there may not be specific requirements, and you must decide the best course of action. In order to understand how to make the best choices and find the best balance, you need to understand how various elements within your animation affect both the size of your SWF and how it will be played back on a typical viewer's computer.

The size of your SWF

Let's first consider size issues. For this, we'll examine "King Klaus," a 40-second animated Christmas card produced by ANIMAX (see the sample file KingKlaus_16kbps.swf). The SWF is 427KB, and sound makes up 160KB of the total file size (when published at 16kbps). This is not surprising, as sound is typically one of, if not *the*, biggest contributors to file size in many of the cartoons produced at ANIMAX. Figure 1-3 demonstrates how the file size changes when the same file is published with different sound settings.

Name ▲	Size	Type
King Klaus04_noSound	267 KB	Flash Movie
KingKlaus_16kbps	427 KB	Flash Movie
KingKlaus_24kbps	466 KB	Flash Movie
KingKlaus_32kbps	505 KB	Flash Movie

Figure 1-3. File size increases when the bit rate of the audio output settings increases.

To get a better idea of what elements contribute to a SWF's size, select the Generate size report check box in your Publish Settings dialog box (File ➤ Publish Settings) as illustrated in Figure 1-4.

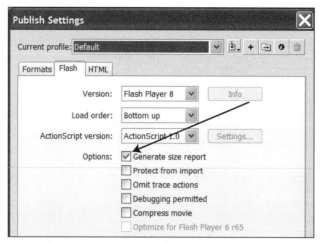

Figure 1-4. Generating a size report in Flash

The size report not only tells you the size of each element in the library but also gives you a frame-by-frame accounting of how size is added to your file. This is important because, as you will see, it isn't just the items in your library that contribute to the size of the SWF; what you do with those elements on the stage and in the timeline also affects it. Let's take a look. Click Control ➤ Test Movie or press Ctrl+Enter, and you will get both a .swf file and an output window with the size report. The top part of the report (see Figure 1-5) lists a per-frame tally of file size.

```
KingKlaus_16kbps.swf Movie Report
----------------------------------

Frame #     Frame Bytes     Total Bytes     Scene
-------     -----------     -----------     ----------------
      1           12477           12477     Scene 1 (AS 2.0 Classes Export Frame)
      2             116           12593
      3             116           12709
      4            1568           14277
      5             301           14578
      6             197           14775
      7             197           14972
      8             301           15273
      9             196           15469
     10             196           15665
```

Figure 1-5. A size report

The size report is very straightforward. The Frame # column corresponds with the frames on your timeline. The Frame Bytes column tells you how much additional size has been added on that frame. In the report in Figure 1-5, you will see that frame 1 of the animation is 12,477 bytes, and that 116 bytes are added in frame 2. The Total Bytes column is the cumulative total. King Klaus is 601 frames long with a file size total of 427KB. The size report, therefore, will list all 601 frames, showing how much file size is added on each successive frame, all of which totals 427KB.

When file size is vital, and you need to optimize your animation, it is very helpful to know what areas of your file are adding the most size. You can quickly see patterns in the size report and how they correspond to your animation. For instance, for each new shot where a new background or character is introduced, you will see a jump in the file size. After the new elements are introduced, you will see the numbers in the Frame Bytes column become much smaller in the successive frame. In the example in Figure 1-5, 12,477 bytes are added on frame 1, and then the bytes added in frames 2–10 average somewhere between 100 and 300 bytes each. The exception is frame 4, in which we first see Santa's knuckles enter the frame holding the stocking. Think of it like this: you are charged for a symbol when it appears on the stage for the *first time.* So if you have a background that is 5000 bytes and you place it on the stage in frame 1 of your FLA, your SWF will increase in size by at least 5000 bytes in that frame. In subsequent frames, you are only charged for *changes* you make to that symbol, such as moving or scaling it.

Looking further down the size report, notice that from frames 242–277, the size increases by more than 1000 bytes per frame, as shown in Figure 1-6. When you go to that section of the animation, you can easily see why.

Within these 35 frames, we see Santa climb up the chimney as a candy cane wipes the screen to reveal Ginger (the gingerbread beauty) dancing for King Klaus. This effect calls for both scenes to be on the timeline at the same time, with an animated mask wiping from one scene to the other, as shown in Figure 1-7.

The more you analyze the size reports of your animations, the more you will come to see how these types of video editing techniques (including dissolves, wipes, fade ins, and fade outs) as well as camera mechanics (including pans, zooms, truck-ins, and truck-outs) not only add to the overall file size but are also harder to accomplish in Flash than they are in

239	278	193382
240	393	193775
241	207	193982
242	1093	195075
243	7245	202320
244	1939	204259
245	1353	205612
246	1297	206909
247	1455	208364
248	1272	209636
249	1338	210974
250	1335	212309
251	1380	213689
252	1344	215033
253	1272	216305
254	1219	217524
255	1312	218836
256	1144	219980
257	1218	221198
258	1256	222454
259	1210	223664
260	1204	224868
261	1146	226014
262	1314	227328
263	1156	228484
264	1044	229528
265	1052	230580
266	1084	231664
267	1048	232712
268	1782	234494
269	2138	236632
270	1650	238282
271	3355	241637
272	1938	243575
273	1542	245117
274	1372	246489
275	1514	248003
276	1503	249506
277	1317	250823
278	307	251130
279	116	251246
280	258	251504
281	154	251658
282	161	251819

Figure 1-6. Identifying frame-by-frame file size increases

other programs—they introduce a level of complexity into your .swf file that makes it increasingly difficult for viewers' computers to play the animation back as you intended. We'll discuss playback issues shortly, but first let's finish our discussion of the size report.

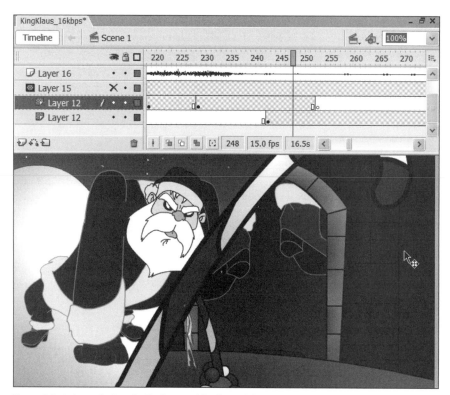

Figure 1-7. Animated wipes in Flash can add substantially to file sizes.

The first part of the size report gives you a frame-by-frame accounting of the files size of the SWF; the second part gives you an item-by-item accounting. Again, this is helpful not only to give you a general sense of how "big" your library items are, but to help you pinpoint specific items when you are optimizing your files. For instance, by looking at the size report, I see that the single largest graphic item in the library is trees f, shown in Figure 1-8, which is 10,708 bytes.

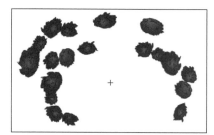

Figure 1-8. This image adds 10KB to the file size.

As we discussed previously, file size for a vector image is related to the complexity of the mathematical formula used to represent it. For an animator, the easiest way to understand this concept is to think about the number of vertices an image has. The more vertices, the more complicated the mathematical formula, and therefore, the bigger the file size. To see how many vertices your image has, click the Subselection Tool (A) in your Tools panel, and select your image. You will see a small square at each vertex. As a point of reference, a circle has eight vertices with a file size of 139 bytes. By comparison, trees f has hundreds (if not thousands). Figure 1-9 shows a close up view of one of the trees.

The playback of your SWF

Animation is a labor intensive endeavor, and after you've poured your blood, sweat, and tears into your cartoon, you want to make sure your audience sees your work as you intend. As described

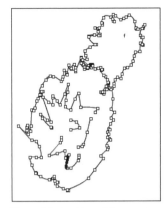

Figure 1-9. Looking at the number of vertices of a particular drawing

previously, if you're delivering your work in .swf format, you will be relying on your audience's computer hardware and software to play back the animation. If you care about that viewer experience, you must understand how your decisions will affect that experience. Let's go back to "King Klaus" and look at it from a playback perspective. I have an HP Pavilion zd8000 Notebook with an Intel Pentium 4 3.2 GHz chip, 1.00 GB of RAM, and an ATI Mobility Radeon X600 graphics card. I am viewing the King Klaus SWF in Flash Player 9. While the animation plays reasonably well, I am disappointed that several sections of the animation drop frames and do not play back as well as I would like them to. As a point of reference, watch the same animation, but this time in the form of an FLV, as opposed to a SWF (http://www.animaxinteractive.com/happyholidays/2006/king_klaus/). The size of this file is 4.12MB—almost ten times bigger than the SWF! At the end of the day, however, ANIMAX chose the FLV over the SWF version of the Christmas card precisely because of these playback issues. Notice, for instance, the pan in the opening scene. On my machine, the FLV plays back the motion perfectly, but the SWF skips frames in order to keep the visuals in sync with the audio, creating a stuttering effect. Later, when Santa turns to climb back up the chimney and we do our candy cane wipe, the SWF drops frames, making it more difficult to see and understand the wipe. When the machine guns fire at King Klaus at the top of the Christmas tree, the SWF seems to freeze at the end of the shot, cutting late to the agonized look on Santa's face. And when he falls from the tree into the snow in the last shot, the slow rotation of the background never plays at full speed.

In the FLV version of the card, the animation plays back very smoothly, but the file size is dramatically larger. Also, the perfectly crisp vector images have been replaced with raster images, which don't have the same quality. Notice King Klaus's suit when the camera pulls back to reveal him standing over the corpse of a dead reindeer.

Hopefully, this will illustrate some of the issues you will face when you choose to deliver your animation in SWF format and how you must balance file size issues against playback issues to make the choices that are right for you. While there are no right choices, there are intelligent decisions you can make to help you achieve your goals regardless of the choices you make. For instance, ANIMAX could have changed its *creative* choices by eliminating pans, wipes, and other camera mechanics that added to both file size and playback problems. Alternately, the team could have chosen to deliver the Christmas card in SWF format and taken a dramatically smaller file size over a smoother playback of the animation. But because ANIMAX is a professional studio that prides itself on good animation, and most of that cartoon's audience has broadband connections, the team was willing to sacrifice small file sizes but *not* creative choices.

Delivery as something other than a SWF

If you decide to deliver your animation in a format other than SWF, you will be faced with a different set of opportunities and challenges. For instance, you may want to create a high-quality QuickTime movie of your animation, but because you are on a PC, you don't have the same number of render options you have when you are using Flash on a Mac. Similarly, Mac users cannot create as many varieties of .avi and .wmv files as PC users can. Combine these limitations with fact that the user base of Microsoft Windows and Apple's QuickTime player aren't as high as the Flash Player, and it becomes more difficult for you to reach your audience. Publishing an .flv is a good option, but ironically, you cannot export an .flv directly from Flash! So if you want to create your animation entirely in Flash and have your audience view it as an .flv through the Flash Player, you will have to go through a few extra steps.

You may also intend to produce your animation for film, TV, DVD, or some other format—all of which Flash is perfectly capable of doing! If this is the case, you will be using other software in addition to Flash. Now that we have discussed using Flash as a delivery tool, let's discuss using Flash as a creation tool.

Using Flash for creation

Flash is an excellent tool for character animation. It gives you everything you need in one easy-to-use interface; it's relatively inexpensive, and its user base is growing steadily. It's easy to see why Flash is becoming the 2-D animation tool of choice for amateurs and professionals alike. Like any tool, results may vary depending on who is using the tool and how they are using it. There are many styles and approaches to character animation, and this book does not purport to describe the *only* method. Rather, it is an illustrative text meant to describe a method and approach that has worked for me. Let's start with an overview of the character animation process in Flash.

A typical cartoon will begin with a script. Next, voices are recorded, character models designed, and storyboards created. After that comes an *animatic*, in which the voice recordings and storyboards are assembled into a movie (either in Flash or some external editing program). If the cartoon is short (generally one minute or less), one animator may create the entire cartoon within a single .fla file. If the cartoon is longer than one minute, a team of animators may work on the project. In these cases, the various FLAs are rarely assembled into a master FLA. Instead, the cartoon is generally assembled in After Effects.

The Flash library system

The Flash library system is perhaps the single biggest reason we use Flash for character animation at ANIMAX. The ability to create a symbol one time and use it over and over again is a very powerful tool in something as labor intensive as character animation. For example, before digital character animation, a traditional animator using pencil and paper would make 24 drawings for every second of animation. That means, in order to create one minute of animation, the animator would need to draw 1,440 frames. Depending on the complexity of the animation, this could take weeks, if not months. By contrast, Flash allows an animator to draw things once and use them over and over again on a timeline without redrawing them. This speeds up the process, allowing the animator to produce more animation, and frees the animator from the tedium of drawing the same (or nearly the same) things over and over again.

As you will read in Chapter 6, ANIMAX's use of Flash libraries falls into two main categories: character layouts and character libraries. The character layout method is a more traditional approach in which animators draw the key character poses they need for each scene. "King Klaus" used this method—animators drew only what was required by the storyboard/animatic. The character library method, by contrast, utilizes a premade character library system, often containing multiple views of a character (e.g., front, three-quarter front, profile, three-quarter back, and back) as well as articulated joints, mouth charts, eye charts, hand charts, and more. This method requires more preproduction time and energy but allows for far greater productivity. Each method has advantages and disadvantages, as you will read in Chapter 6, but Table 1-1 shows the general pros and cons of each.

Table 1-1. Pros and cons of charatcer layout and character libraries

	Pros	Cons
Character layout	Fast and dynamic	Requires more individual drawings and characters can get off model more easily
Character library	Greater productivity	Requires more preproduction time and is less dynamic

Generally speaking, use the character layout method to create something short fairly quickly when animating the same character(s) over and over again is unlikely. On the other hand, if you are working on a longer project or planning to use the same characters repeatedly, create a character library. These libraries typically show the character from multiple angles, as shown in Figure 1-10.

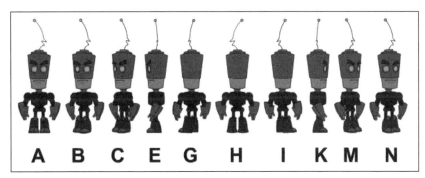

Figure 1-10. Slammo turn-around model   © 2007 AOL LLC

To assist in the frame-by-frame animation process, character libraries are typically broken down into many smaller parts (see Figure 1-11), allowing the animator a high degree of accuracy and control.

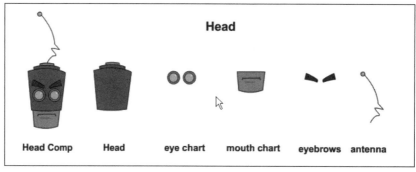

© 2007 AOL LLC

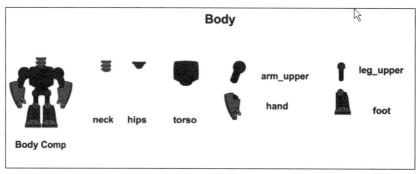

Figure 1-11. The Slammo character library is made up of many individual parts.　　　　© 2007 AOL LLC

In addition to being an excellent character animation tool, Flash can also do just about everything else you may need to create your cartoon. However, there are many instances in which you will want to use other software for portions of your production. At ANIMAX, productions often use Flash for character animation, Photoshop for backgrounds, and After Effects for compositing and editing. Knowing when to use only Flash and when to incorporate other software can make a major impact on your production. Earlier in this chapter, we used "King Klaus" as an example of an animated project that could easily be done entirely in Flash (although, as discussed, the animation was distributed in .flv, as opposed to .swf, format). In this section, we look at another ANIMAX production, "The Animated Adventures of Bob & Doug McKenzie," and describe why After Effects and Photoshop were used in conjunction with Flash.

Backgrounds

It is certainly possible to create backgrounds in Flash. The "King Klaus" cartoon we reviewed earlier in this chapter is a good example. However, there are many instances where you may want (or even need) to create backgrounds outside of Flash. For "The Animated Adventures of Bob & Doug McKenzie" (http://www.animaxinteractive.com/bd/), the art director chose to use Photoshop for the backgrounds, because it gave us the ability to create richer looking backgrounds than we could have created in Flash.

We knew going into the project that we would not be delivering the animation in .swf format, so we were not concerned about the file size of the backgrounds or the impact they might have on the playback of the animation. However, we did need to plan our shots much more carefully in advance than we would have had to if we created vector backgrounds. As you know from earlier in this chapter, vector images are resolution independent, so you can create vector backgrounds and resize them to virtually any size you want. Not so with raster backgrounds created in Photoshop. If you zoom in too close, the image will start to degrade, so you need to make sure you create your Photoshop backgrounds with enough resolution to allow for this resizing. This, in turn, requires planning.

Let's take a look at the opening shot, where the camera flies over the mountains, through the ampersand (&) in the billboard, and down over the town where Bob & Doug live. For broadcast TV or DVD delivery, the resolution of the final output image needs to be 720×480 pixels. However, if you are creating a background and zooming in (thereby enlarging the image) by 400 percent, the resolution of your BG needs to be 2880×1920 pixels.

The billboard in the shot, however, was created in vector format. The camera flies through the hole in the ampersand, getting almost infinitely close to the background image. While this could have been created as a *series* of backgrounds at different sizes, it was easier and more efficient to create this element in vector format.

Because 300dpi Photoshop backgrounds can be quite large (several hundred megabytes), they are difficult to work with in Flash. Importing one of these backgrounds into Flash can take several minutes and may well crash your system. If your system doesn't crash, it may run very slowly, which makes working hard for you. For these and many more reasons, we decided to use After Effects to composite the 5-minute short, as opposed to doing it in Flash.

Compositing and editing

Chapter 9 goes into greater detail about how and when you may consider it advantageous to do your compositing and editing outside of Flash; that chapter focuses on After Effects, although there may be other compositing and editing programs you may prefer. Reasons you might typically use After Effects for compositing and editing include these:

- Your animation is longer than 1 minute.
- You are animating your scenes in separate FLAs (by yourself or as a member or a team).
- You want to incorporate complex camera mechanics.
- You want to incorporate non-Flash assets (such as Photoshop backgrounds or video clips).
- Your delivery requirements indicate something other than a SWF.

In Chapter 9, you can read more about how to use After Effects. Here, I simply want to outline some of the reasons you may want to include After Effects (or some other compositing and editing programs) in your project plan.

Animation longer than 1 minute As a general rule of thumb, I find that projects over 1 minute in length are better composited in After Effects than in Flash. File size is one major reason. Consider that "Bob & Doug" has a total of 52 shots, and that each shot will be animated in its own .fla. The prospect of trying to bring all 52 shots back into one .fla is daunting at best. The file would grow to several gigabytes, and even if that didn't crash the system, it would make the .fla so large as to be virtually impossible to work with.

Animating your scenes in separate FLAs As mentioned previously, it is often preferable to break your animation down into smaller chunks. This is advantageous whether you are working by yourself or with a team of animators. The files are smaller and easier to work with, but if you do try to composite them back into one .fla, you will face several challenges. First, again, the size of your file could get quite large and unmanageable. You will also need to keep your libraries very well organized to avoid naming conflicts. For instance, let's say two animators are working on two different scenes of "Bob & Doug." Both animators create a new hand symbol for Bob and name the symbol Bob_hand (there's a better naming convention for this, but for simplicity in this example, this will do). If you try to composite these two scenes in one .fla, you will get a naming conflict, since a Flash library cannot contain two different symbols with the same name. This could give you some unexpected results, like seeing your animation with the wrong hands.

Complex camera mechanics While it may technically be possible to re-create the opening scene of "Bob & Doug" in Flash, I would never consider trying it. First (and most importantly), Flash doesn't have a camera. For all intents and purposes, Flash's "camera" is fixed, and you must move the world around the camera. This makes it very difficult to achieve anything more complex than a simple pan or zoom. By contrast, After Effects gives you a 3-D camera that you can navigate in X, Y, and Z space.

Even if you don't want to do something as complex as a flying camera, almost all camera mechanics are easier and better in After Effects than in Flash. Consider a simple cross dissolve, where one scene fades into another. Typically, you achieve this effect by putting two scenes on a timeline and overlapping them. Next, you adjust the transparency of the scene on top (from 0 percent to 100 percent transparency over 1 second, for instance). In After Effects, this is very simple and takes only a few seconds to achieve. In Flash, if your timelines are set up properly, it can also be set up quickly, but the result is quite different. Since Flash's transparency affects each individual library symbol, the effect is not necessarily what you might expect. Instead of a nice cross dissolve, you start to see through each library symbol.

Incorporating non-Flash assets You may want to incorporate a wide variety of non-Flash assets into your animation (such as Photoshop backgrounds, photographic images, or even live-action video). While it is possible to do this in Flash, doing it in After Effects is preferable for many reasons. When you import an element into Flash, it becomes part of the library and increases the size of the .fla. When you import an element into After Effects, however, After Effects simply creates a link to that element and does not actually import it. This is preferable for many reasons: file sizes are smaller, changes made to these external elements will update automatically without the need to reimport, and your edits are nondestructive (meaning you do not affect the source elements when you alter them in After Effects). Add to that the ability to import a wider variety of elements and control them with a much higher degree of precision, and After Effects has clear advantages over Flash if you are using non-Flash elements.

Delivery other than as a SWF If you are delivering your animation as something other than a SWF, you will find that After Effects is a much better option. Whether you are going to film, broadcast TV, DVD, QuickTime, or some other format, you will have better control of your final output file in After Effects than you will with Flash. For instance, let's say you need to create a digibeta tape for a broadcaster at 29.97 frames per second (fps). Guess what? You can't do it in Flash, because you can't set your output to 29.97 fps. Also recall that if you are working on a PC you don't have as many QuickTime export options as you do on a Mac, and you don't have as many Windows export options on a Mac as you do on a PC. While Flash is great for publishing SWFs, when you want something else, doing your final exports in another program is often best.

There are so many things you can do in After Effects that you can't do in Flash that it is impossible to list them all. From time remapping to 3-D lights and cameras to a whole host of special filters and effects, After Effects opens up worlds of possibilities that don't exist in Flash alone.

Sound

Flash does have some rudimentary sound-editing capabilities, but we almost never edit sound in an FLA for many reasons. First, Flash does not allow you to record anything directly in the interface. In other words, you would never go into a sound recording booth and record voice actors using Flash as your front-end software interface. For that matter, you would never use a computer mic on your own PC and record directly into Flash. So for recording new sounds, you are *always* going to use some other software, and most likely you'll use that same software to do any sound editing as well.

For some productions, you may be given an animatic by a client, or you may create an animatic outside of Flash. Let's assume we have a 5-minute animatic that was edited in After Effects and rendered as a QuickTime movie. Since it is unlikely that we will ever animate such a long cartoon in one FLA, we will usually cut the animatic into smaller pieces. This will include cutting both the audio and video into shorter shots or scenes and importing them into Flash. Again, this process will happen outside of the Flash interface.

Logically, then, after each individual shot or scene has been animated, we will edit them together outside of Flash. At this point, we will do our final sound mix—adding music and sound effects and fade ins and fade outs, normalizing and equalizing sounds, and so on. Every production is different, and it is outside the scope of this book to discuss sound editing techniques or software, so we will leave it at this: you will most likely need a third-party sound editing program.

Planning your Flash animation

With almost any creative endeavor, there are no absolute rights and wrongs, and so it is with your use of Flash in your production. As we discussed earlier in this chapter, Flash is exceptionally good at some things, and for others—while Flash is certainly capable—you may find doing them in some other program beneficial. Finally, depending on how your particular creative process works, Flash can influence how you approach each stage, be affected by that stage, or both. For instance, if you are doing a project for yourself, you may very well write your script, design your characters, storyboard, and animate directly in Flash and approach every aspect of your production in order to maximize your effectiveness in Flash. On the other hand, you may be working for a client who has already written a script, developed the character designs, and produced storyboards that, while possible to do in Flash, will present certain obstacles. While the remainder of this book goes into specific detail about these various stages of production and how to do them in Flash (and other software such as After Effects), this section is meant to give you a broad overview of how each of the stages impacts (and is in turn impacted by) Flash. This should help you have a better understanding of the strengths and weakness of Flash as it pertains to a typical animation production and plan accordingly.

Like it or not, one of the main reasons people turn to Flash for their animated productions is because it is presumed that Flash is "faster and cheaper" than other forms of animation. While it is true that, with proper preproduction planning, Flash allows you to leverage certain tool sets to great advantage, the idea that Flash is faster and cheaper than other forms of animation is misleading and often false. Is a hammer better than a drill? Is a table saw preferable to a circular saw? It depends on the job you are trying to do, right? Well, the same can be said of Flash. Sometimes, it is absolutely the best tool for the job. Other times, it is not. You will have to weigh many factors as you decide how to produce your project.

A typical animation production has the following stages:

- Script
- Design (character and background)
- Storyboards
- Animatics
- Animation
- Compositing and editing
- Postproduction

In the following sections, we'll discuss how each stage impacts (and can be impacted by) your use of Flash.

Script

The script is arguably the most important element of your production. While it is beyond the scope of this book to go into depth about what separates good scripts from bad, suffice it to say that it will be difficult, if not impossible, to create a good cartoon with a bad script. However, as the purpose of this section is to help you gain a better understanding of *how* to plan your Flash production at each stage of production, I'll limit the discussion to the more technical aspects of how the script will impact your use of Flash in the project.

The script will give you many good indications of how best to approach your Flash production. How long is the script? How many characters are included? How many different locations are required? Is this a "talking head" production with two characters in a room, or do you have a "cast of thousands" engaged in an epic battle? The answers to these questions, plus the artistic style (broadly defined to include character and background designs as well as your style of animation) will affect your approach in very fundamental ways. And since animation productions very seldom happen in a vacuum where budget and schedule are not important factors, the script often becomes the place in which we balance these various elements.

In simplest terms, your production probably has three main constraints: time, money, and quality. (If you *don't* have these constraints and have all the time and money you need, skip this section. And please call me to tell me your secret.) You can usually affect any one of the constraints by making a change in one or both of the other constraints. For instance, let's say you are creating an animated Christmas card. Today is December 1, and you want to distribute your card at least one week before Christmas. Time, therefore is a major constraint. To make sure you finish your project in 17 days, you can control the number of people working on it (the money constraint), or you can simplify the artistic style (the quality constraint). Since people *typically* have tighter money constraints than time constraints, it is usually the quality that gets adjusted first. You can do this in a number of ways:

- Make the card shorter
- Include fewer characters
- Include fewer locations
- Keep the action simple

Obviously, these are just *some* of the things that can affect the quality of your project and are highly subjective. You will have to decide what is right. The point I'm trying to make here is that when you are planning your project you really should consider all of these factors and plan accordingly. Having a good project plan can be the difference between a successful production and disaster, and if you have to adjust your plan to one or more of the constraints, the script is often the best place to start. It's always faster and cheaper to rewrite a script than it is to redo your animation, so make sure you've got the best script you can possibly have, and make sure you can do what it calls for within your time and budget constraints.

Design

Character design may impact (and be impacted by) your use of Flash more than any other single element in your production. A well-designed, well-built character library will allow animators to produce considerably more animation than they could traditionally (or with poorly-designed and poorly-built libraries). Chapter 2 describes what makes a good design for a Flash character and how to build a great character library. This really is Flash's core strength with regard to character animation and *the* area where good planning will help you the most.

Of course, as mentioned previously, designing quality characters and building useful libraries takes a good deal of time and skill. If you are animating something very short, with characters you are unlikely to use again in the future, building extensive libraries will be of limited value, and you may decide to use the character layout method instead (see Chapter 6 for more information). While the layout method does still leverage some of Flash's strengths, the efficiencies you expect to receive by using Flash should be realistic.

On the other hand, when you are animating a longer cartoon, or you plan to reuse the same characters in the future, the importance of having a well-designed and well-built library cannot be overstated. Anecdotally, I've seen animators double or even triple their productivity with well-built libraries. Animators who are able to do 15 to 20 seconds of animation per week (in Flash) using character layouts or a limited library system can produce 30 to 45 seconds of animation (usually at a higher quality) using good character libraries. This is one of the main reasons that more and more TV shows are being animated in Flash. Even a pick-up order of eleven 22-minute shows means that you will need to produce 242 minutes of animation, and the efficiencies that good Flash character libraries bring to a production can save tens, if not hundreds, of thousands of dollars.

Storyboards

What the script does to verbally tell your story, storyboards do visually, as shown in Figure 1-12. Knowing how to tell your story well visually and play to Flash's strengths will give you some latitude in planning your project. As described previously, one of the main choices you'll need to make is how you are going to approach your animation. Will you use the character layout method or the character library method? The answer to this will, in turn, impact how you approach your storyboards.

Figure 1-12. An *Off-Mikes* storyboard panel

Copyright ©2007 ESPN Internet Ventures

For instance, if you are producing a short one-off cartoon and aren't likely to reuse the characters again, you will most likely choose the character layout method. In this method (described in more detail in Chapter 6), you create only the necessary views of the character and articulate them only enough to achieve the necessary action. Because of this, you will have more freedom to storyboard in any way you want, using *dynamic* angles (up angles, down angles, forced perspective, etc.).

On the other hand, if you are working on a TV show, you will want to create good character libraries to make your animation more efficient. Typically, the character libraries are made up of a turn-around model in a straight-on perspective (meaning no up or down angles, etc.). Therefore, in order to leverage the efficiencies of a good character library, storyboards should be made to allow the widest use of the libraries you built and limit the dynamic angles. This is not to say that you cannot storyboard any dynamic angles in a TV show. Of course you can. You can approach those scenes with the character layout method. If you look at a lot of Flash TV shows, however, you will notice that, by and large, they do not use dynamic angles, because they want to get the most efficiency from their Flash libraries.

Knowing how to tell your story well visually, while balancing the time/cost/quality equation, is a skill learned over time. Understanding which things are easy to do in Flash and which are hard will help you create storyboards that give you the best solution. Since cost is often a very real constraint, knowing how to storyboard wisely can save you time while maintaining your quality. For instance, instead of having a character walk through the scene in a wide shot (where you show the entire character) you can storyboard a medium shot where you show the character from the waist up. It may not take much longer to storyboard one version over the other, but when it comes time to animate the scene, the time required to animate the latter option could save hours. Limiting costume changes is another thing you can do to reduce your workload. If you are using the same character from scene to scene, it is always more efficient to use the same library elements. If the character is changing costumes (or changing appearance in any way) you will have to do more work than if the character looks the same. Obviously, sometimes the script calls for these visual differences, or they make for better visual storytelling. However, if time and money are issues, and you need to find areas to simplify, this is a good one.

As described in the "Using Flash for Delivery" section, if you plan to deliver your cartoon as a SWF, you will also need to consider file size and playback constraints, and storyboarding properly is even more important. We discussed how camera mechanics (pans, zooms, multiplane effects, etc.) and editing (fade in, fade out, cross dissolves, wipes, etc.) are extraordinarily hard on the CPU, making it much more difficult to see the animation play back properly. Oftentimes, they also add greatly to the file size of the .swf. When storyboarding for Flash, when the final deliverable is a .swf, you should be aware of the impact of the choices you make and plan accordingly.

Storyboarding directly into Flash is also a great way to leverage the power of Flash. Flash's timeline, drawing tools, stage, and library make a very powerful storyboarding toolset, and a Wacom tablet or Cintiq makes things even better. It also combines storyboard and animatic stages into one step, eliminating the need to scan your pencil-on-paper drawings. Additionally, you can draw a background once, symbolize it, and reuse it in subsequent scenes, eliminating the need to draw the same things over and over as you sometimes do in traditional storyboards. You can also storyboard *in layers*, meaning you can storyboard backgrounds, characters, props, and so forth on their own layers and control them independently. This allows you to plan your animation and camera mechanics much more quickly and easily.

Animatics

When you take your storyboard drawings, assemble them onto a timeline, add sound, and publish a movie, this is called an animatic. This is the stage at which you get your first real look at your cartoon and what lies ahead in animation. Here is an example of some animatics and the animation that followed them: http://www.animaxinteractive.com/offmikes/. Animatics give you a very good idea of what you will need to create for your cartoon and will allow you to make a more accurate project plan, and you should take this stage of your production very seriously. You should really take as much time at this stage as you need to be 100 percent satisfied with your cartoon before proceeding into animation. Don't assume you'll fix it in animation if you are unhappy with certain elements of your animatic. It is much faster and cheaper to revise storyboard panels and retime scenes at this stage than it is once you begin animating, so don't cut corners.

As I mentioned in the "Storyboarding" section, Flash makes an excellent storyboard and animatic tool, and if you can work directly in Flash (as opposed to drawing on paper and scanning your storyboards), you can increase your productivity tremendously. That said, many storyboard artists are more comfortable working with a pencil than a stylus, and there really is no right way to produce your boards and animatics. Do what you feel most comfortable with.

If you are not comfortable working directly in Flash, you may find it faster and easier to storyboard on paper and use something other than Flash to edit your animatic. At ANIMAX, we often storyboard traditionally and create our animatics in After Effects. This is sometimes the best choice, because the editor can begin setting up his timeline with storyboard drawings that will later be replaced with animation. This also allows us to do our scene planning, which is important when we set up our FLAs for animation. Let me give you one example.

The opening scene of "King Klaus" starts with a hand hanging a stocking on the mantle and then the camera pans left to see Ginger (the ginger bread girl) tied to two candy canes. In Flash, we can create a background that is wider than the stage area (shown in Figure 1-13) and then slide the background across the stage to create the pan. If we are doing our camera mechanics in After Effects as opposed to Flash, we must set Flash's document size equal to the width of the entire background and export this larger wider movie to After Effects where we will add the zoom. If you are planning to do your camera mechanics in Flash, you can calculate your background dimensions so your background painter can create the background at the correct size. If you are doing your camera mechanics outside of Flash, you can calculate how large your stage area needs to be. In either case, this information is vital.

Figure 1-13. The black rectangle indicates the "camera view."

Now consider the importance of hammering out all of the important details at the animatic stage versus the animation stage. Let's say you want to change the camera movement by starting wider at the beginning of the shot and zooming in as you pan. You can easily experiment with this variation at the animatic stage with just a little bit of effort. Once you get into animation, however, this could become more difficult. If you are creating your backgrounds in vector format, it may just mean painting your background wider to accommodate the change. If you are creating raster backgrounds (as you would in Photoshop) adding the zoom to your camera move will affect not only the size of your background but the resolution also. And while this is not the end of the world, it will require some reworking and add to the overall cost of your production.

Animation

The vast majority of this book is dedicated to character animation in Flash, so I won't go into great detail here. I will, however, give you an overview of some of the most important elements you should consider at this, the planning stage.

Animation method

We have touched on this several times before, but it bears repeating since your decision on which method you will use will affect your entire project, from script to postproduction. If you are animating a short cartoon and you don't expect to reuse the characters again, you will probably choose the character layout method. "King Klaus" used this method, and even though two animators worked on the project, it was ultimately composited into one FLA file. While not terribly concerned about file size, the animators were concerned about playback and chose to distribute the card via FLV (Flash video) as opposed to SWF. Since the same two animators did everything—from storyboards, backgrounds, and animation to camera mechanics and sound—the storyboards were quite loose, meaning they were just thumbnail sketches indicating scene composition and did not have detailed drawings. If you are working on a small cartoon by yourself or with a small, well-organized team, you can often cut some corners like this and get into animation more quickly.

On the other hand, if you are working on a large project, or one in which you expect to reuse the same characters over and over again in the future, you will most likely want to use the character library method. While this method requires more preproduction time, it will improve your animation productivity tremendously and is perhaps *the* reason why so many TV productions are now turning to Flash. Character libraries also allow a large team of animators to work on the same project at the same time and stay on model. Unlike traditional animation, where each animator creates every drawing by hand, Flash allows animators to use the same set of drawings, reducing the likelihood that the characters will look different from scene to scene. Using this method may also impact how you storyboard. While it is possible to use dynamic angles, you will notice that most TV series using Flash will limit the number of scenes that require new drawings of the characters in order to leverage the efficiencies afforded by Flash. At the same time, since it is likely that a large team of animators—and often animators working at entirely different companies with little or no communication among them—will be working on the same series, having loose storyboards is not recommended. Since animation is such a visual medium, tight storyboards are usually required to avoid any confusion and ensure that the animators achieve the director's vision. Using this method also frequently means that you will *not* be compositing your animation back into a single FLA file and that you will use some other software (such as After Effects). In short, your overall organization structure and production pipeline will be quite different depending on which method you choose, and which method you choose will be suggested, if not dictated, by the kind of production you are embarking on.

Animation efficiencies

Chapter 4 discusses ways to organize your FLA for character animation to help you be as efficient as possible. While every production is different, and every animator has her own way of working, there are certain ways to organize your FLAs to increase your productivity. Chapter 4 will explain how to organize your FLAs optimally for camera mechanics if you are doing them in Flash and ways to simulate camera mechanics if you aren't. It also discusses the 100 Percent Rule, which allows you to size *all* of your library items to a common scale and reuse them more effectively from scene to scene without some of the resizing headaches that can occur. We'll also discuss naming conventions and other organizational tips and tricks that will allow you to be more efficient.

Chapter 5 discusses ways to make your Flash animation more efficient by using plug-ins. Animation of any kind is a labor-intensive endeavor, and Flash animation is no exception. Fortunately, beginning with Flash MX 2004, users have the ability to write their own plug-ins to make repetitive tasks more efficient. While it is not within the scope of this book to show you how to write these plug-ins, Chapter 5 gives you an excellent overview of some very useful plug-ins for character animators and introduces you to the world of JavaScript Flash (JSFL).

Compositing and editing

When you create your cartoon, you will either work (or composite your work) in one master FLA, or you will composite in some other software (such as After Effects). It is important to decide how you will organize your production very early in the process, as that decision can have a major impact on how to proceed. If the cartoon is very short, and you work in one FLA, your main concerns may be file size and playback issues (if you are distributing a SWF). This can impact how you create your backgrounds (raster versus vector) and how you execute your camera mechanics and other transitions (such as fade ins, fade outs, and cross dissolves). If you are working with a small team and compositing your work back into a master FLA, you must keep very strict watch on your naming conventions to avoid library conflicts, which can produce unexpected results. If you are animating in Flash and doing your compositing or editing elsewhere, you must decide whether you are doing your camera mechanics in Flash and plan accordingly. All of these issues are discussed in greater detail later in this book, but you should be aware of them at the outset. If you don't properly plan for these issues, you may find yourself in a position where you have to redo some of your work.

Postproduction

As discussed earlier in this chapter, your postproduction abilities are really quite limited in Flash. For the purposes of this book, postproduction includes sound mixing, color correction, and final output. Your ability to do any of these things in Flash is fairly limited, so if you need to add sound effects, do color correction, and output to anything other than a SWF or popular web-based file (such as QuickTime), it is advisable to do your postproduction outside of Flash.

Making your project plan

Now that you have an overview of the Flash animation process and an understanding of some of the variables you will need to consider, it is time to make your project plan. Remember that project plans are estimates (or best guesses) of what will happen in the future and will never be perfect. Some things are beyond your control, and some things will invariably go wrong, so your plan will need to be flexible. Also, this is not meant to be a text on project management, so while I will briefly discuss scheduling, I will not go into great depth in either topic.

Delivery specifications

The first thing you must determine for your project plan is your delivery specifications. The answers to these questions will impact the rest of your project plan and will be extremely difficult—if not impossible—to get started without them.

Format

Are you making a Film? A TV series? An Internet short? The answers to these questions are fundamental and need to be answered first. You *must* know the file format you are planning to deliver in order to plan properly. Once you know the format, you must also establish all the variables within the format. For instance, if you plan to deliver a SWF, what version are you targeting—Flash Player 9? If you are delivering a QuickTime movie, what codec will you be using?

Dimensions

Sometimes format will dictate dimension, while at other times, they are independent. For instance, if you are planning to deliver a SWF, you could choose virtually any dimension you like. While 550×400 pixels is the default document size in Flash, this size is arbitrary, and you can easily change your dimensions. On the other hand, many formats have a specific size, as Figure 1-14 shows.

You may also want to consider working in a larger size than required, just to be safe. For instance, if you are producing something for the Internet that you plan to deploy at 320×240 pixels, you may want to consider producing the animation at 720×420 NTSC in case you want to put it on a DVD later. When working in TV, you may want to consider producing your work in HD, even if it won't initially be aired that way. While this choice may cost you a little bit in terms of render times and disc space, it could save you a lot of time and effort down the road.

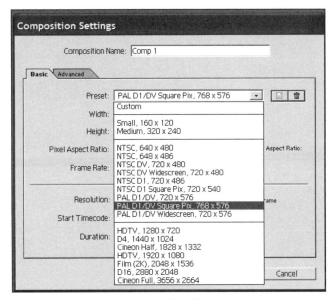

Figure 1-14. Preset dimensions in After Effects

Frame rate

Like dimensions, frame rates are sometimes linked specifically to format but not always. If you are making a film, you will most likely be working at 24 fps. If you are delivering a TV show, your final deliverable will most likely be 29.97 fps (NTSC) and 25 fps (PAL). Keep in mind, however, that the rate you animate at and the rate you deliver at are not always the same. For instance, if you are working on a TV show in the United States, you may set your FLA to 24 fps and convert 24 fps to 29.97 fps in post-production. Further, even though you may set you FLA to 24 fps, you may animate on twos, meaning that you will only set keyframes every other frame, making your effective animation rate 12 fps. For camera mechanics, however, it is advisable to animate your characters and your camera at the same frame rate. For instance, let's say you are working in Flash and your document is set to 24 fps. You have created a clip called animation and placed it on your main timeline. All of your animation is being done inside the clip, and on the main timeline, you are adding a tween to create a pan. This is precisely how the camera pan was created at the beginning of "King Klaus." In this case, you should do your character animation on ones inside the animation clip. If you don't, the camera will move every frame, but the characters will only move every other frame, causing a stutter in your animation.

Aspect ratio

Aspect ratio is similar to dimension, but instead of being measure in actual pixels, it is measured in a percentage of width versus height. For instance, TV is often in a 4:3 aspect ratio, meaning that a TV screen is 4 units wide by 3 units tall. Film, by comparison, is often in a 1.85:1 aspect ratio, which means that the image is almost twice as wide as it is tall. This can be both a technical and an artistic decision. For instance, say your final deliverable is for TV and you are required to deliver a digibeta tape to NTSC D1 specifications (as shown in Figure 1-15).

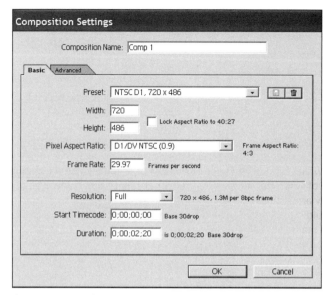

Figure 1-15. Note there are two aspect ratios in an After Effects composition setting.

You will notice that there are, in fact, *two* aspect ratios included in the After Effects Composition Settings window. First, there is the aspect ratio of 40:27, which is a function of the relationship of width (720) and height (486). You will also see that there is something called Pixel Aspect Ratio, which is set at 0.9. It is important to remember that computer monitors use square pixels and TV monitors use nonsquare (0.9) pixels. This refers to the *width* of pixels and not to the height. As it pertains to your use of Flash, you must remember to allow for this difference in your production, or everything that is a circle in Flash (e.g., car tires) will look egg-shaped on a TV monitor. This topic is discussed in greater depth in Chapter 4, but very briefly, to resolve this issue you could set your Flash document size to 648×486, and when you import the footage into After Effects, you could use the Interpret Footage option to tell After Effects that the footage from Flash is using square pixels.

Schedule

Whether you are making a cartoon by yourself for your own enjoyment or producing a TV series for a major network, it is always a good idea to have a schedule. Knowing how long things should take and planning accordingly will help you meet your goals and stay on track. That said, this is not a text on project management, so this conversation on scheduling will be brief but hopefully helpful.

There is a lot of scheduling software out on the market today, and if you are working on a very large project (or lots of little ones), these software solutions can be of tremendous help. However, you do not need to do anything fancy. If you want, you can simply jot down your schedule on a piece of paper or a calendar. It is really up to you. Perhaps the most commonly used scheduling software is Microsoft Project, which is a very powerful tool that goes well beyond helping you build a schedule. However, depending on your project, you may not need all the bells and whistles that come with Microsoft Project, and the price tag may be too high. There are also many free and open source tools on the market, dotProject, netOffice, TaskJuggler and TUTOS to name just a few. For the purpose of this book, however, we'll talk about scheduling in very simple terms without discussing any specific software.

The two major elements of building a schedule are knowing how long things will take and knowing which things can be done simultaneously and which depend on other things. Even if you're working by yourself and know better than anyone what your capabilities are, you are often caught off guard by how long things take. Each project is unique, and you will invariably encounter some unforeseen circumstances along the way. However, you have to start somewhere, so let's look at some *average* time frames to give you a ballpark to work from.

Script

Like every other aspect of your production, there are many variables to consider. Who is writing the script? How long is the script? Is this one in a series of similar projects (e.g., one episode of a TV series) or is this project new and unique? Is there one writer or are many writers working on the script? Are you the final arbiter of when the script is finished, or are there others involved in the decision-making process? There really are entirely too many variables involved to give a precise answer, but this is not something that should be rushed. Try to allow as much time as necessary to write, and rewrite, the script to make sure that it is as good as it can be. You can try to impose arbitrary deadlines (e.g., "I need the script by tomorrow"), but often this results in time wasted later in the production as people try to fix things in storyboards, animation, and postproduction that should have been addressed at the script stage. For the purposes of this book, our schedules will begin when the script is approved.

Designs

As with the script, this is a fairly nebulous area of production and subject to many variables that can change your schedule wildly. How many characters are in the script? How many locations? What is the artistic style? How many designers are working on the project, and is the style one they are comfortable with? Who is making the final decisions? If you are working by (and answering to) yourself only, and drawing in your own style, this could be done very quickly. If a team of designers is working on a show that must go through multiple layers of approval (creator, director, broadcast network, etc.), the process could take much longer. Chapter 2 will discuss in more detail how design considerations can impact your overall schedule and how you can design Flash-friendly characters to animate.

Designs can often begin when you are in the script stage. You may not know all of the characters or locations before the script is final, but chances are you have a good idea who your main characters are so you can begin with them. The design process can also usually be continued as you work through storyboards and animatics (as long as you don't require the boards to be perfectly on model). However, if you are using the character model method of animation, you need to allow time between design completion and animation commencement to build your Flash libraries.

As a general rule of thumb, I usually begin the character design process very loosely, doing a number of quick sketches to flesh out design ideas. If I am working for clients who do not know what design style they are looking for, I often use two or three different designers to work in very different styles to see what style the clients gravitate toward. At this stage, the clients may just want to see one or two of the main characters done in a variety of styles in order to make an initial assessment. Let's assume one day for rough sketches and one day for review. If none of the styles are chosen, I may cycle through this rough sketch stage a few times more, trying different artists and styles until we hit on something that works.

Once a general character style has been decided, I start to work on background designs and fine-tune the character models. The typical process will go from rough sketch to clean pencil drawing to color comp to turn-around model. We'll explore this process in much more detail in Chapter 2.

Storyboards

The further along you get in your production, the easier it becomes to make schedule estimates. While there are certainly a number of variables that will impact how long it takes you to do storyboards, estimating a storyboard schedule is far less nebulous than it is for script or design stages. As a general rule for a typical production, a storyboard artist is usually able to produce somewhere between 1 and 3 minutes' worth of clean storyboards per week.

Animatics

While there is some degree of artistic input here, schedules for animatics are generally more mechanical and easier to estimate than storyboards. And while a more complex storyboard may require more complex camera mechanics, animatics can usually be built fairly quickly. As a general rule, estimate one day for a 1-minute animatic, including scanning and revisions.

Animation

With a well-planned production, Flash animation may be the easiest element to estimate the schedule for. Using the character layout method, you may expect approximately 15 seconds of animation per week. Of course, this is subject to many factors and could fluctuate wildly, but this is a good beginning estimate. For character libraries, most Flash TV shows have animation quotas of approximately 30 to 35 seconds per week.

Compositing and editing

If you are incorporating your backgrounds and camera mechanics in Flash and using After Effects to combine everything, the process can be quite fast. On the other hand, if you are adding backgrounds and camera mechanics in After Effects, it can go slower. On average, you might expect your compositor or editor to handle somewhere between two and four times the footage that an animator handles. Again, this is a ballpark estimate and subject to many variables.

Postproduction

Depending on the complexity of your postproduction requirements, you should estimate somewhere between 10 and 20 percent of your overall production schedule to be spent in this phase. Again, this estimate is very general and subject to many variables.

Sample schedule

Following is a very basic schedule for a 7-minute production. Assume that the script has been approved before the schedule begins. We will use the character library method of animation and do our backgrounds in Photoshop and all camera mechanics in After Effects. The 7-minute short has three main characters, five secondary characters, and twenty backgrounds.

- **Week 1**: Audio recording, rough storyboards, and rough designs
- **Week 2**: Clean storyboards and designs
- **Week 3**: Animatics and character library builds
- **Week 4**: Character library builds, animation, and backgrounds
- **Week 5**: Animation and backgrounds

- **Week 6**: Animation and compositing
- **Week 7**: Animation and compositing
- **Week 8**: Compositing, editing, and postproduction

In this scenario, we would use the following:

- Two storyboard artists for two weeks
- Two character designers for two weeks
- One background artist for two weeks
- Two character library artists for two weeks
- Four animators for four weeks
- One compositor/editor for three weeks
- One producer for eight weeks (at 25 percent time)
- One production assistant for eight weeks (at 50 percent time)

This schedule requires 1,560 hours of labor for 7 minutes of animation. Of course, this is a generic example and may not resemble your particular production process, but (speaking from experience) this may get you into the ballpark for animation that is not particularly ambitious and does not receive many notes for redos. For something that is more ambitious, or for a client who is particularly picky, you could easily double the numbers. But for the sake of this example, let's say that 1,560 is a good estimate. Now, let's assume you are working by yourself, have a full-time job, and are putting 20 hours a week into the project. The 8-week schedule is now a 78-week schedule! Remember that animation is labor intensive and—even with Flash—it requires a great deal of time.

Summary

This chapter has discussed your use of Flash both for delivery and creation and explored some of the main concepts you should be familiar with. We went through a typical animation production and discussed how your use of Flash can impact, and be impacted by, each of the major phases of production. This chapter covered the major elements of your delivery requirements—including format, dimensions, frame rate, and aspect ratios—and made you aware of the major concepts behind each. And finally, we explored a typical animation production, discussed how long each phase may take, and looked at a sample schedule. The remainder of this book will go into much more detail on almost all of these topics, but this chapter has given you a good overview of the character animation process.

Chapter 2

CHARACTER LIBRARIES

By Tim Jones

Character animation is a time-consuming and labor-intensive endeavor. Before computers, animators traditionally drew every frame of animation by hand, which often meant drawing the same thing over and over again. By harnessing the power of Flash's library system, you are able to draw things once and reuse them. This does not mean that once the library is created you will not need to draw anymore! It simply frees you from the tedium of redrawing the same things over and over again.

In this chapter, we will discuss how to create highly-organized libraries for use in character animation. As with most of the topics discussed in this book, these are not hard and fast rules. You may have another way to organize your libraries that works for you, and there really is no right and wrong way to do this. However, I have developed these methods (with the help and assistance of the authors of this book and many other talented animators) over the past seven years and I hope that you will find these methods helpful and effective.

An overview of the character library process

Before we get into the step-by-step details of how to build a character library, it may be helpful to get a quick overview of the process of building character libraries in Flash. It begins with character designs. Most of my characters are pencil-on-paper drawings until I get a design we are happy with, as shown in Figures 2-1 to 2-8.

Figure 2-1. If at first you don't succeed. . .

Figure 2-2. . . .try. . .

Figure 2-3. . . .and try. . .

Figure 2-4. . . .and try. . .

Figure 2-5. . . .and try. . .

Figure 2-6. . . .and try. . .

Figure 2-7. . . .and try again!

Figure 2-8 shows the final character designs of Bob and Doug McKenzie (www.animaxent.com).

Figure 2-8. Final designs of Bob and Doug McKenzie

Next, we make a size comparison chart that shows each character's size relative to the other characters in the project.

Figure 2-9. Size comparison chart for "The Animated Adventures of Bob & Doug McKenzie"

After building the size comparison chart, we create *turn-around models* of each character. These turn-arounds show what the characters look like from different angles. Depending upon your time, budget, and animation style, these can be as limited or as elaborate as you want. A five-point turn is a turn-around model that shows the character from these five views:

1. Front

2. Three-quarter front

3. Profile

4. Three-quarter back

5. Back

31

As you will see later in this chapter, we often flip (i.e., transform on the horizontal axis) the three-quarter front, profile, and three-quarter back drawings to make a complete turn-around model (assuming the character is symmetrical).

Once the turn-around is complete, we scan the drawings, bring them into Flash, and begin building our libraries. When we are done, we will have one master character symbol in our library that contains all of the various library symbols that make up that character. As you will see, this could be hundreds

of individual library symbols. This allows you to have instant access to all the character assets when you drag a character onto the stage and begin animating with it. When done properly, this Flash character library method not only gives you the quickest and most efficient way to access Flash's powerful library system, it also ensures that characters stay *on model* by avoiding placement, rotation, scale, and other errors that may occur when dragging individual symbols from the library and placing them on the stage. In traditional animation, when many different artists draw the same character, differences in drawing styles, inaccuracies in rendering, and deviations from the approved character model could lead to the same character looking different between scenes. Such drawings were said to be *off model*. In Flash, when your animation system requires you to pull various symbols from the library and arrange them in a certain way, you can easily get off model by placing these symbols in the wrong place or using the wrong size.

In the remainder of this chapter, we will be going step by step through the process of building a character library in Flash. To help you, I've created the Generic Man. You can obtain his library by clicking the downloads link on the friends of ED web site.

Figure 2-10. The Generic Man

Size (and weight) are important

Now that you have a good overview of how the process works, let's discuss each step in detail. The first thing you need to consider is what size you are working with. As we discussed in Chapter 1, one

of the advantages of working in Flash is that your artwork is in vector format, making it resolution independent. While it is true that you can work at just about any size and scale your characters according to your needs, you must make sure you work at a consistent size for all of your characters, or you could run into trouble. Consider an example in which Bob and Doug McKenzie were *Flashed* (meaning created in Flash) at different sizes. In both cases, a 1-point line was used, but Bob was created at a much smaller size than Doug. Therefore, when the two characters are put on the stage next to each other, Bob appears to have much thicker lines than Doug, as shown in Figure 2-11

Figure 2-11. Make sure you create your characters at the same size, using the same line weight.

The same thing can occur if Bob and Doug are created at the same size but using different line weights. You can see how important it is to determine size and weight guidelines at the outset of your project to avoid such problems.

Size recommendations

While there are no hard and fast rules to say how large or small you should create the characters in your libraries, at ANIMAX, we like to create our Flash characters fairly large. The reason for this is that the larger the character, the more detail you will be able to see, since you can only zoom in to 2000 percent on the stage. So if you want to be able to zoom in close enough to your characters to fine-tune details like eyelashes, you should start large. As you can see from the Generic Man example, the character is almost 800 pixels tall—at 2000 percent zoom, his eyeball fills your monitor (depending on your resolution settings).

While it is not always easy to relate the size of your characters to the real world (how tall is SpongeBob SquarePants anyway?), you may find it useful to create an arbitrary size relationship between your Flash stage and the real world. For instance, if you set 200 pixels equal to 1 foot, a 6-foot-tall character would be 1200 pixels tall in Flash. While there are no right and wrong scales to work in, it is important that you be consistent when creating your artwork and that each person on the team understands the proper scale to work in.

Weight recommendations

For many practical reasons, we recommend that you begin creating your character with lines (using either the Pencil tool or the Line tool) and convert those lines to fills as one of the last steps in the character building process. Working with lines typically gives you more control over your artwork. They are easier to bend than fills; they respond better when manipulated via the Bezier handles, and they usually have fewer vertices than fills, which keeps the file size lower (if file size matters).

When your work is going to be seen on TV (either through broadcast or on DVD), you should also consider how your line work will appear on an interlaced monitor. Thin lines often deteriorate when shown on an interlaced monitor, so it is always wise to take a look at your designs in their final format as early as possible. If you plan to burn your project to DVD when it's complete, take your first character design, burn it to DVD and watch it on a TV screen to see how it will ultimately look. Even if you don't have animation yet, it is worth looking at the line quality to make sure your character looks the way you want it to before it is too late.

Converting lines to fills

While lines may be easier to work with than fills, they have a definite disadvantage in the way they are displayed when scaled. In terms of character animation, this is typically most noticeable in facial features. When an image is large, it usually looks good whether you've used a line or a fill. However, as you begin to shrink the image, the lines don't scale properly making them appear thicker than they should. Figure 2-12 shows large heads that look fine, but the small head on the left looks very blocky around the eyes. This is because the left head's eyes are made with lines and the right one's eyes have been converted to fills. We recommend that you begin your library build using lines instead of fills. Save the line version of your character in case you need to go back later and make any major changes, and create a final copy of your library by converting lines to fills. If you are using a *thick and thin* style (where the line is thick in some places and tapers off in others), you can then push and pull vertices of the fill to create the line you want.

Figure 2-12. The figure on the left uses lines, and the figure on the right uses fills.

A nose by any other name

A well-organized library begins with a good naming convention, and while there is no right or wrong way to name your symbols, you will quickly find that a haphazard approach will lead to problems and confusion. As you can see, the Generic Man library has 130 symbols in it, and this is a fairly base-level model. As you get into production and begin adding more mouth shapes (e.g., happy mouths, sad mouths, angry mouths) hand shapes, eye expressions, and so on, you can quickly have a model with 300 symbols or more. Without a good naming system, finding the right symbol can be like hunting for the proverbial needle in a haystack. If you open GenericManLibrary_01.fla, you will see the first item in the library is @@man_master_turn. This one symbol contains *every* library item for the Generic Man. The special characters @@ are used at the beginning of the name so that the master turn-around for each character in the library can easily be found at the top of the library. In most cases, you will drag this one symbol onto the stage and access the associated character library symbols from within the master. In some cases, you may need to go back out to the library and pull in individual symbols, but hopefully not often. Therefore, if you had Generic Woman and Generic Baby characters in this FLA file, the first three symbols at the top of the library would be

- @@baby_master_turn
- @@man_master_turn
- @@woman_master_turn

Below the master turn-around symbol, you will find two more turns:

- @man_body_turn
- @man_head_turn

This time a single @ is used so that all the master turns will appear first in the library, then all the head turns and body turns will appear next. From an animation perspective, I often find it useful to have a head turn separate from a body so that a character can stand in one position and turn his head back and forth easily. Below the turns in the library come the regular library symbols. The next symbol you will find is man_arm_a_01.

This symbol really illustrates the basic naming structure for the remainder of the symbols in the library. Let's take a closer look (see Figure 2-13 for more information):

- man: The name of the character comes first. This ensures that all symbols for each character will be grouped together.
- arm: This is the body part. Again, there is no right or wrong way to describe this, just make sure you are consistent (e.g., don't use "body" sometimes and "torso" other times).
- a: This refers to the angle in which we are viewing the character (e.g., front, profile, or back).
- lower: This is a modifier for the body part (e.g., upper, lower, right, or left)
- 01: When there is more than one drawing, number them. Usually, these drawings will become part of a *chart*, which we will discuss shortly.

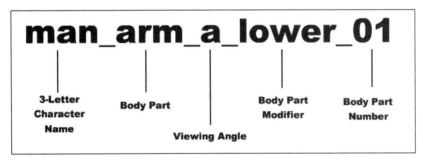

Figure 2-13. Anatomy of a name

Viewing angle

As you can see in the naming convention, I've used a letter to represent the angle in which we are viewing the character. Let's take a look at a standard five-point turn in Figure 2-14 to see how this works.

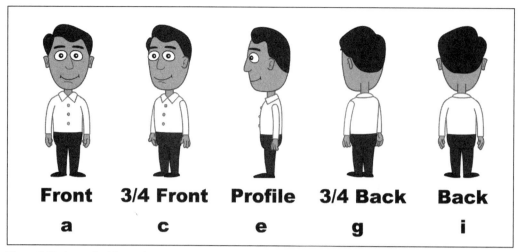

Figure 2-14. A standard five-point turn

As Figure 2-14 shows, all library items made for the front view of a character would use the letter "a" in the library name, while library symbols for the back view would use the letter "i." For instance, the Generic Man's neck, seen from the front, would be named man_neck_a_01, and a back view of his foot would be named man_foot_I_01. These letter designations are arbitrary, and you could use some other system if you prefer. For instance, you could use man_foot_front_01 if you like, but the names get a little long. You could also use a number to indicate degrees of rotation, where the front view equals 0, and the back equals 180. Whatever you do, just be consistent.

You will notice also that I've skipped letters in the preceding five-point turn. I've found that I often want to add in-between views to the heads, especially in the front views, and by skipping, letters I have the freedom to add to our five-point turn if I want to. Most commonly, I will add one head shape between the front and three-quarter front turns. You will notice in Figure 2-15 that the Generic Man's turns go up to letter "O." This is because I've found it is often worth spending a few extra minutes to flip the drawings horizontally in the library, rather than doing it manually in animation every time. For instance, what if you wanted the Generic Man in a three-quarter-turn pose (e.g., viewing angle C), but facing the other way (e.g., viewing angle O)? You could click Modify ➤ Transform ➤ Flip horizontal, and with this particular model, it would be fairly simple to do. Or would it? What about the parting in his hair? Looking at the front view of the character, we can see he parts his hair on the right. If you simply flipped the character horizontally, his parting would now be on the left. This asymmetrical design means that while the rest of the character can simply be flipped, the hair needs to have a new drawing for this angle. To avoid having to deal with this in animation, we typically put the entire character turn in our master turn.

In the Generic Man file, you will see that his current master turn has eight frames, corresponding to viewing angles A, C, E, G, I, K, M, and O in Figure 2-15. This is a standard five-point turn (views A, C, E, G, and I) that includes the flipped images (views K, M, and O). Note that in K, M, and O, while everything else is the same as G, E, and C, the hair is different because of the asymmetrical parting on his right. By addressing this asymmetrical aspect in the master turn (as opposed to addressing it on the fly in animation), you will increase your efficiency. Regarding the missing viewing angles (i.e., B, D, F, H, J, L, N, and P), you may find that you *never* use them. In point of fact, I can't recall an instance where I have ever used angles H and J and only rarely have we felt a need for F and L. On the other hand, B and P are quite often used, especially for the heads. For instance, if a character shakes his head "No" you will find that head positions B and P are extremely useful. If the turn of the head is a little broader, like following the movement of a ball at a tennis match, you will find that positions D and N are quite useful. Quite often, I do not draw the corresponding body shapes for these viewing angles because I often don't feel we need the subtlety of acting in the body that we do in the face, but the viewing angle letters are reserved for these angles nonetheless.

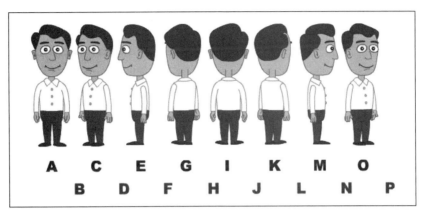

Figure 2-15. A complete turn-around

I have never found it necessary to subdivide the viewing angles into smaller increments than this. That is not to say that I have never needed to animate action that's smoother than what you can get with these angles. For instance, let's assume you don't want to have a character shake his head "No" vigorously, but rather shake his head "No" very subtly, as if he is watching something in disbelief. This subtlety of acting is left for an animator to create—as needed—in animation. Sometimes, she will actually *inbetween* the shapes between angles A and B, but more often, she will manipulate all the symbols (head shape, ears, nose, eyes, mouth, eyebrows, etc.) separately, squashing and stretching the shapes to give the appearance of changing perspective without actually redrawing them. Once the animator creates the subtle head shape, this can be saved into the character library for future use. The point here is that, while the character library is a fantastic tool for the animator, there are some things that are done when creating the initial library, and others that are left to the animator. This can be a fine line of demarcation and will be up to you to decide, but typically, I build a fairly basic model (the Generic Man is a good example of a basic model) and then add to the library as needed in the animation process.

Creating new symbols during animation

As mentioned previously, it is not possible to create every symbol you'll need for animation while building your character library. The purpose of your initial library build is to create and organize those library symbols that will be used *most often*, not to try to create an all-encompassing library that will satisfy *all* of your needs during animation. Invariably, as you animate your scenes, you will find that you need some new drawings that aren't included in your library. Having a good naming convention helps not only in the initial library build in keeping track of all the new items you (and your team) create as you animate, making it possible to easily update your library as you go.

The method we use at ANIMAX is quite simple. When an animator needs to create a new drawing for the character library, he simply adds an asterisk (*) at the beginning of the symbol name, and his initials at the end. For instance, if I were animating with the Generic Man and I needed a new hand symbol, I would name it like this: *man_hand_24_tj.

The use of the asterisk at the beginning of the name will ensure that this new symbol will appear at the top library, making it easy to identify all new symbols in the FLA file. The initials at the end will make it easy to identify who made the symbol and help to avoid any naming conflicts in cases where scenes are being combined into a single FLA. For instance, let's say Dave Wolfe and Al Rosson are both animating scenes using the Generic Man. The project is intended for distribution on the web as a SWF file, so these individual scenes will later be combined into a master FLA. As they are animating, each finds it necessary to create a new hand shape. Let's assume for a moment that they *don't* use the naming convention described previously and simply follow the naming convention used in the initial library build. Since the current library includes the symbol man_hand_chart that includes 23 hand shapes, Al and Dave each create a different hand drawing and name it man_hand_24 and place it in frame 24 of the man_hand_chart. When these two scenes are brought together into one FLA, there will be a naming conflict, and one of the scenes will not look correct (because it will have the wrong hand in it).

Remember that it is necessary to apply this naming convention not only to the individual symbol (e.g., *man_hand_24_tj) but also to its parent (e.g., man_hand_chart) to avoid naming conflicts. Therefore, Dave would change man_hand_chart to *man_hand_chart_dw, and Al would change it to *man_hand_chart_ar. In this way, they could each add a new drawing to frame 24 of the hand chart and avoid any naming conflicts when the scenes are brought together in a single FLA file. Equally important, someone could be assigned the task of going through all the scenes completed every week and adding all the new library symbols to the master character library. This person could easily open up each FLA, look for any symbol at the top of the library that begins with an asterisk, and add those symbols back into the master library. In this way, GenericMan02.FLA would have more symbols than GenericMan01.FLA, meaning that each week all the animators on the team could have access to all the new symbols created last week.

Creating the head comp

In the remainder of this chapter, I'll describe in detail how we build and organize the various symbols within our library system. Two terms that will be used over and over again are "comp" and "chart," so let's begin by defining these terms. *Comp* is used to mean a composite of individual symbols that are grouped together. For instance, man_head_a_comp contains within it the symbols for eyebrows, eyes, mouths, hair, and heads; Figure 2-16 shows an example.

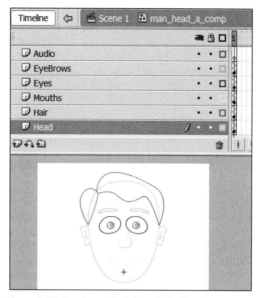

Figure 2-16. A color-coded view of the head comp

It is easy to understand why you would want to combine these symbols together into a *comp* for the purpose of animation. When you rotate the head, you *must* rotate all of these symbols together or risk making your character look like a Picasso painting. Therefore, having all the symbols within one master symbol, with a point of rotation set near the base of the neck, makes logical sense.

A *chart*, on the other hand, is a master symbol that contains *multiple frames*. A mouth chart, for instance, is a symbol that contains multiple frames of different mouth shapes; see Figure 2-17.

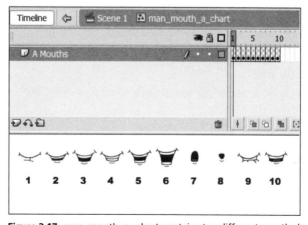

Figure 2-17. man_mouth_a_chart contains ten different mouth shapes.

As opposed to placing symbols on a stage and swapping them for other like symbols in the library, charts are used to speed up the process of animation. Most commonly, I use mouth charts (for dialog), eye charts (for blinks and expressions), and hand charts (for gestures). Depending on your character and the style of animation you are working in, you could use charts for virtually any symbol in your library. If your character drives a motorcycle, you may want to create a chart for hair blowing in the wind. Arm charts can be helpful if your character makes the same gestures over and over again. And torso charts may be the answer if you are animating a voluptuous woman walking down the street and need a series of shapes to indicate the swinging of the hips that you cannot get with a single shape.

Now that we've discussed comps and charts, let's take a look at each element within the head comp more closely.

Mouth charts

As you saw in Figure 2-17, mouth charts contain a series of mouth shapes that you will need if your character has to speak any dialog. This can be as simple as a two-frame chart featuring open and closed mouths for extremely simplistic lip flapping to very elaborate charts that feature every mouth shape you can imagine. If you have never drawn the various mouth shapes that create a mouth chart, or have questions about how to do this, check out Preston Blair's excellent writings on the subject. This former Disney and MGM animator wrote some of the definitive books on the art of character animation, and if you don't have any of his books in your collection, you should.

Creating a series of mouth shapes and putting them into a chart is a fairly straightforward process. As you can see in Figure 2-17, there are ten mouth shapes in the Generic Man's mouth chart, and each shape occupies one frame of the timeline within the symbol man_mouth_a_chart. These mouth shapes correspond to different letters of the alphabet and/or other sounds (such as "th" and "ch") that the character may need to make while speaking dialog. Later, in the animation chapters of this book, we will talk about how to manipulate the chart easily to make your character speak various lines of dialog.

You will notice that in GenericManLibrary_01.fla the jaw does not move with the mouth. But what if you wanted it to? How would you go about creating a mouth chart that included a jaw that moved when the mouth did? Take a few minutes to try it for yourself; then come back and go through it step-by-step with me.

Creating a movable jaw

As you can see in man_head_a_comp, the jaw is not a separate symbol but rather part of the head symbol as shown in Figure 2-18.

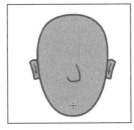

Figure 2-18. There is no separate jaw symbol in man_head_a_01.

In order for the jaw to move with the mouth, the first thing we must do is to separate it from the head symbol and put it with the mouth chart. Here's how to do it:

1. Inside man_head_a_01, select the portion of the lower head you wish to remove, as shown in Figure 2-19. I like to select everything below the bottom of the earlobe, because it makes a natural point of connection, and I run into fewer problems if I need to distort my mouth shapes during animation.

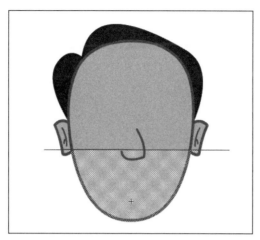

Figure 2-19. Use the line tool to dissect the head just below the ears.

2. Move the lower jaw (both line and fill) to a new layer called Lower Jaw Reference. You will remove this layer later, but you will need it for reference when you put the same symbol inside the mouth chart. Round the top of the fill by grabbing the top edge with your selection tool and pulling upward, so that you will not have any gaps between the upper and lower parts of the head. See Figure 2-20.

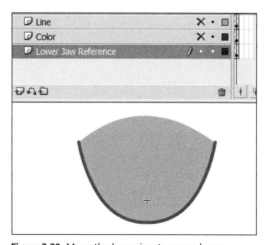

Figure 2-20. Move the lower jaw to a new layer.

3. Now round out the lower edge of the top of the head, and extend the line below the ear slightly, as shown in Figure 2-21. This will ensure a good fit between upper and lower head parts.

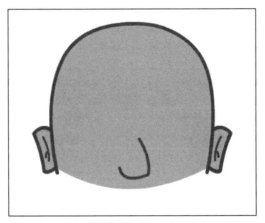

Figure 2-21. Note that the bottom edge of the fill has been rounded and lines have been extended.

4. Your man_head_a_01 symbol should now look like the one shown in Figure 2-22.

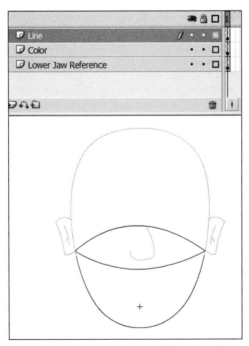

Figure 2-22. See how the upper and lower portions of the head overlap?

5. Symbolize the lower jaw. Since this is happening after the initial library build, I've named my symbol *man_jaw_a_01_tj. Make sure that you align the hinge of the jaw to the center of your stage (see Figure 2-23) so that when you stretch the jaw it will scale properly. You might be tempted to simply cut the bottom part of the head under the nose to create the jaw, but then the point of connection between the upper and lower part of the head would be in the middle of his cheek. This may not be very noticeable if your work is flawless, but imperfections will be more glaring. If you accidentally bump either the jaw or the head by 1 or 2 pixels, a gap, which will draw attention to itself, can occur. Perhaps one or two of these imperfections here and there might not be noticed, but cumulatively, across the dozens of symbols that make up any one frame of your animation, these little things can add up to make for bad Flash animation.

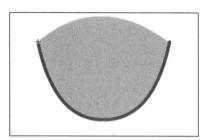

Figure 2-23. See how the "hinge" of the jaw is set to the center of the stage.

6. Go to man_head_a_comp, and make the Head layer an outline, as shown in Figure 2-24.

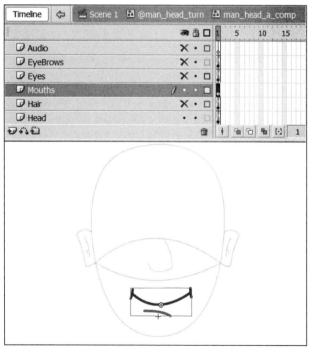

Figure 2-24. Turn the Head layer to outline view so that you can line up the jaw more accurately.

43

7. Double-click man_mouth_a_chart, and create a new layer called Lower Jaw beneath the A Mouths layer. Paste the lower jaw onto this layer as shown in Figure 2-25, and view it as an outline. Now, it should be simple to line up the lower jaw in the mouth chart to the lower jaw in the head chart. Zoom in to 2000 percent for the most accuracy.

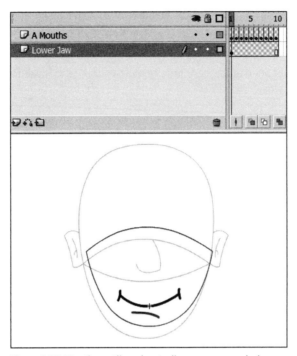

Figure 2-25. Use the outline view to line up your symbols.

8. Put an instance of the lower jaw symbol you have just made on each key frame in the Lower Jaw layer (by pressing F6 nine times). Now, you are ready to move the lower jaw with the mouth. You will not need to create any new lower jaw shapes. Using the Free Transform tool, stretch the chin down or push the chin up to create the shape you need. In just a few minutes you will have a new mouth chart with a moving jaw.

9. But wait! Something doesn't look right. Where is Generic Man's nose?! You will need to remember to move the Mouths layer to the bottom of the man_head_a_comp symbol so that the mouth and lower jaw appear under all other layers as shown in Figure 2-26.

Figure 2-26. Make sure the Mouths layer is at the bottom.

You can download GenericMan_MovingJaw.fla to see how this was done.

Eye comps and lid charts

When it comes to dealing with eyes, you will use both comps and charts. First of all, eyes are handled by comps, because they include multiple symbols that are logically grouped together. As you will see in the Generic Man example, man_eye_a_comp includes Lids, Pupils, and Eye Whites, as shown in Figure 2-27. Notice also that the comp includes both left and right eyes (including lids, pupils, and whites), which are the same images transformed 180 degrees.

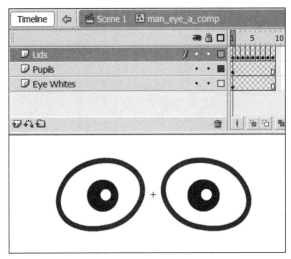

Figure 2-27. Inside the eye comp

Notice, in Figure 2-28, that pupils and eye whites remain the same for all nine frames, but the lids are actually a chart. Let's take a look at man_eye_a_lid_chart.

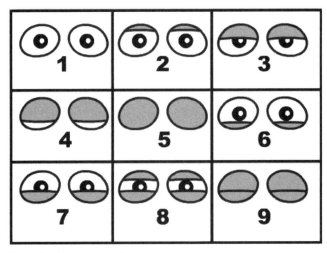

Figure 2-28. The eye chart

As you can see, the eye chart here is used mainly for blinks. Since he is, by his very name, a Generic Man, we have included two kinds of blinks: a top-lid-only blink and a top-and-bottom-lid blink. Later in this book, in the chapters on animation, we will discuss in greater detail how these comps and charts are used effectively in animation. You will learn how to manipulate the pupils to make the character look wherever you want him to, as well as how to use the eyebrows with great effectiveness to get emotion out of your characters.

The rest of the head comp

As you can see, the Generic Man also has eyebrows and hair symbols within the head comp. Currently, the eyebrows have only one frame, but you could easily make an eyebrow comp of different eyebrow shapes to extend the range of emotion you can get from him. You may also wish to make a hair chart if the Generic Man finds himself riding a motorcycle or driving a convertible with the top down. Finally, you may wish to symbolize the ears and nose so that you can manipulate them separately (e.g., for a subtle head shake). Hopefully, you are beginning to see how these various symbols can be organized within a logical, hierarchical structure to allow for the greatest efficiency in Flash.

The body

Like the head, the body is comprised of lots of individual symbols, charts, and comps. In addition to building comps and charts, you will also need to understand how to articulate a character's joints. One of the hallmarks of bad Flash animation is seeing broken lines and awkward joints that can result when trying to manipulate your character's joints. Remember that just because your character looks beautiful as a still drawing, doesn't mean it is a well-constructed model. You need to think about how the character will actually *move* and try to build your library in a way that will give you the most freedom with the least amount of work.

Articulation

Let's take a look at how to articulate an elbow joint to demonstrate this technique.

1. Remember to orient the arm either vertically or horizontally in your library. The arm should never be rotated, as we'll see in Figure 2-29.

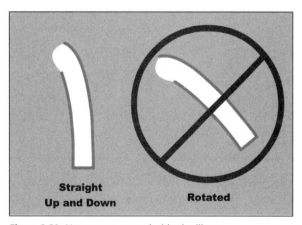

Figure 2-29. Never rotate arms inside the library.

2. Remember that while animating you may want to stretch or foreshorten the arms, so consider how the Free Transform tool works in Flash. For the straight arm, you can easily pull the Transform tool down to stretch the arm, as shown in Figure 2-30.

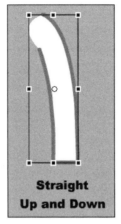

Figure 2-30. It is easy to stretch an arm that is oriented horizontally or vertically.

However, when the arm is rotated, its end is at the corner of the Free Transform tool. When you try to stretch the arm, you end up scaling it larger, which is not what you want to do, as shown in Figure 2-31.

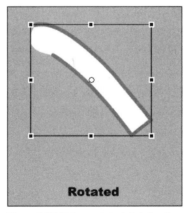

Figure 2-31. When rotated, it is harder to stretch the arm without scaling it.

3. Draw a line across the arm where you want it to bend at the elbow, as shown in Figure 2-32.

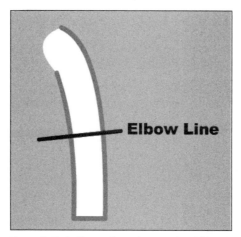

Figure 2-32. Indicate where the arm should bend.

4. Draw a circle on the layer above the arm. Don't worry about the exact size yet, but make sure to hold down the Shift key when using the Oval tool so that your circle is perfect. Convert it to a symbol, and name it Target. Make sure that the circle is centered perfectly on the library stage.

To center the circle perfectly on the stage:

a. Click the circle.

b. Click Window ➤ Info (or press Ctrl+I).

c. Make sure Window Position is the center of the stage

d. Set the X and Y coordinates to 0:0.

5. Inside the Target symbol, make lines along the X and Y axes, as shown in Figure 2-33.

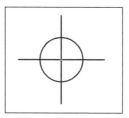

Figure 2-33. Make a target.

6. The target should intersect the elbow line and the arm on both the inside and outside of the elbow, as shown in Figure 2-34. Look at your layers in outline view to be precise.

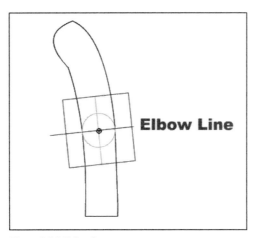

Figure 2-34. Take aim.

7. Duplicate the arm layer, and label the layers Upper Arm and Lower Arm.

8. Copy the Target symbol, and use Paste in Place (Ctrl/Cmd+Shift+V) on top of the Upper Arm and Lower Arm layers. Break Target apart (Ctrl/Cmd+B), and use it to cut out the upper and lower arms, as shown in Figures 2-35, 2-36, and 2-37.

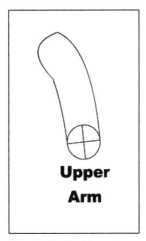

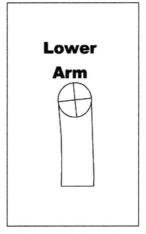

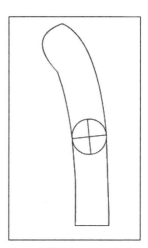

Figure 2-35. The Upper Arm layer

Figure 2-36. The Lower Arm layer

Figure 2-37. The articulated arm

9. Symbolize the Lower Arm layer, and position the crosshairs of the target to the center of the library stage as shown in Figure 2-38.

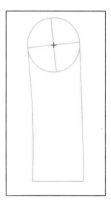

Figure 2-38. The lower arm is now ready to rotate around a circle.

10. Symbolize the Upper Arm layer, and set the point of rotation at the shoulder. At the bottom of the target, convert the line to the same color and line weight as the arm. See Figure 2-39.

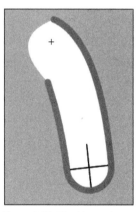

Figure 2-39. The Upper Arm now has a solid line running all the way around the elbow.

11. Put the upper arm and lower arm on the same layer, with the lower arm on top of the upper arm. In outline view, use the crosshairs of the target to align the arms perfectly.

12. Turn the crosshairs of the targets to guide layers so that they are invisible, and see how far you can bend the arm. You should have a wide range of motion without any breaks in the lines as shown in Figure 2-40.

Figure 2-40. The arm has a full range of motion.

You may notice that line at the inside of the elbow extends too far on the lower arm. This can easily be fixed with a *patch*, in which we simply paint it out in one easy stroke.

Figure 2-41. The same arm after a quick patch

Nonarticulated joints

While it is common to articulate joints in your library using the method described in the previous section, you may find yourself in a situation in which this method either does not work or is not the best approach. For example, what if your character design called for sharp, angular elbows or rubber-hose arms, as shown in Figure 2-42? How would you handle these arms in Flash?

Figure 2-42. An angular elbow and a rubber-hose arm

In these cases, it may be a better option to create arm charts, where the whole arm is treated as a single unit. This will require a more traditional approach in which you draw a series of frames for the action required, but by putting these drawings in a chart, you (and others on your team) can reuse the arm animations easily in the future.

The point here is that there is no *one* way to approach your character library builds. If you are finding it difficult to articulate the joints, you can revert to a more traditional approach. At the same time, if you have the ability to control the character design of your project, and time and budget are a concern, you should consider making your designs Flash friendly—by this, I mean that your character is designed to be easily animated in Flash. When in doubt, bring your character into Flash and think about how you will construct the library. Do the joints articulate easily? Is the design symmetrical? Do you have overlapping symbols that will be hard to deal with in animation (e.g., hair that is behind the head but in front of the shoulder)? While technically there's nothing you can do traditionally that you can't do in Flash, chances are you've chosen to animate your project in Flash to leverage some of the efficiencies its library system has to offer, so try not to mitigate these efficiencies with character designs that are burdensome to work with.

Hand charts

Like mouths and eyes, we recommend assembling the hands in your library into a hand chart. Hands naturally rotate at the wrist, so your hands should all be set to rotate accordingly. Hands are one thing you never seem to have enough of. No matter how extensive your hand chart gets, you invariably come across a situation that calls for a hand shape you don't have in your library. The hand chart that comes with the Generic Man includes the hand shapes used most often, but this is far from exhaustive. You will also notice that there is no viewing angle indication for the hands, because you really could use just about any hand in any viewing angle.

Because hands are one of the most commonly created symbols during animation, they are also the most problematic. One of the most common errors when creating new hands is scale. Let's say you are animating a scene and the storyboard shows a close-up of two hands tying a shoe. The natural impulse is to draw the new hand shapes needed for the scene at the scale indicated in the storyboards. However, when you try to incorporate these hands back into the library, you will find that they are way too large. Next, you try to scale the hands down to match the others in your library only to find that the line weight does not match, and you either end up redrawing the hand to work in the library or decide it's not worth the effort and leave the hand out of the chart.

While there will certainly be instances where you may want to draw the hands at a different scale than those in your library (e.g., a close-up has much more detail than the regular hands) being able to capture and reuse as many hands as possible in your library could save you and your team countless hours of work.

In the next chapter, we will discuss many aspects of setting up your FLA files for animation, including the 100 Percent Rule, but as a general rule, we try to create new library symbols directly within the chart in which they appear or at the same scale as the other library items. The 100 Percent Rule encourages you to leave your characters at 100 percent of their original scale (where possible) and either enlarge or reduce the scene symbol they are within. Thus, even when you create new symbols like hands outside their charts, they should be at the proper scale to be incorporated into the master library.

Putting it all together

As you will see later, in the chapters on animation, proper use of this library system requires you to think and work in a specific way. That is not to say it is a rigid system. On the contrary, you will see two very different approaches to animating with this library system, but each of these approaches has certain fundamental similarities. Simply put, the character library system described in this chapter can be thought of as a series of nested modules, and each module gives you a finer level of detail. Look again at GenericManLibrary_01.fla. You will see that there is one symbol on the stage. Now, break the model apart (using Modify ➤ Break Apart or Ctrl/Cmd+B), and you will see two symbols: the head turn-around and the body turn. Click the head, and in the Properties panel, change the first frame to 2. You should now see a three-quarter front head on a front body, as shown in Figure 2-43.

Figure 2-43. Breaking down the Generic Man

You can now see how easy it is to turn the head. At this point, however, you cannot access the mouth chart or eye comp. Break the head apart again twice (once for the head turn and once for the head comp) and now you can access the mouth and eye charts. Note that you cannot access the head turn without dragging a new instance out of the library onto the stage. Break the eyes apart again, and you can access the pupils. You can see how we began with one very large symbol, and by continuing to break the model down, we gain access to finer levels of control.

Let's take a look at this hierarchical structure so that you can better understand how the character library is organized. @@man_master_turn is comprised of a head turn and a body turn, as shown in Figure 2-44.

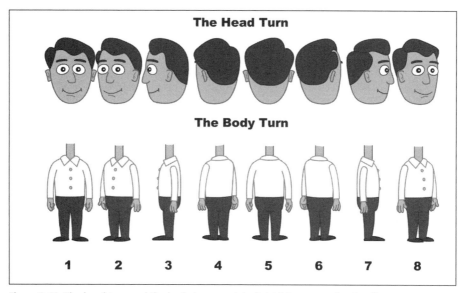

Figure 2-44. The head turn and the body turn consist of eight frames on the timeline

The head turn is a chart of head comps for the various viewing angles. The head comps are comprised of eyebrows, eyes, mouths, hair, and head, as shown in Figure 2-45.

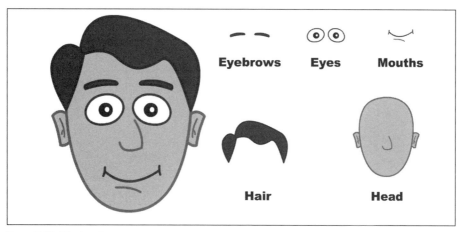

Figure 2-45. The head comp

Like the head, the body is made up of a group of symbols that can be individually manipulated. Obviously, every character design is different, and you will need to organize your character libraries in a way that is logical for your character. Figure 2-46 shows the individual symbols that comprise the Generic Man's body.

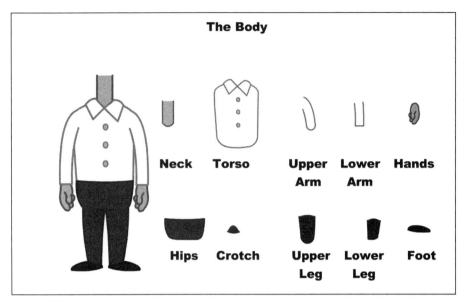

Figure 2-46. The body symbols

Figure 2-47 is a graphical way to think about the library structure.

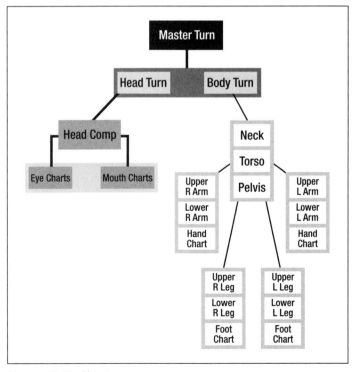

Figure 2-47. The library structure

Summary

In this chapter, we've discussed the most crucial elements of a character library system, including:

- Size and scale
- Naming conventions
- Line weight
- Lines and fills
- Viewing angles
- Comps
- Charts
- Articulation
- Hierarchy

Because each character is unique, it is impossible to perfectly describe a system that is going to work for every instance. One of the biggest challenges, and the most fun aspects, of Flash character animation is developing a character library for a show. It is part art, part science, and a lot like solving a puzzle by finding just the right way to fit all the pieces together.

Symbol-based animation and traditional animation don't have to be mutually exclusive. In fact, I think a hybrid approach—using the symbols when they are appropriate and drawing the rest—is best when balancing art and commerce, allowing you the greatest artistic freedom within your budget and schedule.

If you've chosen to do your project in Flash, you've done so for a reason. Flash's wonderful library system, in my opinion, is perhaps *the* greatest reason to choose it for your character animation project. If you're not convinced yet, wait until you read the chapters on animation and see how you can exploit these character library systems to great effect. But first, read Chapter 3 to learn how to set up your FLA.

Chapter 3

STORYBOARDS AND ANIMATICS

By Barry J. Kelly and Allan Rosson

In this chapter, we will go over storyboards and animatics, why they are useful to your project, and how to implement them into your production. Storyboards are the blueprint of your idea. They are used extensively for both live-action motion picture production and animation.

Previsualization is the first step in making your idea come to life—storyboards are that step. You may have an idea in your mind, just rough sketches on paper, or possibly even a full-length script. Animation can be a rather complex process, and it is advisable not to enter into it haphazardly, especially if you are dealing with a project of considerable size. Storyboarding will help you visualize your end goal.

There are numerous ways to go about creating storyboards. Drawing them is most common, although some have been created using basic 3-D animation or even still photographs. We're talking about a 2-D Flash animated project here so drawing them would definitely be the best choice. You could draw your storyboard panels on paper or create them digitally, in Photoshop, CorelDRAW, or Flash itself.

An *animatic* is simply the separate storyboard images displayed in the proper sequence to tell the story. The images are placed on a timeline in Flash to make a rough edit of your project. This helps to determine exactly what your audience will be seeing and for how long it will be on the screen. You can even add a voice track (if your project has dialog) to determine the timing of spoken lines.

In the following sections, we will go over the specific points that make storyboards and animatics helpful, making storyboards, making animatics, and implementing them into your Flash animation project files.

Storyboards

Storyboards are drawings that convey the basic flow of your story in sequential order. They establish the composition, mood, and pacing of your project, as shown in Figure 3-1. They are extremely useful, because they shape a great number of features of your project at a very early stage.

Figure 3-1. These three panels establish a serious mood and composition.

As mentioned in previous chapters, planning your project well can lead you through your production more efficiently than diving in head first. Of course, you can make your storyboards as detailed or as simple as you like. By making them simple, you can easily change the flow of an entire sequence or scene. Quite often, a director creates drawings known as thumbnail sketches. These drawings might represent a simple action or an entire scene, and though usually of a very rough and simple quality, they can portray an idea very easily. The most important thing to remember is that you are communicating visually, and your images must convey your ideas in the clearest and most direct manner possible. There are numerous ways to go about making your storyboards. In this section, we will cover the traditional way, drawing on paper, and the digital way. Both have their strengths and weaknesses and which to use is totally at the discretion of the artist—unless the choice is defined by the format of the project, meaning the resolution and end format, be it Web, video, film, or High Definition (HD) video.

Drawing storyboards on paper (traditional)

The most common way to make storyboards is with pencil, or whatever drawing tool you prefer to use, on paper. Even if you feel that you don't draw well, give it a try, and do the best you can. You'd be surprised at what you can do. If you aren't satisfied with your own boards, find any reference that can help explain your idea to a more skilled storyboard artist. A common way to begin is to start making frames. Since the animation is being created with Flash, it would be a good idea to make your storyboard panels the same dimensions as your Flash file.

Let's say our Flash animation will be at a width of 640 pixels, by a height of 480 pixels (as shown in Figure 3-2), so we want to make our boards the same size. If you were to draw a box that is about 9×6.5 inches, it would approximate the size of 640×480 pixels, at 72 pixels per inch. You could also draw an exact version on a computer using graphics software, make printed copies of the original frames, and use those to begin your drawings.

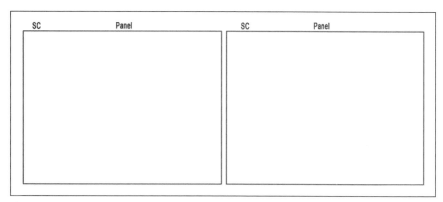

Figure 3-2. These two example storyboard panels were created at 640×480 pixels.

One step that might help would be to draw thumbnails, as mentioned previously, before drawing the final boards. Make a sheet of mini storyboards, with maybe 20 panels on a page. Then scribble-sketch very rough storyboards, to make drawing your storyboards go even faster and easier. This will further help you to clarify the story in your mind. Next, you can draw all of your key points (your keyframes) and actions, as well as indicating any camera movements you want to use in your sequence(s). The number of boards depends on the length of your project and how in-depth you choose to make them.

Acting

Storyboards in live action and animation are used to set up angles, framing, and composition. In animation, acting is a more prominent factor in the storyboard process. By acting, I mean poses and gestures that give off certain emotions motivated by a character's dialog and tone. In storyboards, you'll be mostly concerned with key poses; you wouldn't bother actually animating anything.

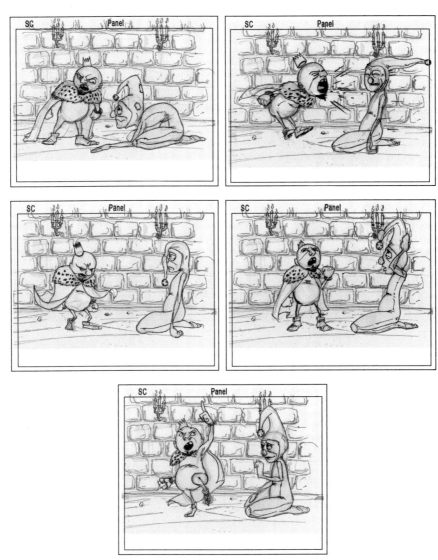

Figure 3-3. Observe the acting within these storyboard panels (these were drawn with fixed BG, which is something easier done in digital boards; see the "Acting in Digital Boards" section later in this section).

Acting-heavy storyboards might be necessary if there are very specific actions that the director wants the animator to follow. The relationship between animation director and animator is very important. It shares many similarities to the relationship of the live-action director and actor. The animator is essentially an actor communicating emotions through the character that he or she has been assigned. Like an actor, an animator may have a strong idea or feeling about how a character should or would behave in a particular situation. The director and animator should always work closely together to achieve the most effective performance. It is in this phase of production that a director and animator will solve most of the problems that may arise.

Storyboards also establish the characters' size relationships to other characters as well as their placement in the environment for the purpose of composition. Storyboards can also give an idea as to what type of backgrounds might be used. In what kind of world will these characters live? What kinds of props or costumes will need to be designed and created? What should the camera angles be? What kind of camera movement should be used, if any?

The storyboard panel in Figure 3-4, for example, gives plenty of information: the background pieces, scale, character placement, and framing are all part of the process of visualizing your idea.

Figure 3-4. This panel shows that the character stands in a large castle full of royal flags and windows, which also tells us it takes place in a medieval time period.

Drawing digitally

Drawing your storyboards in a digital format can prove to be a big benefit for a Flash animation project. Since Flash is digital, you can import them or even draw them directly into Flash so that you can animate in a layer right on top of your storyboards.

This all involves drawing directly into the computer. If, by chance, you can draw flawlessly with a mouse, use that. Otherwise, a tablet would do: a Wacom tablet, a Tablet PC, or a tablet monitor like Cintiq would work best for grasping that drawing feel. These devices may seem strange and will take some getting used to if you're a first-time user, but you'll soon adapt and using a tablet will become very natural for you.

Let's draw our boards directly into an application. You could use Photoshop or CorelDRAW, but in this book, we will draw them directly into Flash.

Drawing directly into Flash

Here, we will go over drawing your boards directly in Flash. Again, since your project will eventually be animated in Flash, it may prove useful to do your boards in Flash.

The storyboard drawings could be made in color or black and white, depending on your preference; black and white is more common and somewhat easier. In this example, Figures 3-5 through 3-10, we will show black-and-white storyboards on the left and the final color frames of the animation on the right. We are going to set a layer of white for the bottom, and then a second layer for our black line work on the top. Let's start by opening Flash and creating a new document; then, follow these steps to create your board:

1. Change the document settings to whatever your final export will be. Let's say it'll be 640×480 pixels on a white background. Since we are just drawing our boards, we won't need to worry about frame rate right now.

Figure 3-5. The storyboard panel displays basic composition of characters in the scene

2. Start by making the bottom layer all white, you can name this layer either White or Base White. Using the square tool, draw a big white square, covering the whole image area. Why do we do this? So that these boards will have an actual layer of white and not just the document background.

3. Next, we'll make a new layer for our black line work. Name it Black or Linework. Then, using the Brush or Pencil tool, draw your image, as in the examples in Figures 3-6 and 3-7.

Figure 3-6. Action begins with arrows indicating character's movement.

Figure 3-7. Action continues.

4. Once you have your black line work, if you want, you can add more gray tones to flesh out your panels. Simply create a new layer in between the Black layer and White layer, and call it Gray Tone. Add shading with the Brush tool, using a light cool gray.

Storyboards also help direct character acting and camera movement by using arrows, motion lines, written notes, and by giving points of direction and composition, like in Figures 3-8 through 3-10.

Figure 3-8. Using arrows and motion lines, the first character is sent out, and the second prepares to exit.

Figure 3-9. The second character anticipates the final action as the photo settles.

Figure 3-10. The second character exits.

Keep the arrows and direction notes on a separate layer if you need them to be removed later. To improve on this and to really communicate your ideas clearly, you can take your boards and cut them together to make an animatic.

Animatics

Creating an animatic is the process of taking your storyboards and cutting them into a video sequence to make your boards even more comprehensible. An animatic displays the rough sequence of your animation, using the most basic keyframes to form a rough cut of what your project may look like. Animatics are essential to an animation project.

Editing animatics for animation is almost determining the final cut of your animation project. Animation is not like live action film and video where footage is shot and one can capture different angles of the same takes, leaving excess footage to cut together later on. Animation needs to be precise. You may not be able to afford a lot of redos, where you reanimate a whole scene all over again. You need to determine what you want, what you will need, and how much you will need. Storyboards show this with images; animatics show even more using timing and quantity. An animatic will be a preview of your piece: it will determine each shot needed, when that shot appears, how long that shot will last on screen, and what action happens in that shot. It ultimately determines exactly what you will need to tell your story or visualize your idea.

In an animatic, you can also add effects and camera moves. An animatic can provide full-motion camera moves to display exactly where the camera goes and when. It can also add effects like transitions, split screens, and whatever your animation may call for.

If your piece has dialog or specific sounds, it would especially help to have that audio in time with the cuts of your scenes—dialog has certain beats and points in the story that reflect the timing and cuts of your piece, determining a specific order to which your events and actions will happen.

Acting in digital boards

Storyboards with heavy acting are better if done digitally. Why? When drawing multiple storyboards on paper, a lot of characters may have to be drawn over and over again that may not need to be. This can be simplified by using outlines of backgrounds (BGs) or characters drawn in previous boards, but in digital boards, once an element is drawn, you can use that one drawing over and over and over again.

Drawing one BG that can be copied and pasted into several boards can save time and really help get continuity across easier. Copying and pasting may also help if you're drawing one character who may only slightly move one limb or if you're showing a new gesture of the face on the same body as the previous panel. A board artist could just copy the body over to a new panel and redraw the head. Using digital boards makes animatics easier to create and read.

Building animatics

If we are going to build an animatic, we need our boards in a digital format. If you drew your boards traditionally on paper, you'll need to scan them into Photoshop or any scanning software that you prefer. Scanning them at 72 dpi may be your default, but for making animatics or for record keeping, scanning them at a higher resolution may help; consider scanning them at 150 or even 300 dpi, so that you have high-resolution copies for your backups.

If you have a large number of boards, scanning may prove to be a long process, but that's one of the tradeoffs when you draw them traditionally.

Keep them named in an orderly fashion. Name them whatever you like, but always add a suffix number on the end to clarify placement. For instance, if the first panel is named Panel 01.jpg, the following would be Panel 02.jpg, then Panel 03.jpg, and so on.

Now, it's time to put your images in a sequence to make them an animatic. This animatic will be the reference for all your animation, and it should be edited as if it were the actual piece finally cut together. It should tell your story or idea visually for others to understand, so they can get an early grasp of your visual scope.

An animatic should be edited for readability first and foremost. It should be easy to understand what is happening; each image should be displayed with enough time to focus or read and still flow along with the story. There may be some scenes that could be animated more quickly than they play out in the animatic, which is fine; that particular scene may be confusing if cut too quickly in its storyboard form. In that case, it should be cut in the animatic so that it's easier to understand.

There are many ways to do this, using any editing or motion graphics application or just Flash itself.

Building an animatic in Flash

You can import your scanned images into Flash and assemble them on a timeline to display them in the proper order. Here, we'll step through the process of creating an animatic in Flash:

1. Create a new Flash document called Animatic.
2. Select the first frame on the timeline. Under the File drop-down menu, go to Import to stage, or press Ctrl/Cmd+R. Then, locate your saved images, and double-click the first one in your sequence. If your images are named correctly, Flash will see this first file as part of a sequence and will ask you if you want to import all of your images as a sequence, as shown in Figure 3-11. Click Yes.

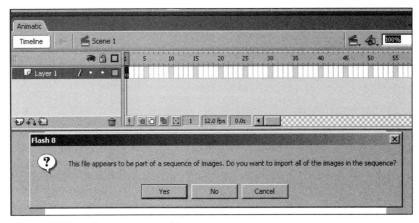

Figure 3-11. Importing a sequence of images

3. Once the images are on your timeline, you will need to decide how long each frame will be displayed. This is where you put on your director's hat. Will your scene be slow and dramatic or fast-paced with quick cuts to generate excitement? It all depends on the needs of your story. To put spaces between these frames, select the frame you want and keep pressing F5 on your keyboard until you have the spaces that you want. To subtract spaces, use Shift+ F5.

4. If you have a soundtrack with music or dialog, you can import that as well on a separate layer below your imported images. To do this, repeat step 2 to add your sound file. Once the file is imported, click the frame of the timeline where you wish to start the sound file. Next, go to the Properties tab of the Actions & Properties panel (Ctrl/Cmd+F3), and click the Sound drop-down menu to select your file. Make sure that Stream is selected next to the Sync label, as shown in Figure 3-12.

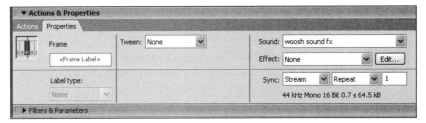

Figure 3-12. Importing a sound file

5. You need to establish enough frames on the timeline for the sound file to play, so go to about frame 100 on the timeline, and press F5 on your keyboard to extend those frames. You should see the sound in the timeline. Shorten or add to the amount of frames depending on the length of your sound. Scroll back and forth along the timeline to hear the sound. If you do not hear it, check your speaker volume, and double-check your sound file settings in the Properties panel.

Building an animatic in other applications

If your boards are in separate image formats (e.g., JPEGs, TIFFs, or PNGs) or if you have audio tracks (like dialog or sound effects), you will find that it is much easier to control them—for example, sliding them to different positions or cutting parts of them—in a more focused editing program. Possible applications for this purpose are Adobe After Effects or Premiere or Apple Final Cut Pro; any of these have the capabilities to import audio and images to cut together as clips in a sequence.

Chapter 10 of this book discusses using After Effects with Flash animation and goes over the After Effects tools and abilities; see that chapter for more specific information on the functions of After Effects and how to apply them to building an animatic.

Whatever program you may choose, you would use the same process to build an animatic:

1. Import the images of your boards.
2. Import any audio tracks, like dialog or sound effects, you may have.
3. Drop your images into the application's timeline, which turns them into clips for editing.
4. Edit together an animatic using your boards and audio.
5. Export the final animatic as video, for example, as a QuickTime movie.

Implementing animatics in your Flash animation file

What makes having an animatic so helpful is the fact that you can import it into Flash. You can implement an animatic directly in your animation files to animate directly on top of them; it's a great convenience to always have your animatic available. Keeping the animatic on a separate layer under your work, you can make it visible or invisible at your discretion to aid you as a guide while you animate and to provide a constant source of reference and inspiration.

Using an animatic from a different format

If your finished animatic is in a video format, like a QuickTime movie, you will have to import it into your Flash animation files. Let's say your animatic is split into separate scenes, so that you have individual clips of animation. You'll have several QuickTime files, one for each scene, and for every scene, you'll need to make separate FLA files that will have the animatic embedded in a guide layer. To set up FLAs with imported animatics, follow these steps:

1. Examine the properties of your QuickTime movie. It's at 720×540 pixels, running at 24 fps, so in Flash, you will create an FLA file with those settings, 720×540 and 24 fps.
2. Go to File ➤ Import; use the file browser to find the QuickTime movie, and select it. Flash will then need to convert it into an FLV (Flash video file), so that it can play in a timeline.
3. When the Import Video dialog box appears, choose the file path where you wish to keep the FLV.

4. The next dialog box, shown in Figure 3-13, will ask you what type of deployment you would like to compress the video for. Since an animatic is for reference use, choose "Embed video in SWF and play in timeline". The following menu will ask you "How would you like to embed the video?". For symbol type, choose Embedded Video, and under Audio track, choose Separate. The options "Place instance on stage", "Expand timeline as needed", "Embed entire video", and "Edit video first" can be chosen at your own discretion.

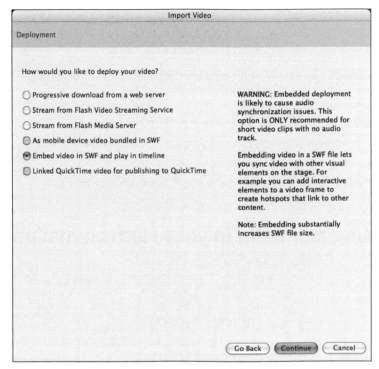

Figure 3-13. Here, you choose your deployment option.

5. Next, you may choose your quality, from Low Quality to Medium Quality to High Quality, and adjust compression, video, and audio settings. Medium quality is usually fine for animatics.

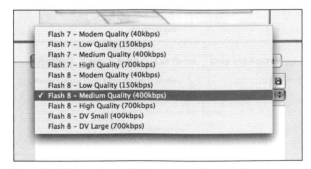

Figure 3-14. The various selections in encoding quality

6. Once Flash is done encoding the FLV, place the animatic video in its own layer, which should remain on the bottom of the layer stack.

7. Make this layer a guide layer: right/Ctrl-click the layer, and select Guide. This is so that this layer doesn't export with our animation.

8. Finally, lock the layer to keep it untouched and underneath your actual work for reference. From here on, you will be ready to begin animation on your project.

Summary

In this chapter, we covered the importance of storyboards as a production tool to plan your animation. We discussed how storyboards can help develop the acting for your characters in a manner that lets you quickly and roughly visualize the progression of your story. We also explored various ways to generate storyboards including thumbnail sketches, drawing more detailed boards by hand and scanning them, as well as drawing them directly into the computer as a more efficient method. Creating an animatic using scanned images and sound files imported into a Flash document was also covered.

The process of storyboarding and the importance it plays in developing an animation project cannot be overstated. The time and care taken to develop a well-constructed storyboard will directly impact and pay great dividends to any animated project.

Chapter 4

SETTING UP YOUR FLA

By Tim Jones

In Chapter 2, we discussed the importance of a well-organized character library and the difference it can make in your production. In this chapter, we will discuss best practices for organizing and structuring your FLA for character animation as well as some of the technical issues you should be aware of before you animate. While some of the more technical aspects (e.g., frame rate, aspect ratios, square versus non-square pixels) are solidly on the science side of the fence, the structure and organization topics discussed here are more of an art and subject to debate. Once again, if you have a method of organizing your FLAs that works for you, by all means use it. If you are new to Flash character animation or looking for ways to improve your production pipeline, I hope this chapter will help.

Before you begin animating, you need to set up your FLA, and in doing so, you will be faced with a myriad of choices. Making the right choices and organizing your FLA properly can make a very large impact on the outcome and success of your project. For purposes of our discussion, these choices fall into two main categories: technical and organizational.

The technical choices you will need to make (and/or be aware of) are

- Aspect ratio
- Pixel aspect ratio
- Image size
- Frame rate
- Title safe and action safe

The organizational issues we will discuss are

- Working in a master FLA
  - File structure overview
  - Shot clips
  - Character clips
  - Compositing scenes
- Splitting up a QuickTime animatic
  - Exporting from After Effects
  - Importing into Flash
  - Frame counters
- Title-safe and action-safe guides
- The 100 Percent Rule
- Camera mechanics

Let's look at each topic in detail.

Technical issues

This section will discuss the technical issues you should be aware of when setting up your FLA. In many cases, these issues will be dictated by your final deliverable. For instance, if you are working on a TV show in the United States, the network will most likely dictate the technical specifications of your deliverable. Having these delivery specs will help you to a point, but you must still understand the underlying implications of how your use of Flash fits into these specs and what you must do to achieve the proper results.

Aspect ratio

As the name implies, an *aspect ratio* (or screen aspect ratio) is an expression of how wide your image is in relation to how tall it is. This ratio is typically expressed as X:Y or X×Y. For instance, the aspect ratio of most televisions is 4:3 (or 4×3) meaning that screen is 4 units wide by 3 units tall. (Note that this aspect ratio is different than the pixel aspect ratio that is discussed later).

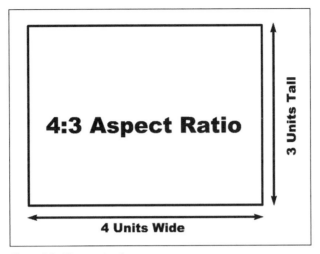

Figure 4-1. 4:3 aspect ratio

As you might expect, there are many aspect ratios you could use, and they vary depending on the medium you are working in. Film and TV have standardized aspect ratios, although even within these media, there are many choices. For work on the Internet, there are even more possibilities (think of all the different Flash banner ads you've seen). The following sections explain some of the most common aspect ratios.

Film

It is common for film aspect ratios to have a denominator value of 1. Therefore, in film, you would describe a typical TV aspect ratio as 1.33:1 as opposed to 4:3. Note that 4:3 and 1.33:1 are exactly the same, just described differently. The most common aspect ratios for film in the United States are 2.40:1 and 1.85:1.

TV

As described previously, TV most commonly has an aspect ratio of 4:3. High-definition television (HDTV) uses 16:9, as does non-HD wide-screen TV.

Internet

On the Internet, it is more common to speak about pixel dimensions, as opposed to aspect ratios, but for purposes of understanding the concept, let's look at a common banner ad size and describe it in terms of aspect ratios. For instance, a leaderboard banner ad is 728 pixels wide by 90 pixels tall, as shown in Figure 4-2.

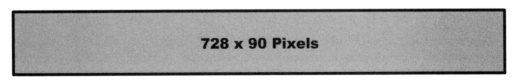

Figure 4-2. A leaderboard banner ad is 728✕90 pixels.

How would you describe the aspect ratio of a leaderboard? Describe it as a ratio of width over height. All of the following are the same:

- 728:90
- 8:1 (actually 8.09:1)
- 56:7 (actually 56:6.92)

In the real world, you would never really talk about a leaderboard ad in terms of its aspect ratio, but I've used this example to help you understand both how to describe any image size in terms of its aspect ratio and to illustrate just how many different ratios are possible.

Pixel aspect ratio

Unlike screen aspect ratios, which describe the size of the screen or image, pixel aspect ratios describe the height and width of the pixels that make up that image. This is important because all pixels are not created equal. Or more specifically, all pixels are not *displayed* equally. The reasons for this are too technical to go into here, but suffice it to say that the same image will appear differently on a TV screen than it will on your computer monitor. This is because televisions (at least older, non-HDTV televisions) display *nonsquare pixels* whereas your computer monitor displays *square pixels*.

Think of it this way: if you make an image that is 100 pixels tall by 100 pixels wide, it will appear as a square on your computer monitor, but will appear slightly squashed on a television monitor (unless you account for this difference).

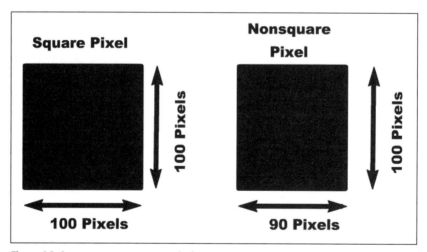

Figure 4-3. Square versus nonsquare pixels

For instance, round car tires that you create in Flash could appear egg-shaped on a TV monitor if you don't account for this display difference in your production. The good news is After Effects and Photoshop can help you make the proper adjustments easily. You just have to remember to do it. Let's walk through one example using After Effects.

Let's say you are animating a TV show for a network in the United States and your deliverable is NTSC DV, 720✕480 pixels. Look at the Composition Settings dialog box in After Effects, shown in Figure 4-4, for this Preset option.

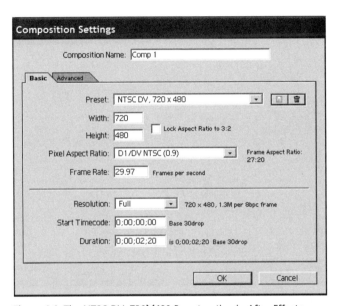

Figure 4-4. The NTSC DV, 720✕480 Preset option in After Effects

Notice that the Pixel Aspect Ratio is D1/DV NTSC (0.9). Since Flash uses square pixels, you must compensate for the difference between square and nonsquare pixels. One way is simply to multiply the width of your Flash document by .9. In this case, 720 times .9 equals 648. Therefore, you could make your Flash document 648✕480 pixels. After Effects automatically assumes images such as JPEGs and PNGs have square pixels, but when in doubt, select your imported footage in the Project window, and click File ➤ Interpret Footage to see how your footage is being handled by After Effects; Figure 4-5 shows the Interpret Footage dialog box.

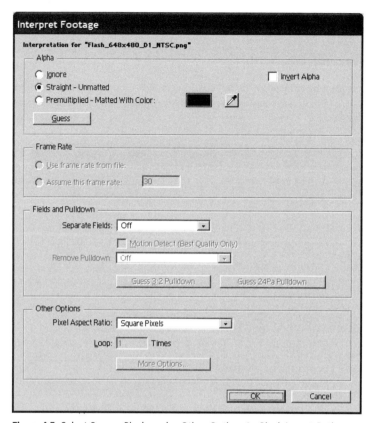

Figure 4-5. Select Square Pixels under Other Options ➤ Pixel Aspect Ratio.

Once you set the pixel aspect ratio to Square Pixels, an image that is 648×480 in Flash will be stretched to 720×480 in After Effects. This may make your image appear stretched on your computer monitor, but on a TV monitor that uses nonsquare pixels, the image will appear correct, meaning that your round car tires from Flash will appear round on the TV screen. To make the image appear correctly on your computer monitor, click the Toggle Pixel Aspect Ratio Correction button at the bottom of the Composition window, as shown in Figure 4-7.

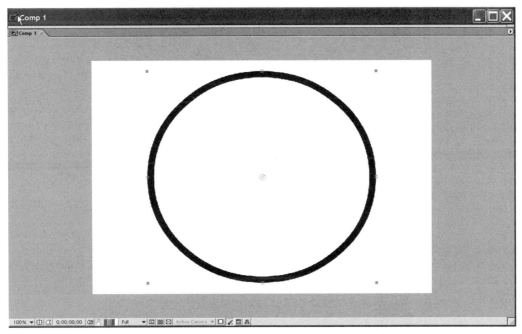

Figure 4-6. A circle that looks egg-shaped on your computer monitor but will look round on a TV screen

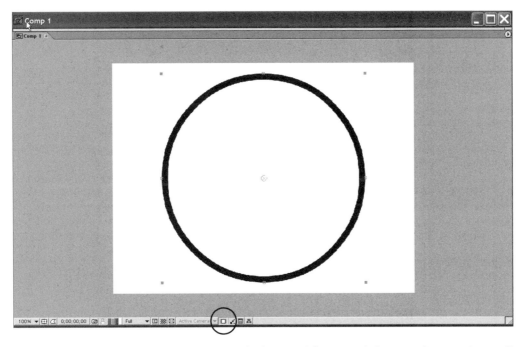

Figure 4-7. Toggle Pixel Aspect Ratio Correction at the bottom of the Comp window to see how your image will look on a TV screen.

Another common way to address this issue is to make your Flash document 720×540, which conforms with the NTSC D1 Square Pixels preset in After Effects, as shown in Figure 4-8.

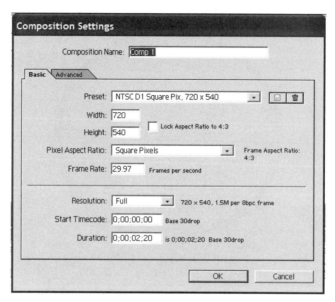

Figure 4-8. The NTSC D1 Square Pix, 720×540 preset

When it comes time to render your scenes, you must then remember to change your render settings back to NTSC DV, 720×480 by selecting Stretch in your Output Module Settings window and selecting NTSC DV, 720×480 in the Stretch to dialog box, as show in Figure 4-9.

Either approach is acceptable and will give you the same output, but you must remember to adjust for the pixel aspect ratio somewhere in your production process to get the proper results.

We have just gone through one of many possible examples of converting square Flash pixels to non-square pixel aspect ratios. Like screen aspect ratios, there are many different pixel aspect ratios, and you should be aware of them as they pertain to your project. After Effects includes many of the most common pixel aspect ratios in the Composition Settings window to help you, as shown in Figure 4-10.

As you can see, it is very important to know not only the size of the image you are working with (e.g., 720×480) but also the pixel aspect ratio (e.g., 0.9).

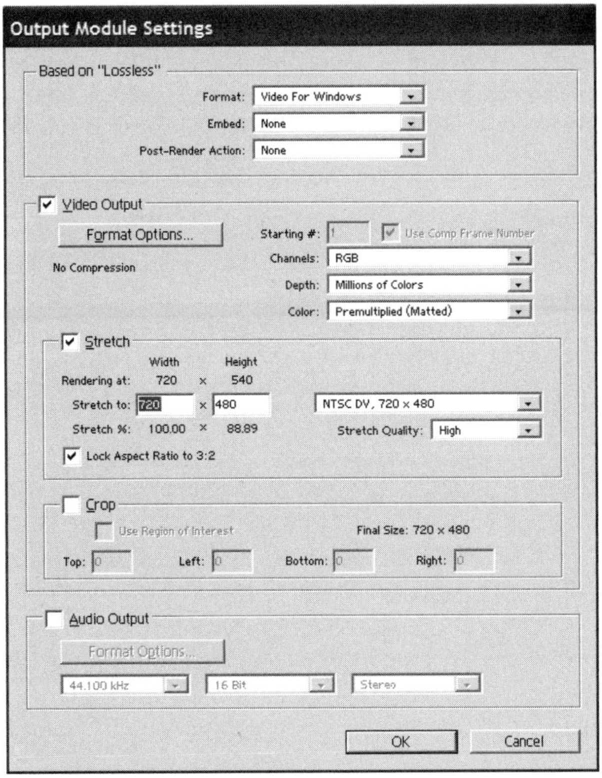

Figure 4-9. Rendering 720×540 square-pixel composition to 720×480 nonsquare-pixel output

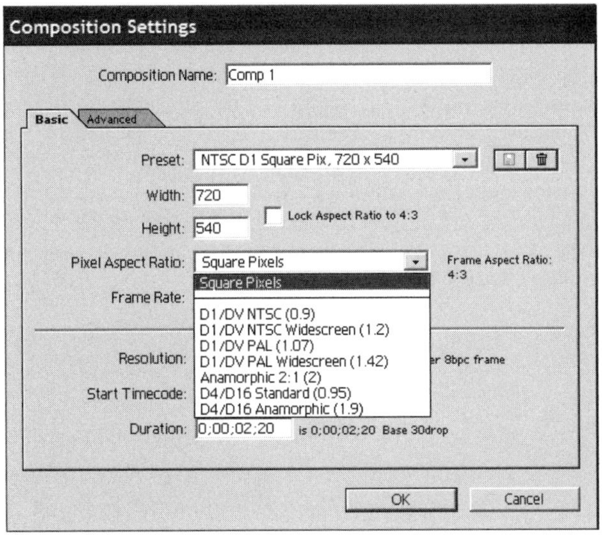

Figure 4-10. After Effects includes some of the most common Pixel Aspect Ratio presets.

Image size

In many cases, the size of your final output will equal the size of your Flash document. For instance, if you want to create a leaderboard ad in Flash, your document size will be set to 728×90 pixels. Do this by clicking Modify ➤ Document or Ctrl/Cmd+J to open the Document Properties dialog box shown in Figure 4-11.

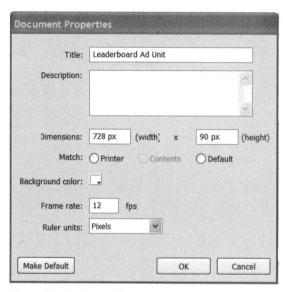

Figure 4-11. Setting the Flash document size

As discussed previously, however, you will need to know the pixel aspect ratio for your final deliverable and adjust your Flash document size accordingly. If the final output is NTSC DV 720×480 (pixel aspect ratio 0.9), your Flash document size should be either 648×480 or 720×540.

As with aspect ratios, the size of your image (and your Flash document) will be dictated by your final deliverable. For instance, if you are animating something for film, your document size will be 2048 pixels wide by 1536 pixels high (commonly referred to as *2K resolution*). On the other hand, if you are producing something for the Internet, you may be working at any number of sizes depending on the project. If you are producing animation for TV, you will probably be working to either NTSC (National Television System Committee) or PAL (Phase Alternating Line) specifications, and the network should provide you with the specifications. After Effects has many of the most common sizes preset in the Composition Settings window; see Figure 4-12.

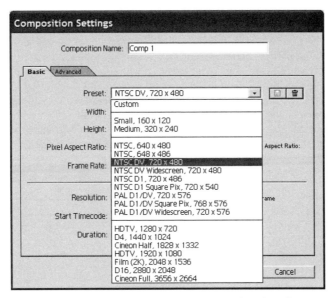

Figure 4-12. The most common sizes are preset in the After Effects Composition Settings window.

Frame rate

Frame rate is the number of frames per second (fps), and as with aspect ratios and image size, it is often determined by your final deliverable. For instance, the frame rate of film is 24 fps; the frame rate for PAL is 25 fps; and the frame rate for NTSC is 29.97 fps. For the Internet, especially when your animation is distributed as a SWF, frame rate is more often determined by the ability of the viewer's computer to play back the file (see Chapter 1 for more details). During the dot-com boom around the turn of the millennium, frame rates for character animation on the Web were often somewhere between 8 fps and 12 fps. Today, with faster computers and more efficient Flash players, character animation delivered as a SWF can be 24 fps (depending on many of the factors discussed in Chapter 1 such as number of characters and complexity of the animation, camera mechanics, and image size).

As with pixel aspect ratios, you will sometimes set your Flash document at a different frame rate than your final deliverable. Let's assume for a moment that your final deliverable is NTSC video. Since you cannot set your frame rate in Flash to 29.97 fps, you animate at 30 fps. The difference between 29.97 and 30 may sound very small, but if you don't account for it you could run into trouble. Since 29.97 fps is 0.1 percent slower than 30 fps, one frame of 30 fps animation will be dropped every 33.3 seconds in a 29.97 fps comp, causing your audio and video images to go out of sync over time. In animation, since you will most likely be animating at 24 fps as opposed to 30 fps, you must make a similar adjustment when importing your animation into After Effects. First, click File ➤ Interpret Footage, and then set the frame rate to 23.976 (0.1 percent slower than 24 fps). When you output your final file at 29.97, you will not have dropped frames of animation, and your audio will stay in sync.

Action safe and title safe

Another important thing to remember when producing animation for television is that most older television sets cut off some part of the image. For this reason, title safe and action safe guides are used to let animators know what is safe (i.e., most likely viewable on the vast majority of television sets). *Title safe* refers to the area inside which all text should appear. This means that if you put text on the screen, you should keep it inside the title safe area to insure that it will be readable on most television sets. *Action safe* refers to the area inside which animators should keep all important action. This means that if you are animating something important (although many animators would argue that *everything* they animate is important) you should make sure to keep it inside the action safe area.

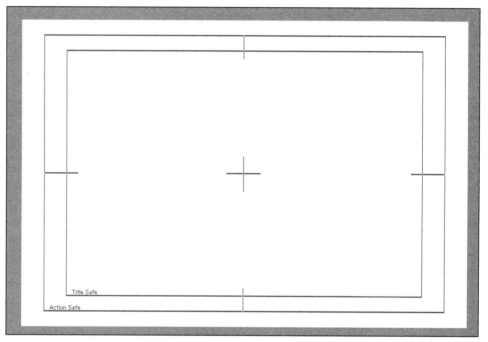

Figure 4-13. This guide shows action safe and title safe regions within an NTSC DV, 720×480 screen.

Unfortunately, Flash does not include these guides, but After Effects does (click the Title – Action Safe button at the bottom of the Composition window). You cannot simply import the guide from After Effects to Flash, but you can make your own in a matter of minutes:

1. Turn the guide on in After Effects, and click Layer ➤ New ➤ Solid.

2. Make a black shape and scale to match the action safe line.

3. Create another new solid, make it white, and scale it to match the title safe line.

4. Now export the file as a jpg image and import it into Flash. Remember to adjust for nonsquare pixels, so resize the 720×480 pixels JPG to 648×480.

5. Use the Line tool to trace the title safe and action safe regions, and you have a new guide template. You'll only need to do this once, and you can keep the template forever.

6. Now, just to make sure it works properly, export your guide from Flash and import it back into After Effects to make sure that the field guides match up (I've included Flash and AE files of this example for your reference on the downloads page of the friends of ED web site).

Remember, title-safe and action-safe guides aren't an exact science. The purpose of these guides is to give you a worst-case scenario for TV viewing areas so that most people will be able to read your titles and see your action. Since every TV is different, these templates are general guidelines, not pixel-perfect borders.

Organizational issues

In this section, we will discuss some best practices for setting up your FLAs for character animation. These are not hard and fast rules and certainly not the *only* way to work. You may very well have organizational methods that work for you, and if so, keep using them. Following are some tips and tricks that I've learned over the years to help streamline our process.

Beginners often jump right in and start doing everything on the main timeline, only to find out later—often when it's too late—that they've created a mess for themselves. The issue usually arises after the first pass of animation has been completed and changes are requested with seemingly simple notes like these: "Let's frame this scene a little tighter." Or, "The size relationship between the characters looks off; make one 10 percent bigger and the other 20 percent smaller." If you've organized your FLA well, these changes can be extremely quick and easy to do. If you've animated everything on the main timeline, on dozens of layers, you may be left scratching your head, wondering how to address the notes.

As discussed in Chapter 1, there are really two main approaches you will use when creating your animation:

- Create one *master* FLA for the entire animation (usually when delivering a SWF for distribution on the Internet).
- Create multiple FLAs (typically one FLA per shot) and composite and edit your project in another program, such as After Effects.

Working in a master FLA

First, let's look at King Klaus04.fla again, which is an example of a master FLA containing the entire project. Notice that the main timeline has only six layers:

- Scene labels: Scene 1 through Scene 21 are labeled on the top layer of the timeline.
- Labels: The playagain label on frame 1 is for the Play Again button on the last frame of the card. We could also put ActionScript on this layer.
- Audio: King Klaus has just one audio layer.
- Mask: This ensures that nothing outside of Flash's stage area will be inadvertently seen.
- Animation01: This layer contains most of the scenes.
- Animation02: This layer is used when two scenes need to overlap, as they do between frames 243 and 283.

The phrase "divide and conquer" is quite appropriate when thinking about how best to organize your FLA. I usually try to keep the main timeline as simple as possible, with the minimum number of layers. This makes it easy to understand the basic structure of the file and to manipulate the various elements with the least amount effort. In this example, all of the animation is displayed in one of two layers: Animation01 and Animation02. King Klaus is divided into 21 individual shots, and each shot has its own graphic clip in the library (see ++shot_01 through ++shot_21). Notice that we use two plus signs (++) at the beginning of the library name to force the shots to the top of the library, making them easier to find and access.

All of the camera mechanics are done on the main timeline and applied to the shots as a whole. All of the animation for each individual shot is done inside the shot clip. For instance, look at the key frames on layer Animation01 from frames 36 to 64 in Figure 4-14.

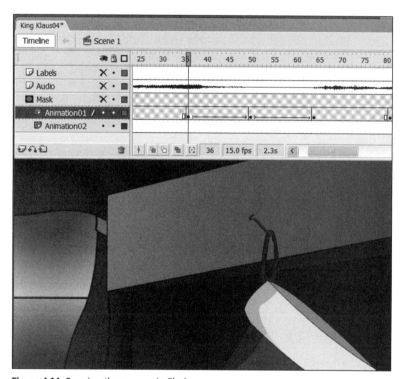

Figure 4-14. Panning the camera in Flash

Here, we are panning the camera left and pulling back (in reality, moving the world in the animation to the right and enlarging it to make it appear closer to the camera).

Double-click ++shot_01 in the library, and you will see the animation of the hand hanging the stocking on the mantle. This, in a nutshell, describes the structural hierarchy that we follow when setting up our FLAs. For elements that you may want to manipulate as a whole (e.g., shots on the main timeline) set them up as graphic clips in the library. We use Graphic (as opposed to Movie Clips), because you can scrub the timeline (meaning to move the play head back and forth) in Flash and see the animation play when they are graphics, but you cannot do the same if they are movie clips.

Don't believe me? Open KingKlaus04.FLA, and scrub the main timeline starting at frame 1. You will see the hand come in and hang the stocking. Now click the instance of ++shot_01 on the stage, and change ++shot_01 from a Graphic to a Movie Clip in the Properties panel. Now scrub the timeline again. Notice that the hand no longer comes into frame. If you publish the SWF, however, the animation will appear, but from a practical standpoint, it is difficult to work this way.

Now, switch ++shot_01 back to a graphic clip (making sure you to set the Options for Graphics dialog back to Play Once instead of Single Frame), and you can watch your animation from the main timeline.

One disadvantage of this approach is that, when published, sound within a graphic clip will not play. Therefore, you must make sure that any audio that is inside your graphic clip is also on the main time-line, and that it is positioned so that it is in sync. Including the audio inside your graphic clip is essen-tial when animating actions where there is a very close relationship between the audio and animation, such as dialog. Having the audio on the same timeline as your images allows you to scrub the audio, allowing you to more easily assign the proper mouth shape to the audio heard across one or more frames.

Go to frame 243 of KingKlaus04.fla, and you can see why we need two layers for animation. Figure 4-15 shows how we wipe from shot 09 to shot 10 using a candy cane. Double-click ++shot_09, and you will see how the candy cane "wipes away" the shot of Santa climbing the chimney from frames 15 through 25. Now, go back to the main timeline, and see how ++shot_10 has been placed on layer Animation02 underneath ++shot_09 in layer Animation01.

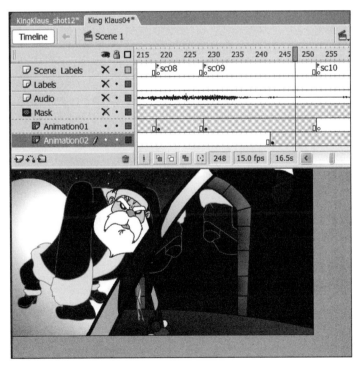

Figure 4-15. A wipe in Flash

This hierarchical structure extends from the main timeline to the individual scenes. Just as each shot is encapsulated into a self-contained clip on the main timeline, we often further subdivide and encapsulate the shots into individual character clips. For instance, look at ++shot_03. Lock all the layers but Klaus, and double-click Klaus on the stage. You are now inside the down chimney clip, and you can see how Santa has been animated inside this clip.

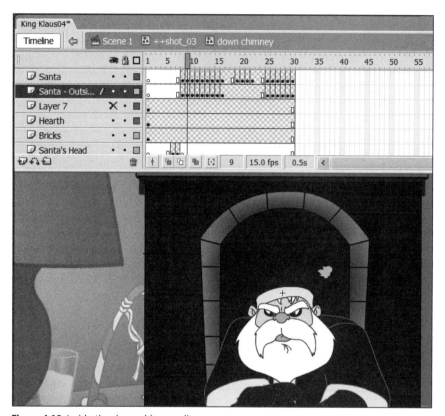

Figure 4-16. Inside the down chimney clip

In this instance, the animator felt it was easier to separate Klaus from Ginger and deal with them separately. In down chimney, notice how the animator moves Klaus from inside the chimney to outside by changing the layers on which he is animated.

You can easily work with a small team of animators—or even divide your scenes into separate FLAs if you are working alone—to help you divide and conquer. The FLAs will be smaller and easier to work with, and if you are moving them back and forth across a network or over the Internet, breaking your FLAs into smaller parts will help keep your file transfer times to a minimum. King Klaus isn't a particularly big file, but you may find your files getting quite large, and you will find it handy (or even necessary) to divide your shots into multiple FLAs. Major contributing factors to file size are audio, video, and raster images. If you have included audio, imported video, or created your backgrounds in Photoshop, these individual-shot FLAs can get very large, very quickly. It is therefore often more efficient to work on individual shots separately from the master FLA. Here's how to create an individual-shot FLA:

1. Create a new FLA, and make sure the settings in the Document Properties window are the same as those for KingKlaus04.fla
2. In KingKlaus04.fla, click frame 301 of layer Animation01.
3. Click Edit ➤ Timeline ➤ Copy Frames.
4. Go to your new FLA; click frame 1 in the timeline, and click Edit ➤ Timeline ➤ Paste Frames.
5. Extend the timeline for the length of the shot (e.g., 32 frames).
6. Change the Layer Name to Shot_12.
7. Save your file as KingKlaus_shot12.fla.

Now, you can animate this scene separately or distribute it to another animator, and later, you can pull the animation back into the master file. For purposes of this demonstration, I have changed the color of Santa's nose in KingKlaus_shot12.fla. Now, it is time to merge shot 12 back into the master:

1. Open both FLAs (KingKlaus04.fla and KingKlaus_shot12.fla).
2. Open the Library window, and click New Library Panel.
3. You now have two Library windows open. In the dialog box at the top of each Library window, make sure that you have one library window open for each FLA, as shown in Figure 4-17.

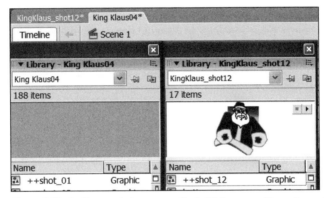

Figure 4-17. Getting ready to copy ++Shot_12 from one library to another

4. Drag ++shot_12 from the KingKlaus_shot12 library to the King Klaus04 library.
5. Click Replace Existing Items in the Resolve Library Conflict dialog box, shown in Figure 4-18.

Figure 4-18. Choose "Replace existing items" to overwrite library symbols of the same name.

Notice now that Santa's nose color is updated in the master file, not just in scene 12 but in *every* scene. Notice also that, since we only changed the color of the nose in the front view, only the front view of his nose has been recolored throughout. For instance, look at frames 221 and 222 of the master file, and notice how Santa's nose is still pink in the profile view and turns white in the front view. The point here is that you must be careful when splitting up scenes and then bringing the back into a master FLA, because you could end up with undesired results if you aren't. If animators simply change symbols inside the individual shots without renaming them, you could run into trouble.

For the sake of argument, let's suppose we only wanted to change Santa's nose color in scene 12. What could we have done differently? Since I changed the color of the nose inside the graphic clip S_nose mouth chart, I can rename that one library item to *S_nose mouth chart_tj and only affect nose color in shot 12. As discussed in Chapter 2, putting the asterisk before the name will move this library item to the top of the library and alert everyone that a change has been made to this symbol. By putting my initials at the end of the name, I've let everyone know who made the change.

Splitting up your animatic

Unless I am delivering a SWF for distribution on the Internet, I rarely use Flash to composite and edit multiple FLAs. Whether it is a 22-minute TV show or a 1-minute short for broadband video, I typically divide my shots into separate FLAs and then use After Effects to composite them. In some ways, this is easier, because I don't have to worry about the naming conflicts (described in the previous example with Santa's nose color) that can occur when working in a master FLA. In some ways, it can be slightly more difficult, because I am often animating in Flash but doing camera mechanics in After Effects. This can make it more difficult to visualize exactly what is happening in the scene. In this section, I will describe how we take a 1-minute animatic (built in After Effects and exported as a QuickTime movie) and break it down into multiple FLA shots. I'll describe how we set up these FLAs, explain the 100 Percent Rule, and describe scene planning methods for animating in Flash and executing camera mechanics in After Effects.

Exporting from After Effects

Quite often, I begin my animation process by taking a QuickTime animatic and splitting into multiple FLAs, typically one shot per FLA file. Take a look at blue_crush_animatic.mov as an example. This is one of the episodes of *Off-Mikes* that ANIMAX produced for ESPN (http://espnradio.espn.go.com/espnradio/story?storyId=2061832).

This particular episode has 13 separate shots, so I want to create 13 separate FLAs—one for each shot. The first thing I do is import my QuickTime file into After Effects and set up a composition. Notice in Figure 4-19 that I set up my After Effects composition exactly as I will my FLA, in this case 648×480 at 15 fps.

Note that even though this series is produced for ESPN.com we work at NTSC specifications just in case it was ever needed for a TV broadcast. Earlier in the chapter, I explained that, because of NTSC's nonsquare pixel aspect ratio, we need to account for the difference in Flash, which is why the width is set to 648 pixels and not 720 pixels (720 × 0.9 = 648). Alternately, I could have set my Flash document to 720×540, as explained previously.

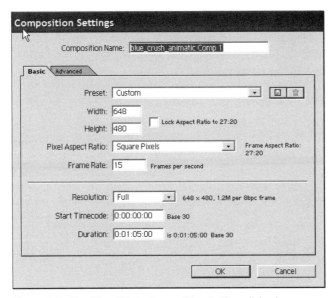

Figure 4-19. The After Effects Composition Settings dialog box

Why 15 fps? I find that 15 fps translates nicely to NTSC (29.97 fps) by effectively being animated on twos. Many productions will use 24 fps when going to NTSC, but at 24 fps, animators will sometimes animate on twos (meaning there is a new key frame every 2 frames) making the effective frame rate 12 fps. When animating at 15fps I animate on ones. I find the fluidity of motion to be decent at 15 fps, and I save 9 frames per second of animation, meaning that I do 540 fewer keyframes in a one-minute short than I would with animation at 24fps.

Since blue_crush_animatic.mov is at 320×240, I transform the size to 200 percent to fit the window. (Yes, this does degrade the image quality, but the animatic is simply to be used for reference in the FLA and does not need to be pristine.) Next, I step through the animatic, writing down the first and last frames of each shot, as shown in Table 4-1.

Table 4-1. The First and Last Frame of Shots in blue_crush_animatic.mov

Shot #	Start Frame	End Frame
Shot01-02	00:00	09:02
Shot03	09:03	11:04
Shot04	11:05	24:07
Shot05	24:08	29:12
Shot06	29:13	33:13
Shot07	33:14	37:03

Continued

Table 4-1. The First and Last Frame of Shots in blue_crush_animatic.mov *(Continued)*

Shot #	Start Frame	End Frame
Shot08	34:04	43:03
Shot09	43:04	45:08
Shot10	45:09	46:13
Shot11	46:14	49:13
Shot12	49:14	57:04
Shot13	57:05	1:04:14

Once you have the beginning and ending frames of each shot, you can open the render queue and export all of your audio and video in one fell swoop:

1. Click Composition ➤ Add to Render Queue.

2. Let's export shot 12, which begins at 49:28 and ends at 57:08. In the Render Queue window shown in Figure 4-20, click Render Settings, and set Quality to Best and Resolution to Full.

3. Under Time Sampling, click Set to open the Custom Time Span window, and set your Start and End times for shot 12.

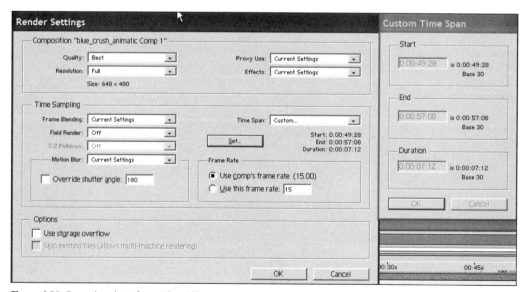

Figure 4-20. Exporting shots from After Effects

4. Click OK, and then from the Render Queue window, open the Output Module Settings window shown in Figure 4-21.

5. Set your file format to QuickTime Movie, and under Format Options, set your Compression option to Animation and the Quality to Best.

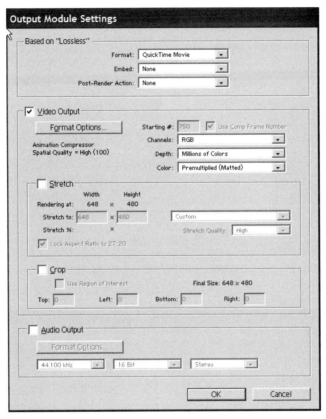

Figure 4-21. Export a QuickTime movie at 100 percent using the Animation codec.

6. Set the Output To destination for your rendered file.

You are now ready to render the video file of the animatic. You'll note that I did not export the video with sound, because you cannot scrub the video file and hear the audio in Flash, so I will need to export a separate audio file.

7. Go back to the Render Queue window. Select shot 12 in the render queue, and press Ctrl/Cmd+D to duplicate the shot.

8. Change the output format from QuickTime to MP3, and change the destination file name to OM_312_audi.mp3—now you have both your audio and video files for your FLA. Follow the same procedures to export audio and video for the other shots, and then render them all at once.

Importing into Flash

Now it is time to set up your FLA. You can open OM_303.fla to follow along. Note the Document Properties window settings are the same as they were in After Effects; see Figure 4-22.

Figure 4-22. The Flash Document Properties window

The main timeline, shown in 4-23, contains only four layers: Audio, Frame Counter, Field Guide, and OM_303_12.

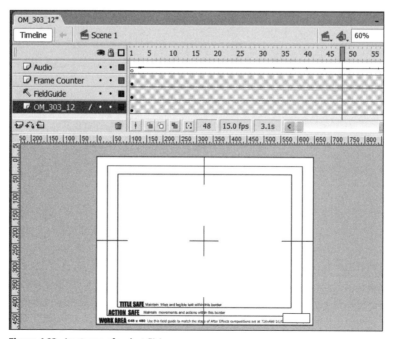

Figure 4-23. Anatomy of a shot FLA

As discussed previously, audio must sit on the main timeline if you want to hear it when you export. I use a frame counter to make it easier to give notes back to the animator from the director (e.g., "Please remove the eye blink starting on frame 20."). We also discussed the field guide earlier. Notice that it is set as a guide layer so that it is visible to the animator but will not be rendered. Finally, OM_303_12 is where all the animation will happen.

Now, it is time to import your audio and video into the FLA and set up your shot:

1. Click File ➤ Import ➤ Import Video, and select the OM_303_12_animatic.mov file you just exported.

2. Next, select Embed video in SWF and play in timeline from the Deployment window, as shown in Figure 4-24.

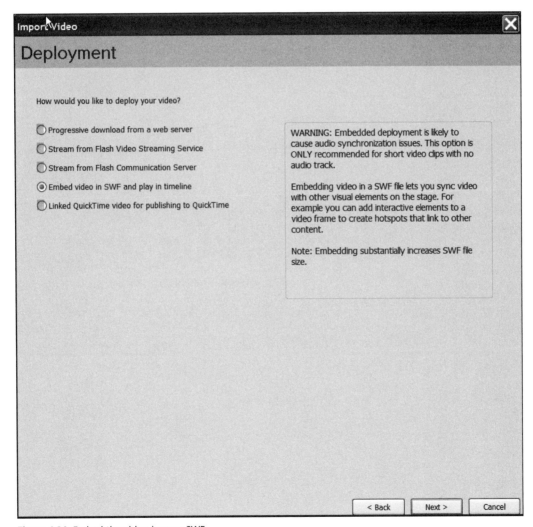

Figure 4-24. Embed the video in your SWF.

3. Set the embedding properties appropriately, as shown in Figure 4-25.

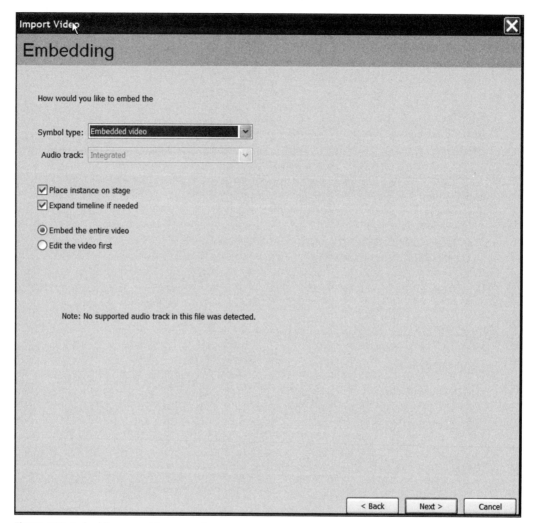

Figure 4-25. Embedding your video properly

4. Set the encoding options as shown in Figure 4-26.

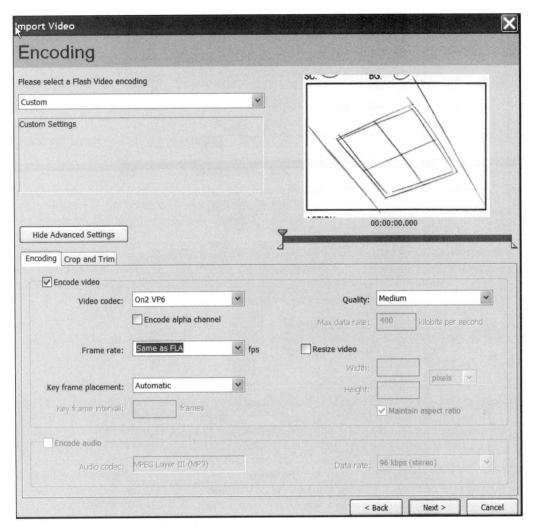

Figure 4-26. Set the Video encoding options.

5. Import your video, and center it on your stage.

6. Now, click the video, and symbolize it, naming it +OM_AN_303_12.swf. Make sure that it is a Graphic clip. The dialog window shown in Figure 4-27 will pop up, asking you if you want to automatically make the length of the graphic clip the same as the video clip. Click Yes.

Figure 4-27. Answer Yes if you get this dialog box.

7. Now, double-click +OM_AN_303_12, and inside the Graphic clip, add the layers Audio, Greeny (the Mike Greenberg animation layer), and Background, and rename the bottom layer animatic. Once you begin animation, you will change the animatic layer to a guide layer so that it will not export, but for now it is fine to leave it as it is.

8. Make sure that the audio on the main timeline and the audio inside the scene clip start on the same frame. When in doubt, you can change +OM_AN_303_12 to a Movie Clip and publish it. Audio inside a movie clip will render, so both audio on the main timeline and audio inside the clip will render. If they are offset, it will be easy to hear.

Your FLA is now set up and ready for animation!

The 100 percent rule

One issue we touched on in Chapter 2 is the problem that can occur when library items for the same character are created at different sizes. This can happen very easily when a team of animators is working on the same project. Typically, what happens is this: An animator begins working on a scene in which the Generic Man is shown in a long shot. The animator takes the character symbol and reduces it to 25 percent and begins working. Later, the animator finds he needs to draw a new hand shape for the scene, and draws one on the fly. Following the proper naming convention, the animator names the hand *man_hand_24_tj. The issue here is that the animator drew the hand to the scale of the character on the stage (25 percent) and *then* symbolized it, so *man_hand_24_tj is actually only one-quarter the size of the other elements in the library. This can become problematic if all of the animators on a project are creating all of their symbols at different sizes. Not only will you have line weight problems (if everyone uses, say, a 1-point line to create their symbols regardless of what size they are), but it will be more difficult to incorporate new symbols into your master character library and reuse those newly created symbols in the future.

The 100 Percent Rule states that, to avoid this problem, you should always animate your characters at 100 percent and then resize them (either within a scene clip or a character clip) to the appropriate size necessary for the scene. Let's look at a quick example. Open 100_percent_rule.fla, and you will see two Generic Man examples on the stage as shown in Figure 4-28.

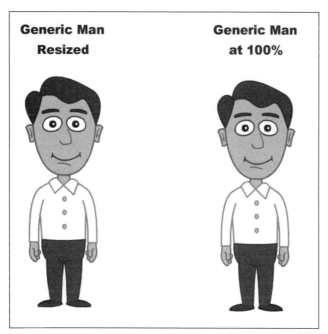

Figure 4-28. They look the same, but they're not.

Generic Man on the left has been resized directly on the stage. Click his symbols, and look at the Transform window—you will see that his symbols are at 25 percent. Generic Man on the right is inside Graphic clip +sc01. Double-click the clip, and check the size of his symbols. See how they are still set to 100 percent? The *clip* has been resized to 25 percent, but the Generic Man inside the clip is still at 100 percent. The point here is that, even though they look identical on the stage, the method of resizing them is important to your work flow. Whenever possible, try to remember the 100 Percent Rule, as it will help you to keep all the new symbols created at the proper scale. To illustrate the point, let's take a look at what happens when we resize Generic Man on the stage and create a new hand for the scene. When that hand symbol is reincorporated into the master library, the scale of the hand is inaccurate, as Figure 4-29 shows.

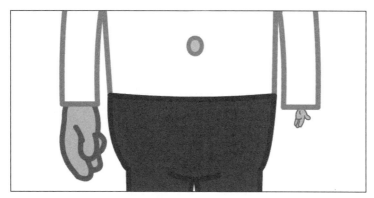

Figure 4-29. What's wrong with this picture?

Camera mechanics

You may wish to animate your characters in Flash and do your camera mechanics, such as pans and zooms, in another program, such as After Effects. In Chapter 10, you will learn how to do these camera mechanics in After Effects. In this section, we will talk about how to *indicate* those mechanics in Flash.

Open CameraMechanicsInFlash.fla to see how we might have handled the opening shot of King Klaus differently if we were going to do camera moves in After Effects as opposed to Flash. The first thing you will notice is that the document size is much larger here than it is in KingKlaus04.fla. This is because if we are doing the mechanics in After Effects we'll need to export the *entire* image and not just the camera view. Therefore, I've sized ++shot_01 to 100 percent and then made the document size just slightly larger than the scene clip (e.g., 2000×500).

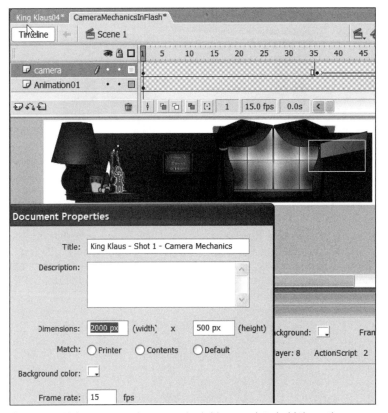

Figure 4-30. Make sure your document size is big enough to hold the entire scene.

Next, I created a layer called camera, where I'll indicate my camera view. Then, I created a symbol called camera by drawing a white rectangle sized 680×364 (to match the document size of King Klaus). After that, I dropped the camera symbol onto the camera layer on the stage and proceeded to *indicate* my camera mechanics. You will see that the camera holds for the first 35 frames, then begins panning over and pulling out until the move is completed on frame 64. Now, the animator knows exactly where the camera should be on any given frame and can plan accordingly. For instance, if we were to animate Ginger struggling to free herself from the candy canes, the animator knows that any animation before frame 60 will most likely not be seen, and therefore, only animates the necessary frames.

When you're done with your animation and ready to do your camera mechanics in After Effects, you need to consider the resolution of your exported images. Let's say we want to export a .png sequence from Flash. Look at your timeline, and see where the camera view is the *smallest*. In this case, the camera appears smallest on frame 1. Another way to think about this is to remember that the camera appears the smallest at the point at which the camera is zoomed in closest to your scene. Recall that when we created the camera symbol, we started at 100 percent of our final document size (i.e., 680×364). Now, click the instance of camera on frame 1 and see that it has been transformed to 50 percent. Remember that if we were doing the camera mechanics in Flash, we would not make the "camera" smaller, we would make the "world" bigger. In other words, we would leave the camera at 100 percent and increase ++shot_01 to 200 percent. (Or more specifically 188 percent in the actual KingKlaus04.fla, but 200 percent is close enough). Therefore, when you render your .png sequence, increase the size of your render to 200 percent. In this example, I've chosen to increase the dpi (dots per inch) from 72 to 150, which gives me slightly more resolution than I'll need.

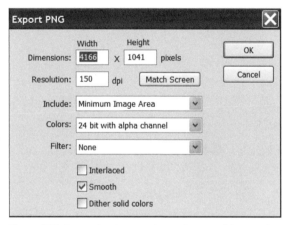

Figure 4-31. Remember to export your images with enough resolution.

You probably will not want to export your image sequence with the camera view included, but you may very well want the camera view in After Effects as a guide. Therefore, you will need to export these layers separately. The easiest way to do this is to change all the layers to guide layers except the one you want to render. There is no render queue in Flash, so you'll need to export your layers manually, one at a time.

Now, you can import your images into After Effects and perform your camera move there. This may seem like a lot of work, but once you get the hang of it, you will find it is an easy, quick way to do your scene planning. You may also be asking yourself why you would go to the extra effort to do this in After Effects, and for this particular move, you may prefer to simply do it in Flash. Once you start breaking your scene into layers and doing multiplane moves and adding rack focus, blur, and additional lighting effects, you'll quickly see that After Effects is a much better tool for the job.

Summary

In this chapter, I've covered technical aspects of setting up your FLA for animation:

- Aspect ratio
- Pixel aspect ratio
- Image size
- Frame rate
- Action safe and title safe guides

I also covered organizational aspects of setting up your FLA:

- Working in a master FLA
  - File structure overview
  - Shot clips
  - Character clips
  - Compositing scenes
- Splitting up a QuickTime animatic
  - Exporting from After Effects
  - Importing into Flash
  - Frame counters
- The 100 percent rule
- Camera mechanics

Whether you're creating a leaderboard ad or animating a TV show, you should now be able to set up your FLA properly for the job. Now, it's time for the fun part—animation!

Chapter 5

PLUG-INS AND EXTENSIONS

By Dave Wolfe

Flash MX 2004 introduced one of the most significant new features for animators, the JavaScript Flash (JSFL) Extension API. JSFL is a simple scripting language based on JavaScript that enables users to write scripts that automate repetitive tasks and extend the Flash tool set. By combining the power of JSFL, XML, and ActionScript, this simple extension API allows animators to create some very useful tools for improving the animation workflow in Flash.

You can download Flash extensions from numerous sites on the Internet, and they can be easily installed by double-clicking the installer file, which will have a .mxp extension. This will launch Extension Manager, enabling you to install the extension into Flash, or to uninstall, disable, or enable an already installed extension (there is a bug in the Mac version of Extension Manager that requires the user to quit Extension Manager before installing another extension).

Extensions fall into five categories: behavior, command, panel, timeline effect, and tool. Behaviors are accessed from the Behavior panel. Commands are accessed from the Commands menu. Panels are accessed from the Windows menu, in the Other Panels submenu. Timeline effects are accessed from the Insert menu, in the Timeline Effects submenu. Tools are accessed from the Tools panel, but first they must be placed there; the installer should do this automatically, but you can do it manually by going to the Edit menu and selecting Customize Tools Panel. The most useful extensions for animators fall into the commands and panels categories, so those are the only extension types that will be covered in this chapter.

In this chapter, we will take a look at some of the extensions available that can improve your animation workflow and save you from wasting time performing monotonous tasks. We'll also take a look at how to use the History panel to record your own command sequences.

Introducing our favorite extensions

The following sections detail some extensions that are particularly useful for animators, and there are many more available on the Internet. Additionally, I've included a few ActionScript tools in the list; although not technically extensions, they can also help improve your animation workflow.

Panel extensions

Let's start by looking at panel extensions. Panel extensions are SWF files designed to run within the Flash authoring environment as new panels. The ability to use a custom user interface combined with the power of ActionScript allows for some very powerful tools you won't want to do without.

AnimSlider

Here are the basic details on the AnimSlider extension, which is shown in Figure 5-1:

- **Author**: Warren Fuller
- **License**: Commercial (free limited version available)
- **Availability**: Flash MX 2004 and higher
- **URL**: http://www.animonger.com/flashtools.html

Figure 5-1. The AnimSlider Pro interface

AnimSlider is an extremely useful set of tools for the Flash animator. The main tool is the AnimSlider itself. It is a frame slider similar to Flash's timeline, but instead of scrolling through frames in the timeline, it scrolls through frames in a Graphic symbol's internal timeline. One common use for this tool is for doing lip sync. Often, the mouth of a character is a graphic symbol set to Single Frame, and changing the frame number in the Properties panel changes the mouth shape. The AnimSlider allows you to quickly scroll through the frames to search for the one you want to display, or if you already know which frame you want, you can simply click that frame on the slider. In addition to speeding up lip syncing, you can also use it for speeding up animation in general. For example, instead of swapping symbols to change hands, you can nest all the hand symbols as frames in a graphic symbol and use the AnimSlider to quickly change which hand is used. It also has some buttons for common tasks, such as duplicating a layer, adding a motion tween, changing a tween's easing, flipping symbols, and so on. There are three commercial versions available: AnimSlider Jr. ($15), AnimSlider ($30), and

AnimSlider Pro ($45). The AnimSlider Jr. has 37 frames available in the slider; AnimSlider has 96 frames, and AnimSlider Pro has 800 frames. AnimSlider Pro also has a four-digit field for typing in frame numbers (instead of a three-digit one), and it can display frame labels and the symbol's name.

Autocolor full

Here are the basic details on the Autocolor Full extension, which is shown in Figure 5-2:

- **Author**: Dave Logan
- **License**: Free
- **Availability**: Flash MX 2004 and higher
- **URL**: http://www.dave-logan.com/weblog/?p=46

Autocolor Full allows you to create a palette of named custom colors and instantly edit those colors across multiple symbols, frames, or files. Small PNG images are used as fills, and by changing the color of the PNG, you change the color of all symbols that use that PNG as a fill. This can come in handy when a client decides to make changes to a character's colors, especially if animation has already begun and col-

Figure 5-2. The Autocolor Full interface

ors need to be changed across multiple files. The author has also made some excellent videos that explain how to use Autocolor Full. The videos can be found on his web site, along with the description of the extension.

Timing chart

Here are the basic details on the Timing Chart extension, which is shown in Figure 5-3:

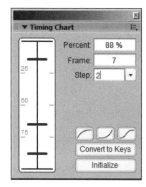

- **Author**: Dave Wolfe
- **License**: Free
- **Availability**: Flash 8 and higher
- **URL**: http://toonmonkey.com/extensions.html

Timing Chart is a tool that makes use of Flash 8's new custom ease feature. It works similar to the timing charts used in traditional animation, where the spacing of the lines on the chart represents the spacing of the drawings made by the inbetweener. To use the extension, first select some motion-tweened frames, and then select the frame step to

Figure 5-3. The Timing Chart interface

use. If you're animating on twos (creating a new drawing or pose every other frame), set the frame Step to 2, if you're animating on ones (creating a new drawing or pose for every frame) then set the frame Step to 1, and so on. When you're done, click the Initialize button. This will populate the chart with sliders representing the spacing of the tweened frames. By dragging the sliders up and down, you alter the spacing of the tweened frames, and thus alter the timing. You can also right-click the chart and flip it, so its orientation is more like that of a traditional timing chart. There are three preset buttons for slow in, slow out, and slow in/slow out. Finally, there is a button to convert the tweened frames to keyframes. This works like the Convert to Keyframes command in Flash, but it uses the frame step to create the keyframes rather than creating a keyframe on every frame.

Command extensions

Now, we'll go over some useful command extensions. A command extension usually has a simple interface or no interface at all. These extensions are the easiest types to make, so there are a lot more of them available.

Break Into Layers

Here are the basic details on the Break Into Layers extension:

- **Author**: Dave Wolfe
- **License**: Free
- **Availability**: Flash 8 and higher
- **URL**: http://www.toonmonkey.com/extensions.html

Break Into Layers will break apart the selected symbol and re-create the layer structure that was inside it. Layer names, colors, and types are retained, and symbols are usually placed into the proper layer. However, there are some limitations. Shapes that are not on the bottom layer should be grouped first, and any layers not containing symbols or shapes should be deleted to prevent symbols from ending up in the wrong layer.

Create Masking Layer

Here are the basic details on the Create Masking Layer extension:

- **Author**: Dave Logan
- **License**: Free
- **Availability**: Flash MX 2004 and higher
- **URL**: http://www.dave-logan.com/weblog/?p=46

Create Masking Layer simply creates a new layer with a black mask around the stage, making sure that whenever users watch your SWF, they only see what you intended them to see, even if they resize the Flash player.

Enter Graphic at Current Frame

Here are the basic details on the Enter Graphic at Current Frame extension:

- **Author**: Dave Logan
- **License**: Free
- **Availability**: Flash MX 2004 and higher
- **URL**: http://www.dave-logan.com/weblog/?p=46

Usually, when you edit a symbol on the stage, Flash automatically takes you to frame 1 of that symbol, which can be immensely frustrating if you were halfway through a 30-frame run cycle and wanted to edit the frame you were currently viewing. Enter Graphic at Current Frame solves this dilemma by automatically moving to the correct frame when you edit a symbol. This command is for editing symbols set to Loop or Play Once.

FrameEDIT

Here are the basic details on the FrameEDIT extension:

- **Author**: Dave Wolfe
- **License**: Free
- **Availability**: Flash MX 2004 and higher
- **URL**: http://toonmonkey.com/extensions.html

FrameEDIT is similar to Enter Graphic at Current Frame, but there are two differences. When editing a symbol, instead of moving the playhead to the frame you were currently viewing like Enter Graphic at Current Frame, it moves the playhead to the same frame number you were on before entering the symbol. This comes in handy, because oftentimes, when animating a head with nested facial animation, for example, the nested animation becomes out of sync as a result of copying, pasting, and moving keyframes. The frame being displayed may not be the frame you want to be displayed, and FrameEDIT will take you to the correct frame. This works best when the main timeline and the nested timelines are the same length. The second difference is in the way it deals with symbols set to Single Frame. When you select a symbol set to Single Frame, it will move the playhead to the same frame that is being displayed.

Frame Extender

Here are the basic details on the Frame Extender extension:

- **Author**: Dave Wolfe
- **License**: Free
- **Availability**: Flash MX 2004 and higher
- **URL**: http://toonmonkey.com/extensions.html

Frame Extender will extend each keyframe on the selected layer by the number of frames a user has entered. For example, you may have animated something with a keyframe on every frame and then realized you wanted the keyframes on every other frame. To extend the keyframes, you would select the layer, run the command, and then enter 1 in the input field. Each keyframe on the layer will then be extended by one frame.

Keyframe Jumper

Here are the basic details on the Keyframe Jumper extension:

- **Author**: Dave Logan
- **License**: Free
- **Availability**: Flash MX 2004 and higher
- **URL**: http://www.dave-logan.com/weblog/?p=46

Keyframe Jumper consists of two commands that will make the playhead jump to the next or previous keyframe on the current layer. This comes in handy when you are blocking out an animation and want to quickly see how the poses work together, especially when you're working on a long scene.

Layer Color

Here are the basic details on the Layer Color extension, which is shown in Figure 5-4:

- **Author**: Dave Wolfe
- **License**: Free
- **Availability**: Flash MX 2004 and higher
- **URL**: http://toonmonkey.com/extensions.html

Figure 5-4. The Layer Color interface

Layer Color is a command for quickly changing the color of selected layers. Flash lets you change colors only one layer at a time, but with Layer Color you can select multiple layers and change them all at once. Layers are selected by either clicking them in the timeline or selecting the symbols whose layer color you want to change.

LibAppend

Here are the basic details on the LibAppend extension, which is shown in Figure 5-5:

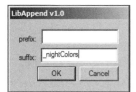

- **Author**: Dave Wolfe
- **License**: Free
- **Availability**: Flash MX 2004 and higher
- **URL**: http://toonmonkey.com/extensions.html

Figure 5-5. The LibAppend interface

LibAppend will append text to the beginning or end of the names of selected symbols in the library. This is handy when building new characters based on previously built characters or making variations of existing characters. For example, if you have a character and you want to make a version with different colors for nighttime, you can select all of the symbols in the library that make up that character, and then run LibAppend and add a prefix of "night." After making the color changes, you can then safely drop those symbols into a scene with the daytime colors and not have to worry about the night colors replacing the day colors. This is also useful for combining FLAs without having to worry about symbol conflicts.

Library Items Renamer

Here are the basic details on the Library Items Renamer extension, which is shown in Figure 5-6:

- **Author**: Sascha Balkau
- **License**: Free
- **Availability**: Flash MX 2004 and higher
- **URL**: http://hiddenresource.corewatch.net/archives/3

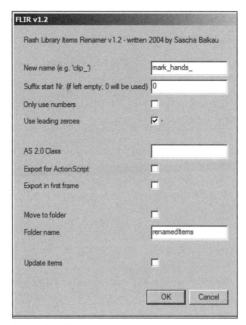

Figure 5-6. The Library Items Renamer interface

Library Items Renamer will rename all selected items in the library at once with a number appended to the end of the name. This is great when you need to rename a lot of symbols that have the same name, such as a series of hand positions or mouth shapes.

Magic Tween

Here are the basic details on the Magic Tween extension:

- **Author**: Dave Wolfe
- **License**: Free
- **Availability**: Flash MX 2004 and higher
- **URL**: http://toonmonkey.com/extensions.html

Magic Tween is a command that adds a tween to the selected frames, and it will determine whether a motion tween or shape tween should be added. This is very useful when working with characters that are made up of a combination of symbols and shapes. However, because it checks the content of an animation layer by layer, using it to add tweens is slower than adding them with a regular motion tween command, so it's best to only use it on characters made up of a mix of shapes and symbols.

111

Merge Layers

Here are the basic details on the Merge Layers extension:

- **Author**: Dave Wolfe
- **License**: Free
- **Availability**: Flash MX 2004 and higher
- **URL**: http://toonmonkey.com/extensions.html

Merge Layers will merge the selected frames of multiple layers into a single layer. This is useful for a number of situations, such as combining multiple shape-tweened lines so they can be filled or flattening a character onto one layer. Tweened frames should be converted to keyframes first, and any layers that you don't want merged should be locked.

MoveRegpoint

Here are the basic details on the MoveRegpoint extension:

- **Author**: Klaas Kielmann
- **License**: Free
- **Availability**: Flash MX 2004 and higher
- **URL**: http://www.adobe.com/exchange

MoveRegpoint will move a symbol's registration point to the same location as the transformation point. This is tremendously useful during character setup. It's good practice to make sure that your registration point is where you want a symbol to rotate from, so that if you need to move the transformation point, all you need to do to get it back to the registration point is double-click it. Normally, this involves editing the symbol, moving the artwork inside, exiting the symbol, and repositioning it. MoveRegpoint takes care of all that with the click of a button.

Multi Swap

Here are the basic details on the Multi Swap extension:

- **Author**: Dave Wolfe
- **License**: Free
- **Availability**: Flash MX 2004 and higher
- **URL**: http://toonmonkey.com/extensions.html

Multi Swap allows you to swap out multiple symbols across multiple frames and replace them with symbols from the library. Sometimes, early on in a production, the assets you're animating with aren't final. You may find that you need to go back to finished animation and swap out older symbols for updated versions. Normally, this is a tedious and time-consuming process, but Multi Swap makes it a piece of cake. To use it, select the symbols on the stage that you want to swap out; select the symbol in the Library that you want to replace them with, and run the command. To swap symbols across multiple frames, you must first enable Edit Multiple Frames.

New Anim Clip

Here are the basic details on the New Anim Clip extension, which is shown in Figure 5-7:

Figure 5-7. The New Anim Clip interface

- **Author**: Dave Wolfe
- **License**: free
- **Availability**: Flash MX 2004 and higher
- **URL**: http://toonmonkey.com/extensions.html

New Anim Clip is a command extension that allows you to nest an animation sequence into a single symbol and keep the animation correctly registered on the stage. Nesting your animation into a symbol allows you to easily rotate, scale, or reposition an entire sequence by dealing with one symbol rather than many symbols across many frames on many layers. This makes it easier to do camera moves and fix composition problems. To use the extension, first select all of the frames that you want to nest, right-click the timeline, and select Cut Frames. Run the plug-in, and a panel will pop up asking for a Layer Name, Symbol Name, and a choice between a Graphic Symbol or a Movie Clip. If you leave the Layer Name or Symbol Name fields blank, the default Flash names will be used (Layer 1, Symbol 1, etc.). When you click OK, you will be editing a new symbol with a single blank keyframe. Right-click this keyframe, and select Paste Frames.

Search and Replace

Here are the basic details on the Search and Replace extension, which is shown in Figure 5-8:

Figure 5-8. The Search and Replace interface

- **Author**: Dave Wolfe
- **License**: Free
- **Availability**: Flash MX 2004 and higher
- **URL**: http://www.toonmonkey.com/extensions.html

Search and Replace will search for text in library item names and replace it with something else; it offers the option of searching all library items or just the selected items. This is very useful for many reasons, but one example is when you build a character based on an already existing character. Let's say the original character is named Joe, and all of Joe's symbols begin with "joe". You've built a character named Bob using Joe's symbols as a starting point, so now all of Bob's symbols begin with "joe". Using Search and Replace, it takes only a few seconds to have "joe" replaced by "bob" in all of the symbols in the library.

Skip Around

Here are the basic details on the Skip Around extension:

- **Author**: Dave Logan
- **License**: Free
- **Availability**: Flash MX 2004 and higher
- **URL**: http://www.dave-logan.com/weblog/?p=46

Skip Around is a set of three commands that allow you to jump forward and backward on the timeline by a set interval of frames. The Set Skip command opens a panel that lets you set the number of frames to skip by. Skip Ahead and Skip Back will then skip forward and backward by the number of frames you set using the Set Skip command.

Symbolize Frames

Here are the basic details on the Symbolize Frames extension:

- **Author**: Dave Logan
- **License**: Free
- **Availability**: Flash MX 2004 and higher
- **URL**: http://www.dave-logan.com/weblog/?p=46

Symbolize Frames will convert the contents of keyframes into symbols with the same name and an incrementing number suffix. This can help speed up a traditional approach to Flash animation by letting you draw your keys and then quickly turn them into symbols for further manipulation. It can also help when building mouth charts, eyelid charts, hand charts, and so on. You can draw each position on a keyframe, and once you're satisfied, turn each frame into a symbol.

Toggle Guide

Here are the basic details on the Toggle Guide extension:

- **Author**: Dave Wolfe
- **License**: Free
- **Availability**: Flash MX 2004 and higher
- **URL**: http://toonmonkey.com/extensions.html

Toggle Guide will toggle the selected layers between guide and normal layer types. Guide layers don't render or export to SWF files, so if you want to keep an element in the Flash file but not export it, changing it to a guide is a good option. Being able to quickly toggle guide layers on and off for multiple layers also makes it easier to export layers for compositing. Use Toggle Guide by either selecting layers in the timeline or selecting elements on the stage.

Toggle Outline

Here are the basic details on the Toggle Outline extension:

- **Author**: Dave Wolfe
- **License**: Free
- **Availability**: Flash MX 2004 and higher
- **URL**: http://toonmonkey.com/extensions.html

Toggle Outline will toggle selected layers between outline and normal view. Changing a layer's rendering mode to Outline lets you work with symbols hidden behind it while still being able to see the symbols on the outlined layer. Like Toggle Guide, use Toggle Outline by selecting layers in the timeline or by selecting elements on the stage.

Trace Sequence

Here are the basic details on the Trace Sequence extension, which is shown in Figure 5-9:

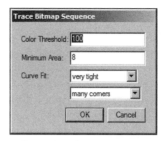

- **Author**: Dave Wolfe
- **License**: Free
- **Availability**: Flash MX 2004 and higher
- **URL**: http://toonmonkey.com/extensions.html

Trace Sequence will trace bitmaps on all the keyframes of the selected layer. If you are using Flash as an ink and paint tool for traditional animation, Trace Sequence will allow you to quickly

Figure 5-9. The Trace Sequence interface

vectorize scanned drawings. If the drawing bitmaps are sequentially numbered, Flash will import them as a sequence of keyframes on the same layer. All you have to do to trace all of the bitmaps into vectors is select the layer and run the command.

Tween 2 Keys

Here are the basic details on the Tween 2 Keys extension:

- **Author**: Dave Wolfe
- **License**: Free
- **Availability**: Flash MX 2004 and higher
- **URL**: http://toonmonkey.com/extensions.html

Tween 2 Keys will convert selected tweened frames to keyframes on twos. Traditional animation for film and television is usually done at 24fps on twos, meaning that each drawing is exposed for two frames of film, effectively making the animation play back at 12fps. Animating on twos at 24fps cuts down the amount of work you need to do, but still lets you animate on ones for fast actions or camera moves. To use Tween 2 Keys, select the frames you want converted to twos and run the command.

ActionScript Tools

Now, we'll turn our attention to ActionScript tools—these are movie clips that you can add to your scenes that don't do anything in the Flash authoring environment but take effect when you view your animation as a SWF.

Camera

Here are the basic details on the Camera extension:

- **Author**: Jarrad Hope
- **License**: Free
- **Availability**: Flash 8 and higher
- **URL**: http://www.fat-pie.com/animationextensions

115

Camera is an extension that creates a movie clip camera symbol that, unlike similar cameras, can be rotated and works with Flash 8's filters. Instead of moving and sizing the artwork on the stage, you just need to move and resize or rotate the camera symbol. When you export your SWF, only the elements within the camera symbol's borders will be shown in the Flash player. Although this does not render to video, there are third-party applications that can render a SWF to video or image sequence.

Frame Jumper

Here are the basic details on the Frame Jumper extension:

- **Author**: Dave Wolfe
- **License**: Free
- **Availability**: Flash MX 2004 and higher
- **URL**: http://toonmonkey.com/extensions.html

Frame Jumper is a movie clip that you can add to your scenes for skipping ahead, jumping back, or looping a range of frames. This is especially useful for really long scenes that you only want to check a portion of. The Jump To buttons will jump to the frame number on the button, or you can type a number into the text field and click Jump To. The Skip By buttons will skip by the number of frames on the buttons, or you can type a number into the text field and click Skip By. Checking the Loop Frames button will loop between the frames in the two text fields below the check box. There is also a Quality drop-down menu that lets you quickly set the rendering quality of the SWF.

Where to download more extensions

There are many sites on the Internet with extensions available, but there are two sites in particular that are updated with commands that are specifically useful for animators. The first is the Cold Hard Flash plug-ins forum at http://bbs.coldhardflash.com. Cold Hard Flash is a blog that is focused on Flash character animation, and the forums are a great place to find and request not only extensions but also a lot of other good Flash tips, news, and job postings. The other site is Adobe Exchange, http://www.adobe.com/exchange (from here, navigate to the Flash portion of the site, and select the JSFL Extensions category from the drop-down menu). Although this site is not focused on animation, a lot of extensions there could aid you in your production.

Making your own commands

An entire book could be written about making your own extensions for Flash. But if you're not ready to dive into programming just yet, Flash has a useful tool that lets you record a series of actions and save them as a command. Let's make a couple commands that will aid you in your future productions.

Many animators get into the bad habit of creating motion tweens by right-clicking the timeline. The problem with this method is that it turns on the Sync option, preventing you from swapping symbols or changing which frame of a multiframe graphic symbol is displayed. So how does an animator quickly add motion tweens without Sync on? By making a command and setting a hotkey for it:

1. Right-click a frame on the timeline, and choose Create Motion Tween from the context menu.

2. In the Properties panel, uncheck the Sync option, as shown in Figure 5-10. You may have to double-click the Properties panel to expand it if you don't see this option.

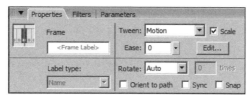

Figure 5-10. Deselect the Sync check box.

3. From the Windows menu, click History Panel from the Other Panels submenu.

4. Holding down the Ctrl key, click the commands for Create Motion Tween and Frame Property; see Figure 5-11.

Figure 5-11. Select Create Motion Tween and Frame Propert in the History Panel.

5. Click the disk icon in the lower right corner of the History panel to save those two actions as a command. Name your command Insert Motion Tween, and click OK.

And that's all there is to it! You can now access your new command from the Commands menu, and you can assign a keyboard shortcut to it for quick access. Let's create one more command. This command will convert a tween to keyframes and remove the tween. Why would you want to do this? Tweens are calculated linearly, but often, you'll need something to move in an arc. Although you can do this with guide layers, it's usually faster to just do it yourself. This command is also useful because shape tweens have been known to corrupt scenes, so it's best to convert them to keyframes and remove the shape tween.

1. Select a frame, and change the tween type to Motion in the Properties panel.

2. Right-click one of the tweened frames, and choose Convert to Keyframes from the context menu.

3. With the frame still selected, change the tween type to None in the Properties panel. It's important to use the Properties panel when removing the motion tween, because unlike using the menus, using the Properties panel won't change other frame properties. This ensures that you don't turn on the Sync option when running our new command.

4. Open the History panel, and holding the Ctrl key, select Convert to Keyframes and Frame Property.

5. Click the disk icon; name your command Key and Remove Tween, and click OK.

If you're interested in making your own extensions, the book *Extending Flash MX 2004* by Keith Peters and Todd Yard (*friends of ED, 2004, ISBN: 1-59059-304-9*) is the best place to start. It covers everything you need to know about programming Flash extensions. The authors assume you have a basic understanding of programming, but the book starts off simply enough that even if you have no programming experience, you should still be able to follow along. The book was written for Flash MX 2004, but everything in it still applies to newer versions of Flash.

Summary

In this chapter, you learned what extensions are, why you want them, and where to find them. We listed several extensions that you may find particularly useful for animation, and you even learned the basics of making your own commands. Many of the boring, repetitive tasks associated with Flash animation can now become a thing of the past!

Chapter 6

FRAME BY FRAME ANIMATION

By Allan S. Rosson

This chapter covers a method for animating frame by frame using Flash symbols in a manner that is closer to traditional animation techniques. Modern technology has, in many ways, eliminated much of the drudgery of doing animation in contrast to how animation was created many years ago. However, the basic techniques and thought processes at the very core of creating quality animation remain the same. In other chapters of this book, the subjects of creating character symbols, character libraries, naming conventions for symbols, and other preproduction issues will be covered in greater detail.

The purpose of this chapter is twofold: to give the reader a better understanding of the mechanics of how to effectively manipulate symbols of a character on a frame by frame basis and to stress the direct relationship between an animator's acting ability and the mechanics behind the movements that are being created.

The following downloadable files accompany this chapter:

- Generic Man Library.fla
- fbf _audio track.fla
- fbf tutorial 01_blocking.fla
- fbf tutorial 02_inbetweening.fla
- fbf tutorial 03_lip sync.fla
- fbf tutorial 04_eye acting.fla

You will be starting with the `fbf_audio track.fla` file as your working file. As you progress through the different stages, you will save your file with a different name before continuing with the next stage. Saving your work in stages is very important so that, in case of a mistake, you can always revert to a previous version. The other four tutorial files are for reference, so you can check your work against these completed stages of this exercise.

A few words on fundamentals

Early in my career, I was told that animation was 95 percent thinking. Now, some 20 years later, I've learned just how true that statement really is! As an animator, you will be making hundreds of decisions while working on any given sequence regardless of the medium you choose. How effective your animation becomes will depend on the tried and tested application and understanding of the basics. If you have traditional training, you have an advantage. The thought process behind creating animation with Flash is no different than any other medium with regard to speed, weight, anticipation, distortion, squash and stretch, and all of the other wonderful things animators talk about. Developing a really good grasp of these basic principles takes time, study, and experience. However, once you have mastered them, you will have the most powerful tools at your disposal, whether you animate with pencil on paper or symbols on a timeline.

A sense of timing

To achieve natural or believable movement, it is very important to allow what you are animating to speed up and slow down. Objects, people, animals and so forth simply do not start and stop on a dime. In the cartoon world, there are exceptions for comic effect, of course, but a good rule of thumb is to always consider slow ins and slow outs. This is simply a matter of adjusting the amount of change from frame to frame to create the feeling that something is either speeding up or slowing down. The less change you incorporate from frame to frame, the slower the speed; the greater the change, the faster the speed. This process may seem elementary, but it is often lacking in an inexperienced animator's work. Often referred to as a sense of timing, this element is one of the most important ingredients to the success of your character's acting.

As you go along, you will discover that the subtle manipulation of this principal will be a vital life-giving property to your work. This principal is also directly related to the weight of anything that is animated. A skilled animator can make a simple circle outline appear to have the properties of the heaviest bowling ball or the lightest soap bubble depending on how it is treated with timing. The bouncing ball exercise (see Figure 6-1) is often thought of as the most simple and effective way of developing a sense of timing: the ball slows down at the highest point of the bounce due to gravity and speeds up as it descends for the next bounce. With this exercise, you can gain a real appreciation of how the physics of motion relate to the principles of slowing in and slowing out, as well as the squashing and stretching of an object.

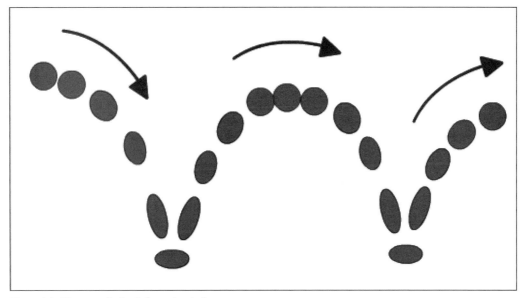

Figure 6-1. Diagram of a basic bouncing ball

You are an actorrrrr!

How natural and believable your characters appear with regard to their animation will depend on your ability to understand who they are as characters and what they are going through both emotionally and physically. There can be a tendency for those who are less experienced in animation to have their characters overact or overreact. This occurs frequently with unnecessary hand or arm gestures. My feeling has always been to not have anything move unless there is a reason for it to move. The reasons for movement can be very simple or quite complex, but they will always be based on either physical laws of motion or believable emotional motivation with regards to character. Watch the way people behave when they express themselves in conversation. You can see how the gestures they make most always support what they are saying. Occasionally, the strongest gesture they make might be no gesture at all!

Reference for acting

Acting styles for live action motion pictures have certainly changed over the years, and it's always a great source of inspiration for animators to study the various eras and pick up on those little things typical of the times. I have always been partial to the classic Warner Bros. style of acting for animation, and my favorite animator has always been the great Virgil Ross. His work demonstrates a complete mastery of both pantomime and dialogue acting. Wonderful examples of this can be seen in cartoons such as Warner Bros. "Rhapsody Rabbit" (1946) and "A Hare Grows in Manhattan" (1947).

The animators of Virgil's time made a study of silent screen comedy. Chaplin, Keaton, and Lloyd were their teachers of comedic timing. I would highly recommend watching as much of their work as possible to anyone interested in creating animation—single-frame through your favorite parts! Study not only the way these actors moved but also when and why.

123

Pantomime acting for animation has its challenges but can be a tremendous amount of fun. If your work is done well, it can be displayed around the world and your idea or message will communicate instantly. Pantomime can be slightly more exaggerated with regard to poses and timing to get the point across, but be careful about going too far, as you might lose the essence of what you are trying to convey.

Acting with dialogue presents a whole other set of challenges. The finer points of analyzing a voice track for acting points will be explored further along in this chapter.

The character library

Let's review character library basics quickly, because you will be using the library quite frequently while creating your animation. Recall from previous chapters that character libraries consist of all the parts or Flash symbols that make up a particular character, usually assembled in a turn-around model consisting of the character in front, three-quarter front, profile, a three-quarter rear, and full rear views. Often, these poses are flipped to create a full 360 degree rotation of the character around the Y axis. All of the symbols that make up a particular character usually follow a specific naming convention. For an in-depth look at how character libraries are constructed and organized, refer to Chapter 3 of this book. When a library is being prepared, great care is taken to ensure that all of the various parts of a character (arms, legs, etc.) connect correctly and that the rotation points on each symbol are correctly placed. In each view of the character, a mouth chart and an eye chart symbol are incorporated into the make up of the character's head symbols (the exceptions being the three-quarter rear and full rear views, as these features would not be seen).

Let's say you are creating a cartoon series consisting of a number of main characters. With a well-built and comprehensive character library, you can be way ahead of the game in terms of how fast you are able to create your animation. A character's turn-around can be saved as a master symbol and will contain most everything needed to animate the character in a very effective way. This is a process of breaking down the master symbol in progressive stages as you animate and will be explored in detail further along in this chapter.

This method also goes a long way in helping to keep your character on model throughout a long sequence. If, at some point in a sequence, your character has gone off model because of too much skewing, sizing, rotation, or distortion of symbols as you are animating, you can always drag an instance of the master symbol back onto your stage from your library. Then, you can break it down to whatever point you need to go back on model. Staying on model is also much easier when you have a team of animators working with the same character.

This would be a good opportunity to download and explore the Generic Man library that we'll be using for the tutorials in this chapter.

Animating a scene

Creating effective animation is difficult no matter how you look at it. It takes patience and persistence. Ultimately, how you chose to work in Flash will be up to you, of course, but I hope this chapter can provide for you some constructive advice that may save you some headaches down the road. This section breaks down the various stages of animating using a character library.

Keeping it simple (as much as possible)

My own standard method of working is basically comprised of four stages, shown in Figure 6-2.

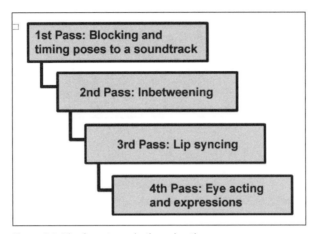

Figure 6-2. The four stages in the animation process

For any given project, I've found that these stages almost always apply to a certain degree. However, every project has different challenges. The more experience you acquire working with Flash, the better you will be able to handle any situation.

A few words about layers and tweens

In the example in this chapter, we will only be using one layer for the animation due to its simplicity. In my own work, I prefer creating new layers only as I need them. If I need to move a character's symbol in front or behind another symbol, I use the Arrange function, under Modify in the main menu, as it gives me more control on a frame-by-frame basis. With very few exceptions, I prefer to not use tweening in my animation, and I tend to discourage it for beginners until they develop their basic skills and a sense of timing in their animation. In Chapter 7 of this book, there are some wonderful techniques for layers and tweening, but I feel that these are advanced techniques and the beginner should approach them as such.

In the next section, we will begin the process of setting up a scene to prepare for animation.

Getting started

Let's begin by opening the Flash file labeled fbf_audio track.fla. As you complete the steps of each stage in the process of your animation, you will be saving your file with a new name before you progress to the next stage. For the purposes of this tutorial, we will be working in the Flash default stage size of 550X400 and a setting of 15 fps (frames per second). As you can see in Figure 6-3, there is an audio file on the main timeline that contains the dialog to which you will be animating.

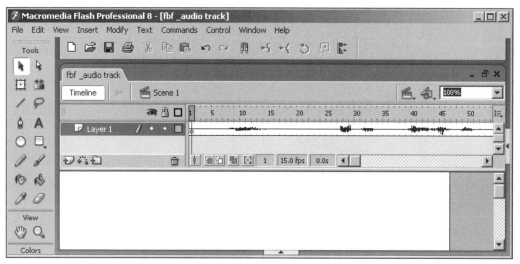

Figure 6-3. The audio track on the main timeline

The first step is to create a new layer on the main timeline above the layer containing the audio track. To do this, click the Layer 1 label to the left of the audio track. Next, click the new layer icon below the Layer 1 label; it is the icon with a plus sign immediately to the left of the trash can. You should now see Layer 2 above the audio track of Layer 1. Layer 2 will contain your animation. You may rename this layer anything you wish by simply double-clicking the Layer 2 label and renaming it. For this exercise, rename the layer Animation. Now we need to bring the character onto the main timeline. Click Window on the main menu followed by Library. When the library opens, click the first symbol in the library list. You should see the character appear in the library window Figure 6-4. You can hide and reopen the library list by clicking the blue strip at the top of the library window.

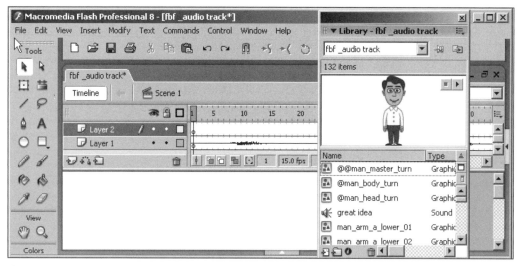

Figure 6-4. Shows the character in the library's window

It's not a bad idea to lock the layer containing the audio to prevent any symbol that you drag from the library from being placed on that layer of the timeline. Locking the layer is also handy for any new action layers that you create where you do not want specific symbols to be placed. For now, lock your audio layer, but keep your animation layer unlocked. Now, click and drag the character from the library window onto the stage underneath the main timeline. As you can see, the character will appear rather large for the size of the stage. Before we resize this symbol and begin animation, we need to convert it into a new symbol and give it a new name. For this example, we will call it *my animation (using an asterisk before the name will place this new symbol at the top of the library list for easy access). To do this, click the symbol that is on the stage and press F8 on your keyboard. You will see a prompt to give this new symbol a name. Also make sure that the Graphic radio button is selected for the symbol type.

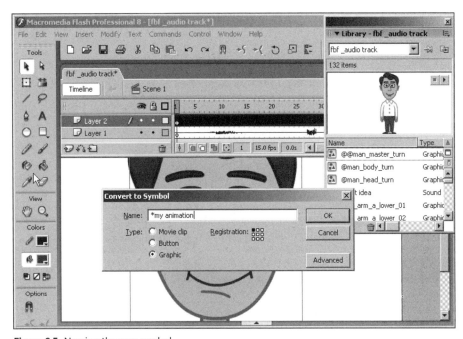

Figure 6-5. Naming the new symbol

In doing this, you apply the 100 Percent Rule, which is covered in Chapter 3. Following the 100 Percent Rule preserves the consistency of individual symbol sizes once a character is broken apart. If this were not done first and you were to break a character's master symbol apart, resize it to fit your stage, and begin animating, most likely any instances of a symbol you drag from the library to your stage will be the incorrect size. They will be the size of the first instance you dragged out before resizing to fit your stage. This is a headache you might like to avoid.

Now, let's resize our character on the stage. Click the symbol to highlight it, and select the resize tool from the top of the tool bar on the left, just underneath the solid arrow. Hold down the Shift key, select a corner of the highlighted symbol, and resize it to better fit the stage. Our character will be speaking dialog and doing some body acting, so don't make him too small. Now, there is one last thing to do to prepare for the first stage of animation. Click the Layer 1 label of the audio track to select the whole layer. Go to Edit ➤ Timeline ➤ Copy Frames, and double-click the character symbol on your stage. You will now be inside the symbol you created for your animation.

Create a new layer by selecting the new layer icon as you did previously. Click the new blank frame. Go to Edit ➤ Timeline ➤ Paste Frames, or right-click the blank keyframe and select Paste Frames from the context menu. You should now have a layer containing the soundtrack for your animation, which is necessary because you will be working on your animation inside this symbol and will be constantly scrubbing back and forth along the timeline to analyze for lip sync. Also, when you test your animation by publishing a SWF file, only the audio on the main timeline will be heard. Make sure you have an equal number of frames for your animation layer by clicking the empty spot of the timeline that is equal to the last space of the soundtrack. Pressing F5 on your keyboard will establish an equal number of frames. You are now ready to begin the first stage of animation. At this point, I highly recommend clicking Save As and renaming your file. I will be using the `fbf tutorial_blocking 01.fla` file for the next demonstration.

First pass: blocking and timing poses

Now the fun begins. The next step is to block out, or set up key poses, to begin the character's acting. In this example, the Generic Man character will be speaking and acting out a line of dialog, "Hey! That's a *great* idea!" I chose this example both for its simplicity and because it provides a variety of acting points I would like to cover.

Take some time and really listen to not only what the character is saying but, more important, how it's being said. This is where your talents as an actor will come into play. When I receive a new scene to animate, the first thing I do is to listen very carefully for all of the places that have the greatest emphasis on a word or a phrase. I'm visualizing in my mind how the character looks while speaking the dialog. If I hit a place where I'm not sure what should be happening, I get out of my chair and act out the dialog to try and find the most natural actions that will support what is being said. This can make you feel kind of silly at first, but you'll get used to it. The funny thing is, as you gain more experience, you may find this practice not as necessary, because you will instinctively know how a line of dialog should play out.

Later in this chapter, as we get into the actual lip sync, we will talk about some finer points of animation that will really help bring life to the character.

Let's take a look at the character's turn-around. Double-click the character that you have set up in your *my animation symbol. This takes you inside the character's turn-around symbol. By clicking the red tab and dragging it back and forth along the timeline, you will see the character do a complete rotation displaying how he looks from eight points of view. Now, try double-clicking the character's head symbol. You now have a complete head turn. By double-clicking any blank area of the stage, you will return to the previous symbol's timeline. By double-clicking various parts of the character's body, the hands for example, you will find that the symbol may contain numerous parts that can be called up in the Properties panel and used for animation on any given frame. This is how we will create rough poses for the character.

Click the first frame of your animation layer, and place a key frame there by pressing F6 on your keyboard. Click your character's symbol to highlight it. Press Ctrl/Cmd+F3 on your keyboard to bring up the Properties panel. To close or reopen the Properties panel, click the small arrow at the bottom middle of the stage. Select the frame of the turnaround symbol that shows the character's three-quarter front position, so the character is facing slightly to the right. To do this, change the frame number in the properties panel to 8 as this frame corresponds to the character's three-quarter front position. Now, press Enter. By the way, you will be selecting various mouth shapes and eye blinks later on using this same steps. Keep the selection you have made for the character's three-quarter front position at the single frame setting (see Figure 6-6).

Figure 6-6. Selecting a frame in the Properties panel

Break the symbol apart once by pressing Ctrl/Cmd+B on your keyboard (see Figure 6-7). This frees the various symbols that make up the character's three-quarter front position to be posed in a more appropriate way.

Figure 6-7. Breaking a symbol apart for posing

If you select the head symbol and then select the rotation tool, you will see that the pivot point for the character's head is placed in a manner that allows for a natural rotation near the neck. Figure 6-8 shows where I've started placing key frames along the timeline to indicate a pose at an important place in the dialog. On key frame 8, the character's body symbol is broken apart once to gain access for posing the arms and hands. Figure 6-8 shows the words of dialog on a layer to better indicate why key frames were placed at those specific locations.

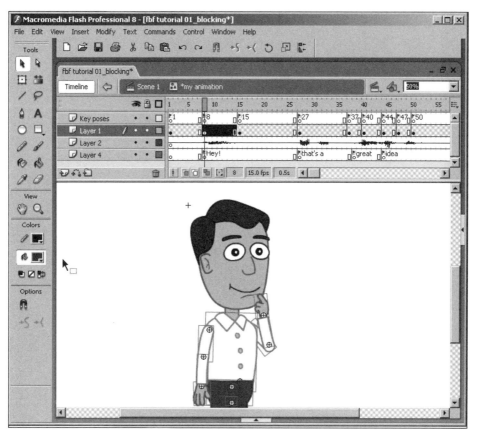

Figure 6-8. The dialog shows where key frames are placed.

As with the head symbol, you will notice that all the symbols that make up the arms and hands have their pivot points properly placed so that shoulders, elbows, wrists, and hands can join up easily as pieces are rotated to create poses. This sequence consists of six primary poses to act out the dialog. They are on frames 1, 8, 27, 37, 40, and 50. The other key frames I have placed help me to keep in mind how I want the main actions to follow through.

Look carefully at the poses that I've set up on these key frames and listen to what's being said at those places in the dialog. On frame 27, as the character begins to say "that's a," his head turns toward camera, and he gestures with his finger in the air as though a thought has just come to him. On frame 37, when he begins to say the word "great," his whole body goes into what is referred to as an *anticipation*; this is an action that starts the character moving in the opposite direction of where he will eventually go. For acting purposes, it is used to emphasize or accent certain places where the dialog is also being emphasized. As you reference the blocking tutorial file, scroll back and forth along the timeline between frames 27, 37, and 40. Watch how these simple poses support what the character is saying. The poses on frames 44, 47, and 50 are used to slow or settle the character down as we get to the end of the sequence.

As you study the different tutorial files, you may see subtle changes in the development of the actions. As I said early on, you will be making hundreds of decisions as you work on your animation to determine what your character will be doing or how fast or slow an action should be. This stage in the process is still very early, but it's very important. Your decisions here will have an effect on everything that follows. What do you want to emphasize? Is your character happy, or sad, or angry? Strive to find the simplest and most effective way to communicate your character's emotions. For example, if your character is sad, the head could be lowered and the shoulders stooped slightly. At this stage, it is also very important to not break apart the character's head symbol. Doing that makes it very difficult to move the character's head as one unit. It also prevents you from calling up the different head turns that are arranged inside of the head symbol. It is best to break apart the head symbol only when you have completely finished the next stage of inbetweening and you are ready to proceed to the stage after that, which is lip sync. When you have finished creating your rough poses, save your changes. Then click Save As, and rename this file as your inbetweening one.

Second pass: inbetweening and body acting

OK, here is where you really start to apply some animation basics. For this section, please refer to the inbetweening tutorial file fbf tutorial 02_inbetweening.fla as you work on your own file. Inbetweening isn't just a process of linking together the basic poses you've created; it's where you actually start to put life into your animation. At this stage, listening to the audio becomes even more important. As you listen, you'll find that additional movements suggest themselves. Again, you are also making countless decisions about how fast or how slow movements should be made to support the acting in the most effective way possible.

At the beginning of this sequence, from frames 1-15, I had the character rise up and come down as he says "hey." It's a little thing, but it supports what he is saying in a very subtle way; it's as though he were rising up on his toes to make the point. To do this, place a key frame, by pressing F6 on your keyboard, on frame 2 of your Animation layer, and by using your arrow keys, begin nudging the character upward over successive key frames until you reach frame 8. We know from our blocking stage that the highest point the character will go for this move is frame 8 and then he will come down again until frame 15. Notice in the tutorial file how the movement here is slower at the beginning, speeds up slightly through the middle section, and again slows down when the character comes to a holding pose on frame 15—the progressive movements are tapered using subtle changes between frames at the beginning, more noticeable changes in the middle section, then again less drastic changes at the end. This creates the slow in, slow out that is referred to near the beginning of this chapter; it is one of the most vital aspects of your animation, and its use should be on your mind at all times while you are animating each and every frame.

Now, what else is happening here on these frames? The character is raising his hand and arm up to reach his chin on the second pose. Again, notice how the movement is faster in the middle of the move and slows down as he comes to rest. You'll also notice that at frames 5 and 6, where the largest change in the move happens, I chose to change the hand symbol to the pointing finger, which will be used when slowing into the second pose and will keep the action smooth. Notice also that, during these frames, the character's head is slightly rotating to meet up with his hand on frame 15. At this point in the sequence, we've come to what's called a *hold pose*. The character has eased into a natural position and is ready to go into his next action of turning his head to the front view as in Figure 6-9.

Figure 6-9. Character's head turn after hold pose on frame 15

Reaching our next pose won't be too difficult at all, and we can do it smoothly in two frames! Here, the character will be turning his head to the front view as he says the next part of the line. We want to try to make this transition as smooth as possible.

Here's a quick tip on moving the head symbol from the three-quarter front to the front view and to minimize a jumpy or popping look in the animation. With the head in three-quarter front on frame 24, the last frame of the hold pose, I made a keyframe on frame 25 and moved the head slightly in the direction I wanted to go. Then, I made a keyframe on frame 26 and switched to the front view head by highlighting the symbol, and through the Properties window, I selected the front head view. On frame 27, I continued moving the head slightly in the same direction with less of a change until the head came to rest. By doing this, you are slowing in and slowing out of these movements: you are using the actual change of the three-quarter front view to the front view of the head as the fastest part of your timing and softening that transition at both the beginning and ending of the move.

Also, notice the hand movement to the new pose on frame 27. As the hand starts to move on frame 25, it actually rotates slightly counterclockwise from the wrist in order to give more of a believable looseness to the wrist joint. This is known as a *whip action*, and in this case, its use is very gentle. Again, the hand's view changes on frame 25 through the Properties panel, and the hand stops on 27.

From frame 27 to frame 33, you can see we have another holding pose. While you are animating, try to resist the feeling or temptation that you should have something in motion at all times for the sake of animation. It just isn't necessary. What will really give life and a believable appearance to your work are the natural pauses that occur between the actions that you are creating. Without these pauses, there are no natural starting and stopping points on which to base the timing of an action. A perfect example would be the next bit of action we will be creating for frames 34 through 50. I commented earlier that you may notice some modification to the poses as the tutorials progress. The pose on frame 37 of the inbetweening tutorial was modified and made stronger than the pose in the blocking tutorial. We are using this pose to create an anticipation, which can be seen in Figure 6-10. On the timeline, you will see that this is the pose where the character actually begins to say the word "great." To move into this pose, however, means starting a few frames back. The timing here is critical. We don't want the movement to be too slow by starting too far back or too abrupt by not starting soon enough. A good way to gauge this is by scrolling back and forth on the timeline to get a feel for when the move should start. I have it starting on frame 34.

Figure 6-10. The character's anticipation into the word "great"

Notice how in the fbf tutorial 02_inbetweening.fla the character's head changes again during the fastest part of the action to the three-quarter position on frame 36. The hands are now changing to the closed fist position, and the arms are rising up in contrast to the lowering of the head and torso.

As the character's body begins to rise up on frame 38, see how the head is continuing to rotate slightly downward? This is another example of a very gentle whip action. Notice the speed with which the character goes from frames 37 to 40. This is the highest point of this action (see Figure 6-11) and the strongest emphasis on the word "great." The arm movement supports the emotion of how this word is being said.

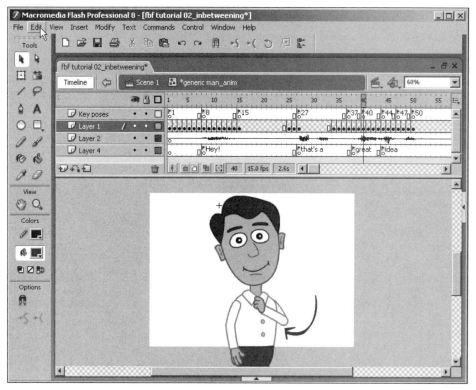

Figure 6-11. The character's highest point and the arching motion of the arm

On frame 41, the character begins to settle down from the extreme pose of frame 40 and continues to settle and relax until we reach frame 50 (see Figure 6-12). Notice the slight tilt of the head in frames 45 through 50; this helps to emphasize the word "idea" and to increase the relaxed feeling in the character's head and neck.

How are you coming along? As you review your work, check all of the actions that you have created to be sure that their movements follow a smooth path. Check your timing as well. Are you slowing in and out of your poses effectively? When you are satisfied with this stage, click Save As, and rename your file Lip Sync to prepare for the next stage of lip syncing the dialog. At any time during these tutorials, you can easily publish an SWF file of your animation by pressing Ctrl/Cmd+Enter on your keyboard. This file will be a compressed version of your animation.

Figure 6-12. Shows the character's last pose

Third pass: lip sync

Before we get into the actual lip sync, let's have a look at the character's mouth chart (see Figure 6-13). This diagram shows all of the mouth shapes that are in the character's front view. The frame numbers that go with each mouth shape correspond with the frame numbers of the other mouth charts that complete the character's head turn. For example, the "O" sound on frame 7 of the front head view would be the same type of mouth shape for frame 7 on the three-quarter head view, and likewise for the profile. You'll soon become acquainted with which mouth shapes go with which frames, as they are consistent.

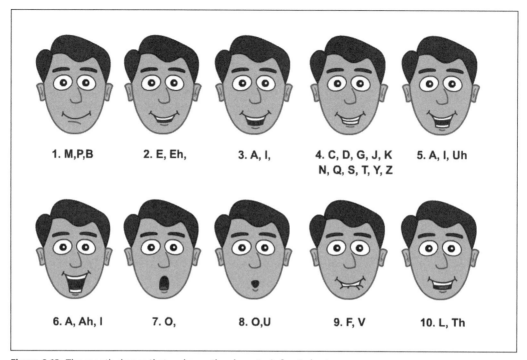

Figure 6-13. The mouth shapes that make up the character's front view

When you are ready to do the lip sync, double-click the character's head symbol. This will bring you into the head turn-around symbol. Go to frame 8, which should be the three-quarter view head that matches the head on the first frame of your animation timeline, and double-click it. You should now see all the symbols that make up the character's three-quarter view head. Click the mouth to highlight it. Then double-click it. Now, you should see all the frames that make up the character's mouth shapes (see Figure 6-14). These ten frames will enable you to animate any vowel sound or consonant needed for any dialog you choose.

Scroll back and forth along the timeline to see how the different mouth shapes work. Frame 1 represents the letters "M," "B," and "P." Frames 2 and 3 can be used for "E" or the beginning of an "A" sound. Frame 4 can be used for "C," "CH," "D," "G," "K," "T" . . . well, you get the idea. Frames 7 and 8 are, of course, "O" sounds. Frame 9 is for "F" or "V," and frame 10 is for "TH" or "L" sounds. Each head symbol position contains a mouth chart with the exception of the three-quarter back and the full back views, since the mouth would never be seen in these positions. You can call up these mouth charts through your Properties window the same way you have been doing with the different head positions or hand shapes. To return to your Animation timeline, you can double-click a blank portion of the stage until you reach your animation timeline, or click the symbol label for your animation just to the right of the Scene1 label at the top of the timeline.

Figure 6-14. The frames that make up the character's mouth chart

Lip sync

As you listen to the dialog and scroll back and forth along the timeline, you'll be listening for the exact beginning and ending of words and phrases. Once a selection is made, the mouth position will be perfectly registered with the character's head no matter where the head is moving, because it was once part of the original head symbol. This is why I feel that it is important to not break apart the head symbol until you are satisfied with the general head and body acting of the character. Every stage of this process supports the one following. If you break apart too soon and try to move around the separate symbols of the head, you'll be in danger of going off model, which can be a real headache.

It is not necessary to try and match every single syllable of a word with a different mouth shape. This can sometimes give the mouth a chatty appearance that is not convincing or natural. Sometimes, it might seem that some words on your audio track are slurred or spoken too quickly. With practice, you'll discover which mouth shape will work best to carry over two, three, or even more frames without ill effect. You'll be listening to your dialog until you can recite it in your sleep! Actually, pouring over the dialog track especially during the blocking and inbetweening stages can reveal many interesting things that might otherwise go unnoticed. As you listen, try to pick up on every breath, every pause, every inflection—these are the things that can help you decide how to act out your scene.

Now, let's do some lip sync. Scroll along the timeline of your animation until you hear the character begin to speak the first word, "hey." Now, click the head symbol to highlight it, and press Ctrl/Cmd+B on your keyboard twice: the first time will break the head symbol from the head turn-around symbol, and the second break will give you access to the mouth chart. At this time, you will also have access to the eye chart and eyebrow symbols, but do not try to animate those yet. Focus on just the lip sync for now. Select, from the Properties window, the mouth shape that best fits the word "hey." Review the frame selection process from Stage 1's blocking pass in Figure 6-6. Since it is an "A" sound, maybe frame 2 or 3? In Figure 6-15, I actually placed this mouth a few frames earlier than when the actual sound started, to give the feeling that the character was getting a bit of a breath.

Figure 6-15. Selecting the proper mouth shape to begin the word "hey"

Lip sync is actually the easiest part of this process. By this time, you have already established the body acting for the character, and now, you are just matching the mouth shapes to the appropriate frames. You will find that you may need to establish key frames on the timeline throughout those frames that were once the holding or rest positions for the character, as the character's mouth might be moving on those frames. Refer to the lip sync tutorial file to see how I used certain mouth shapes to, in a sense, slow in and out of certain words. When you are satisfied with your work on the lip sync, save your changes by clicking Save As to rename your file Eye Acting for the next and final stage of the process, the eye movements.

Fourth pass: eye acting and expressions

Congratulations! By making it this far, you have seen your animation progress from just a few poses of a static character to a character that's begun to take on real personality through the movements you have created. Now, we get to the stage of this process that will really bring life to your character. For this section, please refer to the fbf tutorial 04_eye acting.fla.

The eyes have it!

It never fails to amaze me what this final stage can do for a character's animation. Even after all the body movements and the lip sync are finished and everything seems to be working really well, there is still something missing. The body movements can communicate what the character is doing or maybe feeling; the lip sync can communicate what the character is saying; but the eyes, the eyes are the secret ingredients that have the ability to communicate what the character is actually thinking! I really believe this step in the animation process deserves the utmost care and consideration. I've seen numerous Flash animated sequences that were well animated in every respect except when it came to the eyes. For me, eye charts are the last symbol to be broken apart in this process. Let's look at the eye chart to see how best to make use of it.

Double-click the character's eyes from the timeline of your animation. Figure 6-16 shows the separate layers and elements of the character's eye chart. Scroll back and forth along the timeline to see the different positions of the eyelids. Recall that breaking apart the head symbol to gain access to the mouth charts during the lip sync process also made the eye charts and the eyebrow symbols accessible.

I usually start the process of eye acting by finding all the places in the animation where I want the character to blink or to have closed eyes over a succession of frames. Head turns are usually a very good place for blinks. Try to start the blink just before the head begins the turn. During this process, you don't need to break apart the eyes just yet. Doing so will separate the pupils. If you do break the eyes and pupils apart, you can still make the eyes blink, but you will have more pieces to keep track of as you go from frame to frame. I recommend first calling up the eye shapes you want through the Properties panel to set up where you want the blinks to happen.

When you are satisfied that your blinks are working, you can go ahead and break the eyes apart to release the pupils. It's really the combination of the movement of the pupils in harmony with the eye blinks that gives life to the character. Also, when the character turns his head, try to use the pupils to lead the head in the direction of the head turn. If the character's head is not turning but the eyes are moving from left to right, it's very effective to have the character blink during the transition of the eye movement. In this case, the eyelids would be closed briefly at the pupils' midpoint positions. As the eyelids open, they reveal the pupils' new positions.

Figure 6-16. The eye chart showing separate layers

My approach for this sequence was to start on frame 1 with the character's eyes in a half-closed, relaxed expression, the eye position shown in Figure 6-16. By frame 15 (see Figure 6-17), the eyes blink as the pupils look upward as if in thought, and the eyebrow positions support this expression. From frames 23 to 29, another blink happens, as the pupils change their position. Notice how the pupils lead the turn of the head here, as the character's head turns to look toward camera. The eyebrows lower slightly halfway through the blink (see Figure 6-18), and then rise to support the expression by frame 29. Going into the anticipation on frame 37, notice that I used the squinting eye shapes and positioned the eyebrows at a downward angle (see Figure 6-19). This angle is most often associated with an angry expression, but here, I am using it to create a contrast with the extreme expression that will follow. Frame 40, where the word "great" is emphasized the most, the eyes fly wide open with eyebrows angled in the opposite direction from frame 37 to create a more excited expression (see Figure 6-20). As the character is settling in frames 41 through 54, the eyebrows lower and relax, and finally in frames 55 through 60, we see one last blink that ends the sequence (see Figure 6-21).

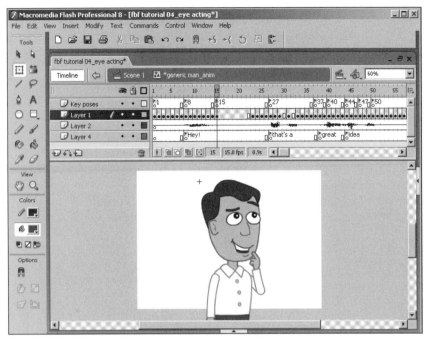

Figure 6-17. The positions of pupils and eyebrows strengthen the expression.

Figure 6-18. The eyes blink as the head turns toward camera.

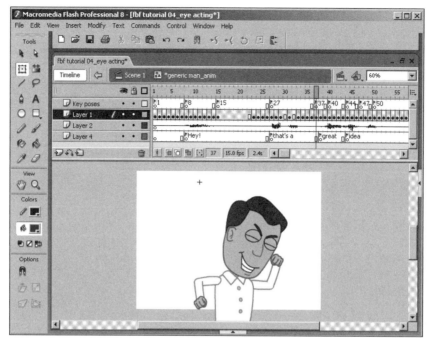

Figure 6-19. The eye expression during anticipation on frame 37

Figure 6-20. The contrast in the eye expression from the previous pose

Figure 6-21. The last eye blink

Summary

For those readers who might be new to using Flash or creating animation, I hope that this chapter has been helpful in showing you some techniques for reaching your desired results. I've covered preparing your file for animation, blocking out the rough actions and acting for your character, the effects of slowing in and slowing out for the timing of movements that are created, lip syncing dialog, and finally, bringing the character to life by the movements and expressions of the eyes. This four-pass animation method has served me extremely well in my own work. It certainly is not the only way of doing things, and I encourage you to develop and explore your own methods.

Whichever way you choose to approach your work, please keep in mind that the ingredients that will give your animation life and personality will not come from the computer; they will come from you, from your experimentation and observation of the life around you. Strive to make your animation natural and believable for your characters through simple and direct action that is tempered by the subtlety of timing. Keep thinking about how all these things—the poses, the timing of inbetweens, lip sync, and the expressions of the eye—work together in harmony to create one result. In working with a great many animators over the years, I've always enjoyed seeing how each one brings a unique personality to the work. Good luck with the rest of the projects in this book!

Chapter 7

ANIMATING WITH TWEENS

By Dave Wolfe

One of the most frequently used and misused features of Flash is the tween. Tweens are the frames between your keys and breakdowns, coldly calculated by the computer. Many animators leave too much of the work to the computer, resulting in floaty, amateurish animation often derided as "tweeny" or "Flashy." However, properly used tweens can save time and look just as good as if you had done all the work by hand.

The examples in this chapter make use of several extensions that have been created to enhance Flash's animation workflow. These aren't necessary to follow along with the examples, but they do make life a little easier. Take a look at Chapter 5 for more information about extensions and to find out where to download the extensions used in this chapter.

Pros and cons of tweens

The biggest benefit to using tweens is the amount of time they can save. Although they are rarely usable without some tweaking, they can still get you pretty close, especially when it comes to subtle movements. With the custom ease ability introduced in Flash 8, you have even more control over your tweens and can get away with fewer keyframes. Another one of the benefits to using tweens is that, because the character must have each body part on a separate layer, it is a piece of cake to lock or hide certain body parts or props that you don't want to work with.

The necessity of putting each body part onto a separate layer is also one of the drawbacks to using tweens and makes it impossible to use the Arrange commands to change the depth or Z order of the symbols; the symbol on the top layer is always going to be on top. When a character is turning, for example, dealing with all the symbols that need to change which layer they're on can be difficult, and adding more layers for them clutters your timeline. A character with many pieces will also take up a lot of space in your timeline, and if you have multiple characters interacting with each other, all the layers and overlapping body parts can become a nightmare.

For these reasons, I prefer to take a hybrid approach to animating. Characters are usually separated into layers, and if multiple characters are needed, each gets its own layer folder, allowing me to easily hide or lock the entire character. When a character needs to perform an action that would require lots of symbols changing their Z orders, I flatten the character into one or two layers and animate frame by frame for the duration of that action. Once the character has reached a point where the Z order of the symbols doesn't need to change anymore, the symbols can be distributed to layers so that tweens can be used again.

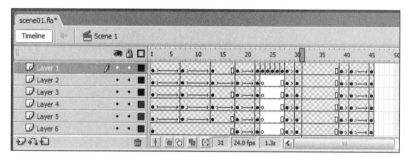

Figure 7-1. Switching from tweened animation to frame by frame animation enables you to use the advantages that each style offers.

Analyzing the scene

Before you jump right in and start animating, it's a good idea to study the scene you'll be animating and plan ahead. If you're working on a sequence of scenes, take a look at the storyboard/animatic to make sure you don't animate yourself into a corner; you need to make sure that the scene you're animating works with the other scenes, the scale is consistent, and poses all hook up correctly.

Breaking down the audio track

A good place to start when analyzing your shot is the dialog. The tone of the voice, the rhythm, the volume, and the phrasing all tell the animator a great deal more than just the words alone. The way the words are spoken dictates the character's mood and feelings, which are essential to making the right acting choices. The dialog is also a tremendous tool for timing, which will be covered in more depth later in this chapter.

When you play the audio track, pay attention to which words or syllables are accented. When does the speaker raise or lower her voice? Is the character excited; is she speaking quickly and jumbling words together?

It may help to write the dialog on a piece of paper, and above the text, draw a line that represents the accents in the speech. The line curves upward when the character raises his voice or puts strong emphasis on a syllable. The line curves downward when the character lowers his voice or intensity. These curves are basic acting guides for the character's intensity. With a little experience under your belt, this exercise won't be necessary, but you may still find it helpful when tackling tough scenes.

Figure 7-2. The wavy line graphs the intensity of the actor's performance.

Making good acting choices

Animation involves acting, and bad acting leads to bad animation. Although you don't necessarily need to take acting classes, it doesn't hurt to study films and cartoons that have good acting in them. The important thing is to really think about how the character would react in a given situation. Take an angry character, for example. When Clint Eastwood gets angry, he squints his eyes, grits his teeth, and speaks calmly but with iron in his voice. Someone like Adam Sandler, on the other hand, is not so subtle about his anger. He yells, turns red-faced, and may throw a temper tantrum. You need to keep your characters' personalities in mind when deciding how they will perform a certain scene.

When breaking down the dialog, you can see or hear where the emphasis lies, and in most cases, that's where the emphasis in the acting will be. For each line a character speaks, there are usually only a couple stressed words, and you put the key poses in sync with them. If you try to squeeze too many poses into a segment of dialog, your characters are likely to end up looking like they're having seizures. Don't feel like the character needs to be constantly moving.

There are also minor accents in dialog, and this is where you can put small movements in your animation to keep the characters from looking like they're just going from pose to pose. Usually a head tilt or other similar action, or maybe some slight hand movement or a shoulder shrug, is all that's required. These types of subtle movements are also good for other characters in the scene who are listening to the speaker or perhaps just milling about in the background; they need movement to keep from looking dead without taking attention away from the speaker. Often, you don't even need to move the body for these subtle accents. A character's facial expressions can add a lot, and sometimes, having a character blink or raise a single eyebrow is more powerful.

A tremendous resource for acting and animation information is the blog of John Kricfalusi, the creator of *Ren and Stimpy*. He's a controversial figure, but whether you love him or hate him, his blog is chock full of excellent information on what makes a cartoon good. Visit `http://johnkstuff.blogspot.com`, and dig through the archives; there's a lot there, but the time you'll spend sifting through them is time well spent.

Thumbnailing the scene

Drawing little thumbnails of the action is a quick way to rough out some ideas visually. Rather than waste a lot of time trying out different poses with your Flash character, draw a series of small, quick roughs of the action you have in mind. In the time it takes to do one or two poses in Flash, you can have the entire shot roughed out. This lets you quickly spot where things aren't working and try several ways of solving the problem.

When you're planning out the animation, keeping a few animation principles in mind is a good idea: the squash and stretch or elasticity of the character, the silhouette or outline of the character's shape, the line of action or centerline of the character, and the arcs or path of action the various parts of the character follow as they move. The silhouette and squash and stretch are often taken care of naturally when drawing the rough poses, but some animators may forget about planning their arcs or reversing the line of action to make the characters' poses look more interesting. Reversing the line of action is a way to make the movement in the animation look more interesting and add contrast to the poses. By reversing the direction of the line of action between poses, you can avoid repetitive looking poses and add more dynamic movement to the character. Although these issues are usually resolved by the time the animation is complete, you can save time by taking care of them in the planning stage.

Thumbnails can be drawn on paper, or you may find it easier to thumbnail directly in Flash using a Wacom tablet, Cintiq monitor, or Tablet PC. Although drawing on paper can be a nice break from the computer, there are advantages to drawing your thumbnails directly in Flash. First of all, you can use the timeline so that your thumbnails can be used as a kind of animatic or pose test, letting you see right away if the timing is working and if the poses flow from one to the next naturally. Another advantage to thumbnailing in Flash is that, if you draw the characters with roughly the correct proportions, you can save a lot of time by using your thumbnails as a posing guide for the Flash model.

Figure 7-3. Using thumbnail drawings to plan your animation can help you avoid problems before they arise.

Timing and animation

Now, it's time for the fun part—animation! If you're animating to dialog, then the basic timing is practically done for you; at this point, the timing is just refining what you already worked out when breaking down the audio track. Usually, the major poses should hit right on or slightly before the major accents in the dialog. When your character starts moving into the pose and how quickly he settles will depend on the style of animation you're going for, the way the actor reads the dialog, and the personality of the character you're animating.

If you don't have a soundtrack to animate, that doesn't mean you have to fly blind. In the olden days, animators would use a musical beat as a timing guide, and you can do the same thing today. You don't need to have music in the scene to do it; you just need to pick a beat. 120 beats per minute (bpm) is a good beat to use for most situations. That would mean you have a beat every 12 frames if you're running at 24 frames per second. You don't need to have something happen on every beat, but you should try to start and end your actions on a beat or a half beat. And you don't need to stick with 120 bpm; you may want to experiment with slower beats for a sad character or a faster beat for a hyperactive character. In most cases, you don't want the beat to take precedence over the dialog. Make the actions match the dialog first, and use a beat for any actions that don't correspond to dialog. If you're animating an entire project all by yourself, you can use the beats as a way to time out the whole piece and sync it perfectly with the final music. Even if you're just animating a few scenes that are part of a larger production, you can use a beat as a guide for your particular scenes.

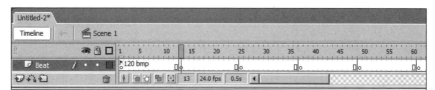

Figure 7-4. A guide layer at 120 bpm with keyframes every 12 frames that indicate where the beat falls

Blocking the animation

Once you have the scene set up, it's time to block the character's action. The blocking pass is the first pass at your animation, where you work out the timing of the major poses. This is when you should spot potential problems and fix them before you've done all the animation. Do any of the characters' outlines fall directly on lines in the background, creating tangents? Do the characters get in the way of background elements? Do any of the characters get in the way of other characters in the scene? Is there enough acting room for all the characters? These are things that should be addressed in the storyboard and layout stages, but sometimes, you'll need to make a few small changes to make the scene work better.

Using your thumbnails as a guide, select the master turnaround, pick the correct view of the character, break it apart, and distribute it to layers. The extension Break Into Layers (see Chapter 5) is useful for this; it will not only break apart the symbol but distribute it to layers for you, using the same layer names and colors as the symbol's nested timeline.

Your character may need to turn at some point in the animation. If this is the case, before you break apart the character, create a keyframe at the approximate frame where the turn will occur. Next, select the character, and in the Properties panel, change the First frame to the appropriate view of the character. Figure 7-5 shows the turn-around of the character used in this chapter's examples; the character is designed by the AnimSlider extension author Warren Fuller to make use of the View buttons found on the AnimSlider panel, but the AnimSlider extension (see Chapter 5) is not required to use the character. The front, or A, view is frame 1; the three-quarter, or C, view is frame 38; the profile, or E, view is frame 75, and so on. The frames in between the views are used to store special poses of the character.

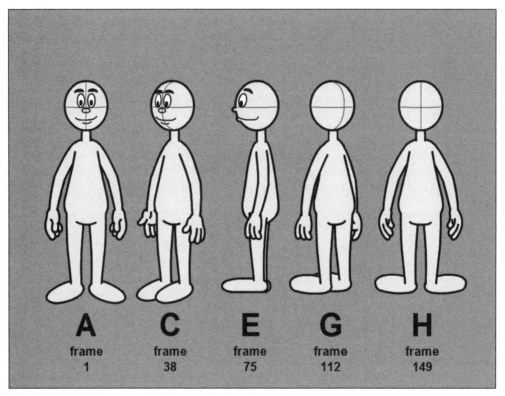

Figure 7-5. The full turn-around of the example character

Once the character has been broken apart and distributed to layers, refer to your thumbnails once again, and start posing the character. You probably won't be able to match the thumbnail poses exactly, but try to get as close as possible, even if you have to draw some new symbols. As you go over your blocking pass, make sure to check that your timing works and that each pose flows nicely into the next pose.

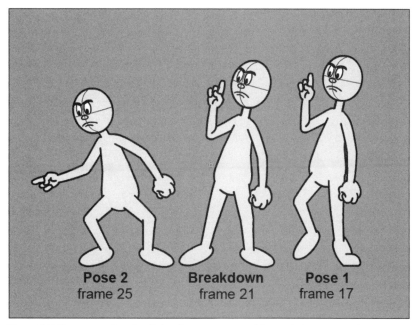

Figure 7-6. Using your thumbnail drawings as a pose guide can help you save time.

Adding breakdowns

A *breakdown* is a pose that falls between two key poses. Its purpose is to help describe the action and prevent mechanical-looking inbetweens. The breakdown pose is where you might add some squash and stretch or overlapping movement. You can make some body parts lead others, break joints, and come up with more interesting ways to go from A to B than just using generic inbetweens.

The breakdowns are what can really set your animation apart from the boring, floaty, or tweeny look of the beginner. Some actions won't require a breakdown, but you should always look at your start and end poses to see if there's something you can do to make the transition more interesting. This is when a tablet comes in handy again; you can sketch out more rough poses to see what works and what doesn't. When you're happy with the rough breakdown, you can use it as a guide for posing the Flash character, just like you did with the thumbnails. You may even want to get into the habit of doing some breakdowns when you're in the thumbnailing stage.

Open the file ch07_xmas03.fla. Frame 21 is an example of a breakdown drawing (see Figure 7-7). Frames 17 and 25 are the two keys, and with the correct ease settings, you could simply tween between the two of them and make the transition look alright. But adding the breakdown on frame 21 gives us a more interesting transition between the two key poses. Frame 17 slows out of the start pose and leads with the right foot, which lands quickly and pulls the rest of the body down into the pose on frame 25. Having the foot move more quickly and reach its final position before the rest of the body prevents the mechanical and dull look that happens when everything moves at the same speed and starts and stops on the same frames.

Figure 7-7. Breakdown poses provide a more interesting transition between two key poses.

Adding inbetweens

Adding the inbetweens is a simple process: select the frames you want to be inbetweened, and select Motion from the Properties panel's Tween pull-down menu. You'll almost always want to add some easing to the tween; otherwise, the spacing between each frame is completely even, and the animation will look dull and mechanical. A positive ease value will have tighter spacing toward the end keyframe, and a negative ease value will have tighter spacing toward the start keyframe. Flash calls these ease out and ease in, respectively. That will likely sound backward to animators new to Flash, since, traditionally, easing out of a pose would mean tighter spacing toward the start pose, and easing in would be tighter spacing toward the end pose.

Working with those values can be limiting and force you to use extra keyframes to enable you to ease in and out of a pose. Flash 8 introduced a new feature called Custom Ease. Next to the Ease slider in the Properties panel is a button labeled Edit. Clicking this will open the Custom Ease In / Ease Out window, which displays a graph representing the motion from the beginning keyframe on the bottom left and the ending keyframe at the top right (see Figure 7-9). Rather than creating multiple keyframes to alter the timing of your tween, you can now simply click the graph to add a control point and move it around to adjust the ease. You can add multiple control points by clicking the graph again, and you can remove control points by holding the Alt key and clicking the point. The play button lets you preview the effect of your curve, and you can use the Ctrl/Cmd+C and Ctrl/Cmd+V shortcuts to copy and paste curves among different tweens. You also have the option of using one curve for all motion properties (position, rotation, scale, color, and filters), or you can have a unique curve for each motion property. This makes it easy to give a more interesting and varied timing to your animation by using different ease settings for each property and having some parts of the animation reach their end poses before others.

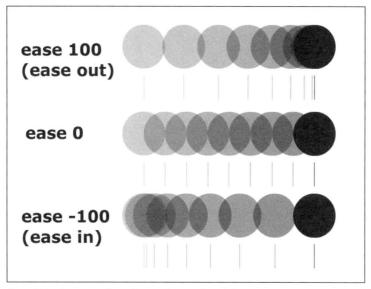

Figure 7-8. The ease values change the spacing of the tweened frames.

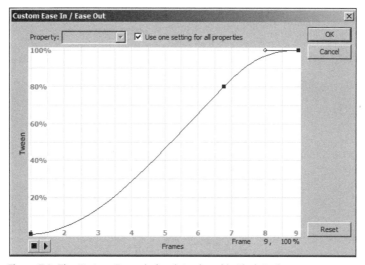

Figure 7-9. The Custom Ease window introduced in Flash 8 gives you more control over your tweened animation.

Taking advantage of custom ease

Let's do a quick exercise to get familiar with the Custom Ease In / Ease Out window. We're going to use a custom ease to make a character's head rotation settle after the position.

1. Open the file ch07_customEase.fla.

2. Go to frame 7, and keyframe all layers; then, go to frame 13, and keyframe all layers (see Figure 7-10).

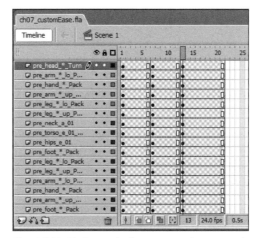

Figure 7-10. Keyframe the layers to set the start and end of the action.

3. On frame 13, select all the body parts except for the legs and feet. Using the Free Transform tool, move the pivot point to the hips, and rotate the upper body forward, as shown in Figure 7-11.

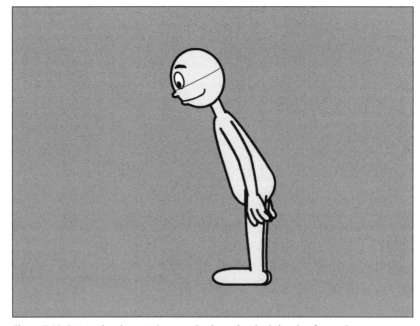

Figure 7-11. Rotate the character's upper body so that he is leaning forward.

4. Select all the keyframes on frame 7, and add a motion tween. Even though the Sync option won't cause any trouble for this exercise, it's best to get in the habit of using the Motion Tween command you made in Chapter 5.

5. With the keyframes still selected, change the ease in the Properties panel to 100. Play the animation to see how the ease affects the motion of the body. Changing the ease to 100 slows into the second pose; it looks OK, but having everything start and stop on the same frames is boring.

6. Now, let's add the overlapping action on the head. On the head layer, select the keyframe on frame 13, and drag it to frame 17 (see Figure 7-12).

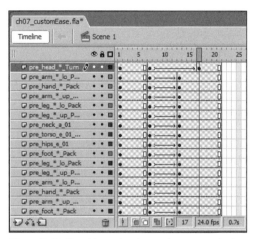

Figure 7-12. To add overlapping action, move the last keyframe of the head to frame 17.

7. Select the keyframe on frame 7 of the head layer, and in the Properties panel, click the Edit button, shown in Figure 7-13, to open the Custom Ease In / Ease Out window.

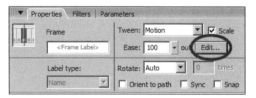

Figure 7-13. Click the Edit button to open the Custom Ease In / Ease Out window.

8. The graph you are presented with (see Figure 7-14) is what an ease of 100 looks like; it starts with a fairly steep curve that flattens out as it approaches the end keyframe, indicating that the symbol moves quickly out of the start pose and slows into the final pose. Copy this curve by pressing Ctrl/Cmd+C, and uncheck the box labeled Use one setting for all properties.

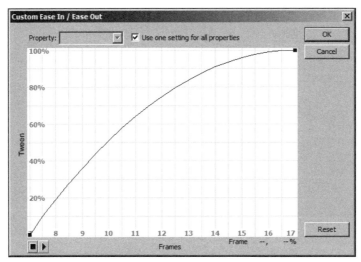

Figure 7-14. The curve representing an ease out setting of 100.

9. In the Property menu, make sure Position is selected. Click an empty section of the graph to make sure the graph is active, and press Ctrl/Cmd+V to paste the curve. The frame numbers are listed along the bottom of the graph; click the curve at frame 13, and drag the new control point up to 100%. Use the Bezier handles to shape the curve between frames 7 and 13 so that it resembles the ease 100 curve, as shown in Figure 7-15. This will make the head position reach its final pose on frame 13 along with the rest of the body. You can click the play button or press F2 to preview the effects of your new curve.

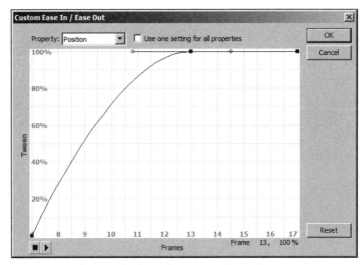

Figure 7-15. Add a control point at frame 13, and move it up to 100%.

10. In the Property menu, select Rotation, and paste the ease 100 curve again. You can leave the curve as it is, or if you want, you can adjust the Bezier handle for frame 7 so that there's a bit of a slow out, as shown in Figure 7-16.

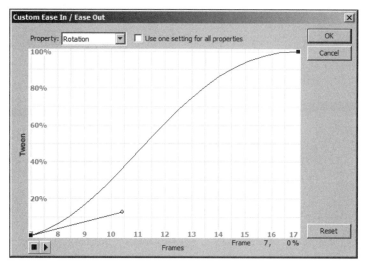

Figure 7-16. Adjust the Bezier handle to slow out of the keyframe.

Click OK, and play your animation to see the results. The character should lean forward, and after he stops leaning forward, the head should continue to rotate for a few frames. Look at the file `ch07_customEase_final.fla` to see the final animation.

Fine-tuning tweens and timing

As you go through your keys and breakdowns and start adding tweens you may run into situations where you need to make some adjustments to your timing. In most cases this should be done by adjusting the spacing of your tweens, not by rearranging your key poses. You may also notice that sometimes the tweened symbol doesn't follow the path you had in mind. Flash tweens the position of symbols in a linear path rather than in the more natural arcs you want in most of your animation. Another problem you'll run into is that when you change the displayed frame for single-frame symbols, such as hands, they pop from one position to the next in an unnatural way. Let's take a look at how to deal with these problems.

1. Open the file `ch07_xmas03.fla`, and double-click the character to edit him in place. You'll notice that his right arm and hand are behind his chest. Most of the animation takes place with him turned the other direction, and when he turns around, his right arm and hand should go behind the body. You can change the body to outline mode, as shown in Figure 7-17, to see the arm more clearly as you adjust the tween. This can be quickly accomplished with the Toggle Outline extension (see Chapter 5); select the two symbols that make up his chest and run the Toggle Outline extension. You should create a keyboard shortcut for quick access to the command.

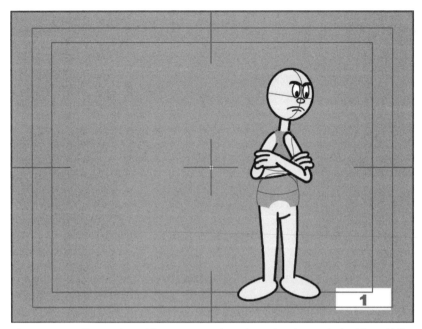

Figure 7-17. Outline mode enables you to see through overlapping symbols without hiding the symbols on top.

2. Let's start adding motion tweens and see what we end up with. Frames 1–6 are held so that the viewer has a chance to register what they're seeing. Go to frame 7; press Ctrl/Cmd+A to select all the symbols, and use the motion tween command you made in Chapter 5 to add a motion tween (see Figure 7-18).

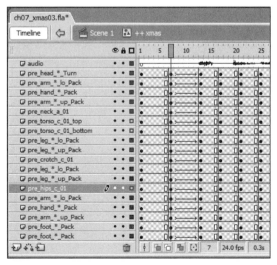

Figure 7-18. Add a motion tween to the keyframes on frame 7.

3. Frames 13–16 are where the transition from three-quarter right to three-quarter left view takes place. This will be taken care of once the layers are merged. Select all the layers on frames 17–24, and add a motion tween.

4. The next breakdown pose is at frame 33, but the length of time that passes between frames 25 and 33 is too long for a tween. The difference between the two poses is small; it's mostly just the right arm settling before he goes into his next pose. Four frames for his body to make the transition should be plenty. We'll add some keyframes for the right arm to settle later. At frame 29, select all the symbols, create a keyframe, and add a motion tween. Next, select all the symbols on frame 33, and add a motion tween.

5. Six frames is just a little bit too long for the anticipation on frame 47, so at frame 43, select all the symbols and keyframe them. Next, select all layers of frames 47–56, and add a motion tween.

6. Once again, the length of time between frames 57 and 67 is too long for the anticipation. Instead of four frames, this time six frames will make for a stronger anticipation before he slams his fists down. Select all the symbols on frame 61, and keyframe them. Then, select all layers on frames 61–81, and add a motion tween.

That's it for adding the tweens, but we obviously can't leave it at that. The timing is way too even; body parts don't stay together; there's a flipping leg symbol; the hands don't change their displayed frames at the right times, and the right arm needs to settle better when he points his finger.

7. The first thing we want to do is adjust the timing by changing the ease values. Select all the layers on frame 7, and change the Ease to 100, as shown in Figure 7-19.

8. Set the keyframes on frame 17 to –100, and the keyframes on frame 21 to –50. This will make him slow out of his anticipation and overshoot the pointing pose with more force.

Figure 7-19. Change the Ease to 100.

9. The pointing arm could use a bit of delay and a settle. Select the keyframes on frame 25 for the right upper arm, forearm, and hand, and move those keyframes to frame 27. You may notice that when you select multiple symbols the transformation point moves to the center of the selection. This usually isn't where you want the center of rotation to be. Click the transformation point, and move it to the appropriate joint, in this case, the shoulder. Add keyframes for the arm symbols on frame 25 and rotate the forearm and hand up a few degrees to slow out of the raised pose. The arm could also use a keyframe on frame 23 to slow out some more and help prevent the hand from flying off of the arm during the tween. To figure out where the arm and hand should go, it helps to draw a curve on a guide layer to use as a reference when adjusting the path of action the hand and arm will follow (see Figure 7-20).

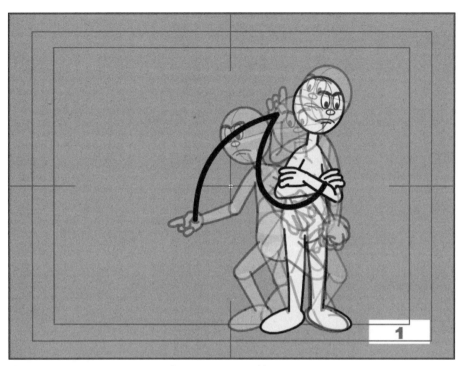

Figure 7-20. Draw arcs on a separate layer to use as a guide.

10. On frame 29, rotate the right forearm and hand up slightly to begin the settle. Keyframe the right arm on frame 31, and make the forearm and hand settle a little higher before the forearm and hand drop to the pose on frame 33, shown in Figure 7-21. The rest of the body's Ease should be set to –100 on frame 29 and 100 for frame 33 as the character settles into frame 41. The breakdown here is in frame 33, slowing the character out of the pointing pose before he slows into the pose on frame 41.

11. Change the Ease for the rest of the tweened frames to 100. If you play the animation, you can see that it's starting to look better. The Ease for frame 67 could be changed to –100 to give the pose on frame 75 a more forceful impact.

Changing the ease values has helped the timing a bit, but using the Custom Ease In / Ease Out window can make a big improvement here. Now that you've learned how to use the Custom Ease In / Ease Out window, the next few steps will explain an alternate way to adjust your custom ease curves. If you're coming from a traditional animation background, you may prefer to use the Timing Chart extension (see Chapter 5) to set your custom ease curves. If you choose not to use the Timing Chart extension, you can still follow along using the Custom Ease In / Ease Out window.

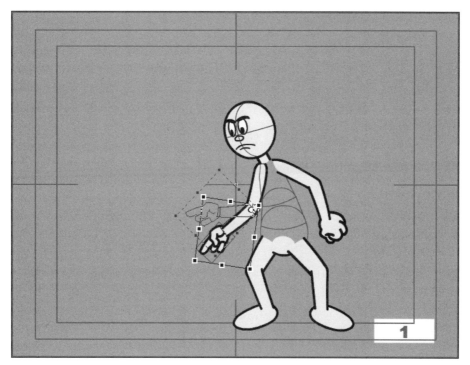

Figure 7-21. Vary the timing of the action by adding a settle to the right arm.

12. Select all the layers on frame 7, and open the Timing Chart extension from the Window menu, in the Other Panels submenu (see Figure 7-22). This animation will eventually be on twos, so change the Step value to 2, and click Initialize. Two horizontal lines will appear evenly spaced on the chart. These lines are sliders that represent the inbetween frames 9 and 11. In the default setup, the top of the chart represents the ending pose or keyframe, and the bottom of the chart represents the starting pose or keyframe. If you right/Ctrl-click the chart, you have the option to flip it so the orientation is more like traditional animation with the start pose at the top and the end pose at the bottom. The 25, 50, and 75 percent marks on the chart will let you know which way your chart is oriented.

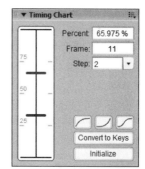

Figure 7-22. Animators with a traditional background may be more comfortable adjusting custom ease with the Timing Chart extension.

13. This action could use a stronger slow in, so drag the frame 11 slider to about 90 percent and the frame 9 slider to 58 percent. If you prefer to use the Custom Ease In / Ease Out window, you can get the same effect by adding control points on frames 9 and 11 and dragging the control points to 58 percent and 90 percent, as shown in Figure 7-23. Since this animation will be on twos, you don't need to worry about smoothing out the curve with the Bezier handles.

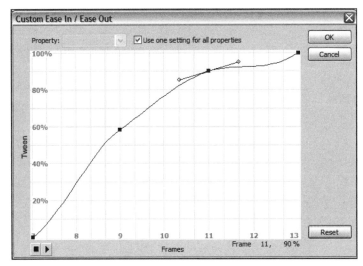

Figure 7-23. The custom ease curve does not need to be smoothed out, because the animation will be on twos.

14. The next actions that could use some tweaking with the Timing Chart are the accent and settle in frames 43–59. Select all the keyframes on frame 43, and click Initialize on the Timing Chart. Drag the frame 45 slider to 75 percent.

15. Select the keyframes on frame 47, and click Initialize on the Timing Chart. For the action taking place between frames 47 and 51, we're going to want both slow out and slow in, so drag the frame 49 slider to 15 percent and the frame 51 slider to 95 percent.

16. The settle in frames 53–57 could also use both slow out and slow in. First, we're going to need some more time for this to settle, so drag the keyframes on frame 57 to frame 59. Next, select the keyframes on frame 53, and click Initialize on the Timing Chart. Drag the slider for frame 55 to 8 percent and the slider for frame 57 to 83 percent.

17. The final part of the animation, when he slams his fists down, could use some adjusting as well. Select the keyframes on frame 61, and click Initialize on the Timing Chart. Drag the frame 63 slider to 58 percent and the frame 65 slider to 92 percent for a nice slow in to the anticipation pose.

18. The part where he slams his fists down needs to be pretty forceful, so a strong slow out and a slow in that's almost the final pose should do the trick. Initialize the keyframes on frame 67, and drag the frame 69 slider to 2 or 3 percent. Drag the frame 71 slider to about 25 percent, and drag the frame 73 slider to 95 percent.

19. Finally, the settle needs to slow out and slow in as well. Instead of using frame sliders for this, the slow in/out curve preset on the Timing Chart should do the trick. Select the keyframes on frame 75, and click the right-most curve button; the tool-tip that appears when you hover your mouse pointer over the button should say slow in/out, as shown in Figure 7-24.

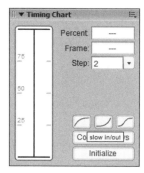

Figure 7-24. The curve presets

The timing is starting to look a lot better now, but some things are still missing: Body parts are still separating from each other; the turn from three-quarter right to three-quarter left view isn't complete; some arcs could use finessing: the hands still need to change their displayed frames earlier; and finally, some symbols need to have their Z orders changed. Let's take one final pass at the animation to fix all these problems.

20. Before we make all the final adjustments, the tweens need to be converted to keyframes. This animation is going to be on twos, so let's use the Tween 2 Keys extension (see Chapter 5) to make life a little easier. Select frames 7–81 on all layers, and run the Tween 2 Keys extension from the Commands menu. After running the Tween 2 Keys extension, your timeline should look like the one shown in Figure 7-25.

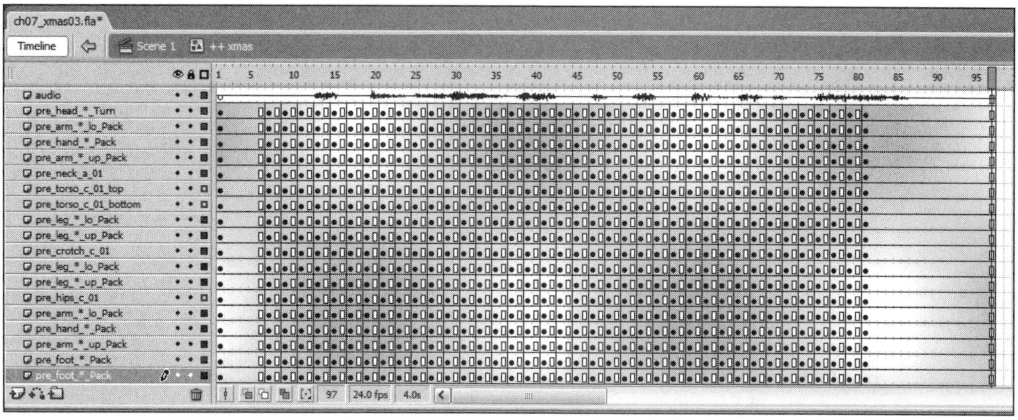

Figure 7-25. The timeline after the Tween2Keys extension is executed

21. The beginning of the animation, when the character turns around, has some symbols that need their Z orders changed. The easiest way to do this is with the Merge Layers (see Chapter 5) extension. Make sure all the layers are unlocked, select the frames 1–13, and run the Merge Layers extension from the Commands menu. After running the Merge Layers extension, your timeline should look like Figure 7-26. If you want, you can clear the blank keyframes to reduce screen clutter.

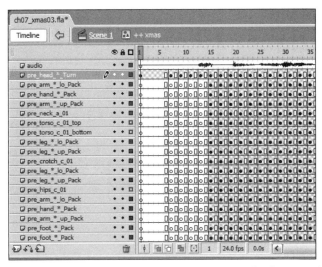

Figure 7-26. The timeline after the Merge Layers extension is executed

22. Select the right forearm and hand, and use the Arrange commands (Ctrl/Cmd+Up) to bring those symbols forward, as shown in Figure 7-27. It would also look better if the right arm leads the action by sweeping out early, instead of moving at the same rate as the rest of the body. Remember to make sure that the hand follows a nice arc and that the spacing isn't erratic.

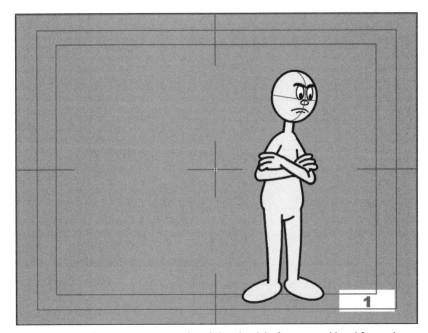

Figure 7-27. Use the Arrange commands to bring the right forearm and hand forward.

23. It's time to make our inbetween on frame 15. Select all the keyframes on frame 17, and hold down the Alt key to drag and copy the keyframes to frame 15. Slightly lower the torso, head, and arms; tilt the head forward a bit; and lower the right arm a little to slow into the pose on frame 17.

24. Frame 13 could also be changed to help with the slow in to frame 17—raise the body, straighten the legs, and swing the right arm out a bit more. This is also a good time to change the hand position. An open hand with the palm out would make a good transition from the backhand to the pointing hand. Select the right hand symbol, and type 40 in the First frame box in the Properties panel. Alternatively, if you have the AnimSlider extension, you can click the L3/4 button to have the slider show frames 38–74, and click frame 40. The AnimSlider Pro shows 100 frames, so if you have that, you can directly click frame 40.

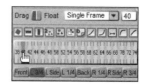

Figure 7-28. The AnimSlider extension speeds up the process of setting the first frame property of graphic symbols.

25. As you advance frame by frame through the pointing gesture, you'll see the right hand and forearm separate from the upper arm. For each keyframe in the action, move the forearm so that the elbow is connected, and move the hand so the wrist connects properly, as shown in Figure 7-29. As you make these adjustments, remember to pay attention to your arcs; if necessary, adjust the upper arm and forearm so that the hand's path of action follows a smooth arc. It would also look nice to rotate the hand up a little as it comes down to give it a bit of drag. Keep it subtle, though; we don't want him looking like a rag doll. You should also reconnect any other body parts, such as the thigh and calf, that you see starting separate.

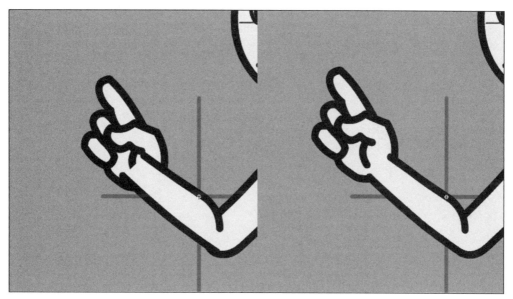

Figure 7-29. Don't leave poorly connected joints after converting a motion tween to keyframes.

26. As the character begins settling from frame 27 to frame 41, the pointing hand needs to turn into a more relaxed hand. Frame 1 of the hand symbol looks good, but how do you decide when to change the displayed frame? Usually, you want to change the frame when the hand moves the greatest distance, so you can hide the sudden change in shape. As the hand slows into frame 41, it moves the greatest distance from frame 33 to frame 35. Usually, frame 35 would be the right frame to change hands, and in this case, it would look fine—but you can get a nicer arc in the finger tips by keeping frame 35 a pointing finger and changing to the relaxed hand on frame 37. The distance the hand travels from frame 35 to 37 is enough that the sudden change in hand shape isn't a distraction.

From this point, you should be able to go through the rest of the scene and fix the problem areas. You can also add some squash and stretch to the character and maybe a dry-brush streak or blur for fast actions. Take a look at the file ch07_xmas06.fla to see the final body animation.

Facial animation and lip sync

Now that the body acting has been taken care of, it's time to make his lips move. The audience is going to pay the most attention to the face, so it's important to get the right expressions, eye direction, and properly synced mouth shapes.

1. Open the file ch07_xmas06.fla, and double-click the character to edit it in place. Nearly all of the dialog happens with the three-quarter face, so on the first frame, copy the head, and paste it into a new layer. Drag the copied head out of the acting space of the character, and click the Reset button on the Transform panel. This will reset the duplicate head symbol to 100 percent with no rotation, allowing you to animate the facial features without having to worry about the head being squashed, skewed, or tilted at a weird angle (see Figure 7-30). You can delete the duplicated head layer after the facial animation is complete. Because the duplicated head is still the same symbol as the original head, the animation done within the duplicated head symbol will also appear on the original head.

If you attempt to edit the head, you'll notice that it's still the head turn-around symbol, not the actual three-quarter view head. Exit the head symbol, and break it apart once. If you select the head and look at the name in the Properties panel, you should see that it is named *DW pre_head_c_01_C (it's actually *DW pre_head_c_01_Comp, but the Properties panel isn't wide enough to display the full name). That symbol is the three-quarter view head symbol that we want to animate.

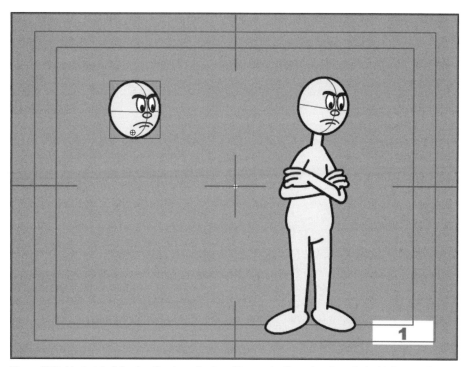

Figure 7-30. Nested facial animation is easier to edit on a duplicate head symbol with its transformation reset.

If you edit this symbol, you'll see the layers for the eyes, mouth, nose, and so on. For the facial animation to play back correctly on the character, you'll also need to break apart the original head that has been animated, and it needs to be broken apart on each keyframe. Instead of breaking apart the head one frame at a time, you can use Edit Multiple Frames. Lock all layers except for the original head layer, and turn on Edit Multiple Frames. Click the Modify Onion Markers button, and click Onion All from the menu, as shown in Figure 7-31. Because the first 14 frames have been merged, you'll need to drag the left onion skin marker to frame 15, where the body parts have all been separated onto different layers. Then press Ctrl/Cmd+A to select all the head symbols and break them apart once. Turn off Edit Multiple Frames, and break apart the original head on each keyframe from frames 1 through 13. Now, we're ready for the facial animation. Unlock the other layers, and double-click the duplicated head to edit it in place.

Figure 7-31. The Modify Onion Markers menu

2. Let's start by leading the action with the eyes. The pupils should start to move screen left on frame 5. Go to frame 5, select the head, and run the FrameEDIT extension (see Chapter 5). This will edit the head in place and take us directly to frame 5. Select the pupils, and keyframe them. Pupils tend to dart around quickly, but there should still be some slow in before the final position. Move the pupils so they're almost all the way to the left of the screen, and on frame 7, keyframe the pupils again, and move them to their final positions against the edges of the eyes.

3. As the character turns around, he could use a blink, so on frame 7, bring his eyelids down, but don't close them all the way. On frame 9, the head turns to the front view, so we'll finish the blink later.

4. On frame 13, we switch back to the flipped three-quarter view. We'll start by keeping the eyelids partially shut as he comes out of the blink. Raise the eyebrows to help emphasize the body acting as well as the intensity in the voice. The character is looking forward now, so move the pupils back to the other side of his eyes.

5. Lower the eyebrows on frames 17–21 as he begins to settle his pose. Slow out on frame 17, and use frame 19 to slow into the final position on frame 21.

6. When the character says "for Christmas" he goes down in anticipation of an upward gesture. This is another place where a blink followed by raising the eyebrows can help emphasize the body acting. Start closing the eyes on frame 43, and on frame 45, they should be completely shut. Hold the eyes shut for four frames, and begin to open them on frame 49 as the upward gesture begins. This is also when the eyebrows should begin to rise.

7. The eyes should be completely open on frame 51, and the eyebrows should be slowing into the peak position. Frame 53 is when the body gesture is at its peak, so this is when the eyebrows should be at their peak. If the upward gesture is held for a few frames, sometimes having the eyebrows peak a frame or two after the body can look nice. Because this gesture settles down immediately, the lag in the eyebrows would get lost, so in this case, the eyebrows will peak and settle on the same frames as the body.

8. The final gesture to emphasize is when he slams his fists down. Another blink so soon would look a little odd, and this gesture will look more intense if he keeps his eyes open. His expression could look a little more menacing though, so on frame 73, angle the eyebrows down to make him look more angry. Because the change from 71 to 73 of the body acting is so large, you can just pop the eyebrows into this position without any inbetweens.

9. Exit the face symbol, and watch the animation play. We have two problems. First, the nested animation doesn't appear to be playing properly. The first 13 frames of the animation are merged, so you'll have to go to each keyframe one at a time, select the head, and change its First frame property to match the frame you're on (see Figure 7-32). For example, on frame 7, the head's First frame should be 7; on frame 9, the First frame should be 9, and so on. Starting at frame 15, however, the head is on its own layer, so there's a much less tedious way to synchronize the head symbol with its nested facial animation.

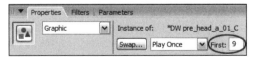

Figure 7-32. The First frame property needs to be changed to synchronize the body animation with the nested facial animation.

10. Go to frame 15, select the head, and make sure it's First frame is set to 15. Then on the head layer, select frames 15–81. Right/Ctrl+Click a frame on the timeline, and click Synchronize Symbols from the menu, as shown in Figure 7-33. Synchronize Symbols uses the first selected frame as a starting point (in this case, frame 15) and synchronizes all the following keyframes using the First frame setting for the symbol on that frame. In this case, the First frame is set to frame 15, so two frames later, the next keyframe is 17 (15 plus 2), and so on for each selected keyframe. When you do your own animation and you find that you need to merge layers, it's best to keep the head on its own layer and merge the layers below it and above it separately. This way, you can still use the Arrange commands to send symbols forward and backward and the Synchronize Symbols command for the head.

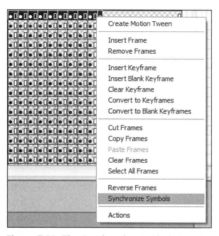

Figure 7-33. The Synchronize Symbols command is a way to quickly synchronize a nested timeline to the current timeline.

11. The second problem you should notice when you play back the body animation is that frames 9 and 11, where the front view of the head is used, have the eyes wide open, but in frame 7, he is beginning to close his eyes. Go to frame 9, select the head and run the FrameEDIT extension, which will edit the head in place and take us to frame 9. Close the eyes, and exit the symbol.

Now we need to do the lip sync. When doing lip sync there are a few general guidelines to follow. The mouth shape should almost always come a frame or two before the sound; otherwise, the mouth shape will look like it's appearing late. Vowels should usually pop open, but you can slow out of them if there's time. You should try to hold consonants for at least two frames to give them time to register. Don't try to animate every single syllable of a word; listen to how the line is said, and pay attention to the way the word is pronounced by the actor. The sounds that are most clearly heard should take precedence over the sounds that are slurred or not given much emphasis.

12. Let's start with the "A" sound in "what." If you scrub through the audio, you can see that the sound is first heard on frame 12. The mouth shapes should precede the audio, so make a keyframe for the mouth on frame 11, and change its First frame to 5 in the Properties panel.

13. Now that we know where the "A" sound needs to be, let's figure out where the "W" sound should go. Putting it two frames before "A" would work fine, but if you put it four frames before, on frame 7, it becomes a sort of anticipation for the word he's about to say. It fits with the animation, and there are enough frames for it to work, so keyframe the mouth on frame 7, and change the First frame to 8.

14. Frame 15 is where the "T" sound happens, but closing the mouth two frames ahead is too early; the "A" sound has a pretty strong emphasis, so the mouth should stay open longer for it. Because this character is animated on twos, putting mouth shapes on even-numbered frames can cause a strobe effect when the body and mouth animation aren't in sync. In this case, it will look better to have the "T" mouth shape appear on the same frame as the sound. Keyframe the mouth on frame 15, and change the First frame to 2.

15. To make a smoother transition from the wide-open to completely shut mouth, make another keyframe for the mouth on frame 13, and break apart the symbol (see Figure 7-34). Squash the mouth and jaw up a little, deselect the jaw, and stretch the mouth a little bit wider. You may need to adjust the position of mouth to get a smooth transition from the "A" to the "T" mouth shape.

Figure 7-34. By breaking apart the mouth chart, you can alter the shape of the lips and jaw independently to create smoother transitions between mouth shapes.

16. The mouth shapes for "D" and "T" are the same, so the next shape to worry about is the "OO" sound. Frame 19 is when the "D" sound is first heard, and that's a good place to put the "OO" mouth shape. The mouth chart on this character has two shapes that would work for this sound. Because the character is almost yelling, a more open "OO" shape might look better, so keyframe the mouth on frame 19 and change the First frame to 7.

17. He holds the "OO" sound for a bit, and then makes a sort of "E" sound as he pronounces the letter "y" in "you". On frame 23, keyframe the mouth, and change the First frame to 4. That "E" mouth is too extreme for this situation, so break apart the mouth, and deselect the lips. Change the jaw symbol's First frame to 3, deselect the jaw, and select the mouth. Squash the mouth down so it's not as open, and make it a little skinnier too.

18. The transition to the "OO" shape should occur on frame 27. This sound is held for a while, which gives us the opportunity do a little more animation with the mouth than just switching to the "OO" shape and holding it. Keyframe the mouth on frame 27, and change the First frame to 7; the mouth was broken apart previously, so to get our mouth comp back, simply drag and copy one of the earlier keyframes to frame 27. Keyframe the mouth on frame 29, and change the First frame to 8. Keyframe the mouth again on frame 31, and break apart the mouth. Deselect the jaw, and move the lips to the left a little bit. Go back to frame 29, and break apart the mouth. Deselect the jaw, and move the lips down a little bit. Now, we should have a little arc with the lips as he transitions from the "E" shape through the more open "OO" shape and into the final smaller "OO" shape.

19. The mouth is already in the right shape for the "W" sound in "want," so hold that shape until frame 37. On frame 37, keyframe the mouth, and change the First frame to 5. The "T" sound should come on frame 41, so keyframe the mouth on frame 41, and change the First frame to 2.

By this point, you should be able to finish the rest of the lip sync on your own. Don't forget to do the lip sync for the front view of the head on frames 9 and 11. One more thing you can do to make the facial animation look a little smoother is to slide the facial features left and right for the head turn, as shown in Figure 7-35. This will make for a much smoother head turn, instead of just popping from three-quarter view to front view and back again. You may want to try using one of the AnimSlider extensions to speed up the lip sync. Instead of having to memorize all the mouth positions and type the frame numbers into the Properties panel, you can simply click the frame number you want on the slider or scrub the slider to preview all the mouth shapes. To see the final animation, open ch07_xmas07.fla.

Figure 7-35. Moving the facial features to one side in the front view head smooths the transition from the three-quarter view head.

Using shape tweens

Shape tweens are a way of calculating inbetweens for two shapes instead of calculating inbetweens for symbols. With a symbol you can tween the scale, rotation, skew, position, or color. Shape tweens give you more flexibility in that the shape itself can change more dramatically and still be tweened by the computer. There are limits to the complexity of shape tweens, and there are a number of problems that you may run into.

Despite the problems associated with shape tweens, they can be very useful in certain situations. For example, if you want to make a character's eyes slowly close or squint, shape tweening the lids is a simple solution. You can also use shape tweens for mouth shapes or even entire characters. Let's take a look at how to use shape tweens and deal with common problems by animating a simple blob character, shown in Figure 7-36, that uses a face comp made of symbols and a blobby body that is a shape.

Figure 7-36. A simple character made up of symbols for the face and a shape for the body.

1. Open the file ch07_ShapeTween01.fla. If you play the timeline, you'll see that the keys and breakdowns are already there. All you have to do is select the frames and add tweens. This is the type of character that benefits from the Magic Tween extension. Select the frames you want to add a tween to and run the Magic Tween extension. Magic Tween will check the contents of each layer and determine whether to use a shape tween or motion tween.

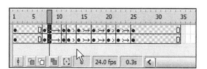

Figure 7-37. The Magic Tween extension is a way to quickly add shape and motion tweens to mixed characters.

2. Change the Ease value to 100 for all the frames except 17–19. The character should slow out of the peak of its jump, so make the ease –100. Again, extensions can save some time. Flash doesn't allow you to change the ease of motion tweens and shape tweens at the same time. The Timing Chart extension and the three commercial versions of AnimSlider have ease presets that work on shape and motion tweens simultaneously.

Play the animation, and you'll see that the shape tweens on frames 13, 18, 19, and 21 don't look quite right (see Figure 7-38). Flash is having a hard time determining how the tween should be calculated, so we'll have to use shape hints to give Flash a little assistance.

Figure 7-38. This shape tween on frame 21
is not being calculated correctly.

3. Hide the face layer, go to frame 12, and select the body. Open the Modify menu, click Shape
and then Add Shape Hint. A red circle with the letter "a" appears in the middle of the shape.
This is a shape hint: by placing this circle on the same part of a shape in the beginning and ending keyframe, Flash has a better idea of how you want the shape tween to be calculated. Add
three more shape hints, and place them around the character as shown in Figure 7-39. You can
use the Ctrl/Cmd+Shift+H keyboard shortcut to add shape hints more quickly. Sometimes,
you'll see your shape hint disappear immediately after adding it. To make it visible again, go to
the View menu, and click Show Shape Hints.

Figure 7-39. Placement of shape hints for
the start keyframe.

4. Go to frame 14, and you'll see your shape hints are once again in the center of the shape. The
shape hints should correspond to the same part of the body on the starting and ending
keyframes, so move the shape hints around the body as shown in Figure 7-40. Now, when you
look at frame 13, the body should look a lot better.

Figure 7-40. Placement of shape hints for the end keyframe

Follow the same process for the keyframes on frames 17, 20, and 22. Adding the shape hints to frame 20 may seem confusing at first, because the shape hints for the tween on frames 17–20 will overlap with the shape hints for the tween on frames 20–22. Another problem you may run into occasionally is when a shape disappears for the duration of the tween. This situation is most common when dealing with rounded shapes that don't have corner points for the shape hints to snap to. You can usually solve the problem by removing one of the shape hints by right-clicking it and selecting Remove Hint from the menu. The remaining shape hints may need to be distributed a little differently. Also, keep in mind that shape hints work best when placed in a counterclockwise order starting from the bottom-left of the shape.

To see the final result of our shape hints, open ch07_ShapeTween02.fla.

Summary

In this chapter, you learned what tweens are, why you would want to use them, and when to use them. You learned how to make use of shape tweens and shape hints, and how to use the custom ease editor to take full advantage of the power tweened animation offers. You should now have a good idea of which approach to Flash animation you want to take. Whether you prefer a frame-by-frame approach, tweens, or a combination of the two, it's important to keep practicing what you've learned and to strive to take your Flash animation to the next level.

Chapter 8

ANIMATION SPECIAL EFFECTS

By Allan S. Rosson and Dave Wolfe

This chapter will cover a number of different effects and techniques you can use to enhance the animation that you have created. Some of these techniques can be accomplished entirely in Flash, while others may require additional work using After Effects. Some of the effects that we'll be going over are deceptively simple in their execution but can yield maximum impact with how they are perceived. The special effects we will be dealing with are highlights and shadow modeling on a character as well as water, fire, smoke, and debris.

Highlights and shadow modeling

To achieve a more rendered look for a character, the use of highlights and shadows, or shadow modeling, is often used. These give the character the feeling of additional depth and dimension. This is especially useful when you have a scene that calls for a more dramatic mood or lighting scheme. The actual processes for creating highlights and shadows are identical; the only differences occur in the final rendering of color and transparency depending on what is a highlight and what is a shadow. Using the Generic Man character from previous chapters, we will go through the steps to create a shadow model. The background of this example was made darker to better illustrate these steps.

Preparing the shadow model layer

For this example, please refer to Chapter 6, and use the FLA file called fbf tutorial 04_eye acting. Inside the character's animated symbol, we will create a new layer just above the character's animated frames:

1. To do this, start by clicking the layer 1 label to the left of the frames. Next, go to Insert ➤ Timeline ➤ Layer, or click the Insert Layer icon under the list of layers. Name this new layer Shadow. It is important for this new layer to be just above the layer containing the animated frames.

2. Once again, click the layer label just below the new layer you just made. Now, go to Edit ➤ Timeline ➤ Copy Frames, or press Ctrl/Cmd+Alt+C. Next, select all of the Shadow layer, and go to Edit ➤ Timeline ➤ Paste Frames, or press Ctrl/Cmd+Alt+V (see Figure 8-1).

Figure 8-1. Selecting and duplicating the entire layer of animation

You should now have an exact duplicate layer of your original animated frames.

An alternate and faster way to copy the animation frames to a new layer is to follow the first step to create a new layer, then select your animation frames, and while holding down the Alt key, click and drag your animated frames to the new layer. Just be sure that the frames line up correctly, or the actions will be out of sync.

3. Now, we want to lock and hide all the layers except the Shadow layer. To do this, click the dots underneath the eye and lock icons that correspond to the layers that are to be locked and hidden. Click the Shadow layer name to select all the frames on that layer. Click the Edit Multiple Frames icon, which is below the timeline. Slide the brackets that appear at the top of the timeline so that they include all of the frames on the Shadow layer. Next, using Edit ➤ Select All or pressing Ctrl/Cmd+A will make sure that all of your frames are selected to do an edit multiple frame function (see Figure 8-2).

Figure 8-2. Using the Edit Multiple Frames tool

179

4. Use Modify ➤ Break Apart or press Ctrl/Cmd+B to break apart all those symbols along the time-line. You may need to do this a couple of times to be sure that all of the symbols are broken down completely.

5. Next, go to Modify ➤ Shape ➤ Convert Lines to Fills. Also perform this function at least twice to be sure that any lines that make up the character's parts are now converted to fills.

6. Last, set the color selection, which is on your toolbar next to the paint bucket, to black. This will change all of the fill colors of the shapes on the selected frames to black, as shown in Figure 8-3. Do not turn off the Edit Multiple Frames feature until you have completed these steps. You now have a complete silhouette of all the frames of your character's animation. The next step will be to create the modeled shapes for the character's shadow.

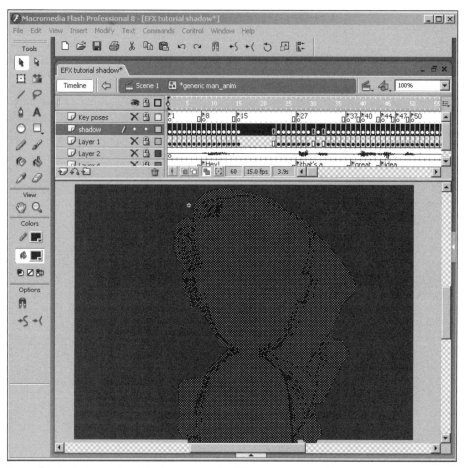

Figure 8-3. Symbols completely broken apart with all lines converted to fills and fill areas changed to black

Modeling the silhouette

This section will show you how to edit your animated silhouette so that you can create both a modeled shadow and a modeled highlight. Some of these steps require little effort, and others will take more time and patience. The results will be worth it and will give your character a more dramatic and rendered look.

1. Make sure the Edit Multiple Frames feature is turned off and the layer with the original animation is visible again. Keep all layers except the Shadow layer locked. Scroll back and forth along the timeline to see how well the silhouette matches the original animation. You may notice little places that don't fully cover the original animation. This happened during the breaking down process when some of the vectors that make up the images may have been shifted or reduced in numbers when lines were converted to fills. These defects should be minor and won't be too much trouble to fix as you go along.

2. I strongly suggest that you save this Shadow layer as a separate animated symbol to use again before you alter any of the frames for the shadow modeling. This will save you the trouble of re-creating the silhouette when you make your highlight layer. To do this, make sure all layers are locked except the Shadow layer. Click the Shadow layer's title bar to select all frames. Next, go to Edit ➤ Timeline ➤ Copy Frames or press Ctrl/Cmd+Alt+C, and then click Insert ➤ New Symbol or press Ctrl/Cmd+F8. When the prompt comes up, name this symbol Highlight, and be sure the space next to Graphic is selected before pressing Enter.

3. Select the first frame on the timeline, and go to Edit ➤ Timeline ➤ Paste Frames or press Ctrl/Cmd+Alt+V. All of your silhouette frames should now appear inside your Highlight symbol.

4. Go back to your main timeline, and double-click the character to get back to your Shadow layer. Now, click the Show Layer as Outline icon for the Shadow layer. Now you can see the silhouette throughout the timeline as it relates to the original animation. I'm choosing the right side of the character to model for this example.

5. Using the Pencil tool, choose a color that will be easy for you to see when the outline function is turned off. Draw a line that follows the contours of the character's face and body on the right side. Make sure that your line completely isolates the portion of the shadow that you want to keep, so that when you delete the excess later, you won't accidentally lose any of your modeling (see Figure 8-4).

6. When the outline feature is turned on, the Pencil's line color will be the same as the outline of the silhouette. You will see the color you chose for the Pencil line when you turn the outline feature off. When you are happy with that line, go to the next frame of animation, and create another line for that frame, and so on. This will test your abilities as an animator, as you will essentially be modeling the shadow line to the character as you go through the frames. It is a somewhat tedious process, but half of it was eliminated when you created the original silhouette. If you like, you can create a separate layer above the silhouette to draw these contour lines and copy and paste them progressively from frame to frame changing them as you go; this technique can help preserve consistency. However, you would still need to copy and paste those lines individually onto the silhouette frames, as we are using those lines to cut away the portion of the silhouette that is not wanted.

Figure 8-4. Outlined silhouette with a contour line for modeling

7. When you have completed all of your contour lines and they animate smoothly, turn off the outline feature, and go back to select the unwanted portion of the silhouettes and delete them. Also, make sure you delete the lines you drew so that you are left with only the modeled shape. A good way to do this after you have deleted the unwanted portion of the silhouette is to select the frame you are working on so that both the modeled shape and the line are selected. Now, hold down the Shift key, and click once inside the modeled shape. This will deselect only the shape, leaving the entire line selected. You can now delete the line.

8. Next, we need to modify the transparency of these modeled shapes to give them a more natural appearance as a shadow model. A great way to do this is to save this entire shadow layer as another symbol. This is the same process as we used in steps 8 and 9 to create the highlight symbol. This time, name the new symbol *Model Shadow. The asterisk is used so that the symbol will appear near the top of your library list for easy reference. Now, create a new layer, and name it Highlight. Place this layer above the Shadow layer on your timeline. Next, drag the *Model Shadow symbol from your library onto your stage, and place it so that it registers exactly with the shadow layer frames underneath (see Figure 8-5).

Figure 8-5. The unwanted portion of the silhouette is deleted, leaving only the modeled shape.

9. Hide and lock the Shadow layer. Click the shadow model symbol on the stage once, and using Properties panel ➤ Window ➤ Properties or pressing Ctrl/Cmd+F3, you can change the Alpha setting on this symbol to give it a transparency: set it to 30% (see Figure 8-6). Now you should have a transparent modeled shadow that animates in register with your original frames. Scroll back and forth along the timeline, and check to see that your modeled shadow does, in fact, register with the frames of your character's animation. When you are satisfied with the place-ment and transparency of your modeled shadow symbol, you can delete the Shadow layer underneath. Be sure to save your file periodically.

10. By using exactly these same steps, you can create a highlight model layer for the left side of the character that indicates the direction of the light source. The only difference would be to use a light color, such as a pale blue or yellow, in Edit Multiple Frames mode after converting lines to fills. It all depends on the mood you wish to create (see Figure 8-7).

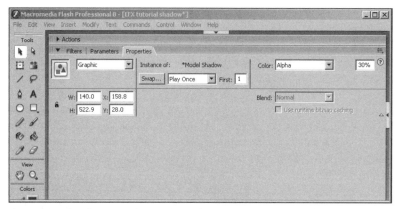

Figure 8-6. Using the Properties panel to select alpha transparency for the
*Model Shadow symbol

Explore this technique. By creating silhouettes in this way and saving them as symbols, you can create drop shadows on a wall, or by stretching and distorting the symbols, you can even create long shadows underneath a character for a more mysterious effect.

Figure 8-7. A character with modeled shadow and highlight

Water

Animating water can be a real challenge. Because of its fluidity, there really is no easy cheat or short cut, and animating it will take some time and a little patience. However, using some of the tools in Flash can ease some of the burden. In this example, we will have the Generic Man character fall into a body of water and create the resulting splash. To achieve this effect, you will be using a combination of your drawing skills and some of the wonderful tools in Flash to create distortion. The splash effect we made lasts 15 frames. The figures provided in this section will cover the most important aspects of this effect, and we will describe how to create it step by step. An FLA and a SWF file called 9128ch08_Splash are available for download from www.friendsofed.com, so you can view the finished sequence frame by frame to study the features of this particular effect.

1. Start by copying and pasting the Generic Man master symbol from the library onto the stage of a new file. Name your new file Splash Effect. Create a new layer on your timeline to hold the splash effect itself. Using the Rectangle tool draw a rectangle that will occupy approximately the bottom third of your stage, similar to what you see in Figure 8-8. Make sure to have the layer for the water below the layer containing the character.

Figure 8-8. A simple rectangle shape as the body of water

2. Break apart the Generic Man's symbol using Ctrl/Cmd+B, and pose him in a similar fashion to what is shown in Figure 8-8. Refer to Chapter 6 for more information on the workings of this character's library.

3. Figure 8-9 shows the character's impact on the water's surface. At this point, make a new layer between the character and the water layers to begin drawing the actual splash effect. Using your Pencil tool and choosing an appropriate outline color, draw a shape similar to the one shown in Figure 8-9.

4. Notice also that the body of water has distorted slightly upon the character's impact. To create this distortion, first highlight the frame that contains the body of water. Next, click the Free Transform tool or press Q on your keyboard, and click the Envelope tool at the bottom right under the magnet on your toolbar; you will see a series of handles surrounding your selection. Place your cursor on the top middle handle on the body of water selection, and pull down slightly. The handles distort the shape of the water. The Envelope tool is a wonderful feature in Flash, and we used it extensively for this effect and suggest you experiment with it to get the feel of it. If you don't like any of your changes, you can always press Ctrl/Cmd+Z to undo them and then reselect the Envelope tool to try again. The shape that you draw for the splash is very important because you will be creating progressive key frames (pressing F6 on your keyboard) along your timeline and distorting the splash shape with the Envelope tool as you go, rather than trying to redraw the shape for each and every frame as you might do if you were drawing on paper. Animators call this type of animation the straight ahead method as opposed to using pose-to-pose or traditional keyframing. The straight ahead method works well here, because you can keep the integrity of the original shape as you guide it though the transformation of the splash. Tweening is not recommended, because the distortion is limited, and the water would end up looking flat and stiff. Do not symbolize this shape, as you need to be able to manipulate the lines and fills to create this distortion.

Figure 8-9. Creating the character's initial impact on the water surface using the Envelope tool

5. In Figure 8-10, the character is sinking below the surface as the initial splash shape grows larger and engulfs him. At this point, a ripple wave begins to form as a result of the impact. The surrounding water continues to distort slightly. Notice the darker fill color inside of the splash shape to provide some dimension. With each progressive frame, we are using the Envelope tool to distort the splash's shape and size. We are also controlling and distorting the shape of the water as it moves up and out along an arching path on either side.

Figure 8-10. The splash grows, and ripples start to form.

6. Here is where it really starts to get interesting. In Figure 8-11, as the larger shapes of the water become more affected by gravity, they begin to stretch, get thinner, and pull themselves apart, so holes start to form in various places. To create the holes, use your Pencil tool to draw the shape of the holes at appropriate places on the splash shape. Then, simply delete the fill inside the lines you have drawn. Be careful to make these holes follow a logical shape so as to fit the overall splash shape. As you continue to make progressive frames and distort the splash shape, you can trace larger holes around the previous ones and again delete what was inside the lines. You may find that you need to make additional layers to manipulate all of these shapes easily. In our finished example, we had nine layers for the different components of the effect. Our general rule of thumb is that we make new layers only as we need them.

7. At this point, the main event is beginning to subside, but now a secondary splash begins to form (see Figure 8-12), because the water wants to rush in on itself to replace what was originally displaced. This is a good place to begin making the main splash shape progressively more transparent. You can do this by clicking inside of the fill color of the main splash and going to Window ➤ Color Mixer or pressing Shift+F9.

Figure 8-11. Holes begin to form as gravity stretches and thins out the shapes.

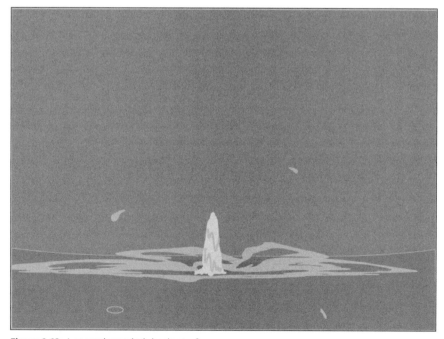

Figure 8-12. A secondary splash begins to form.

8. In the Alpha selection, you can change the transparency of that fill color from 100% down to 0 (see Figure 8-13). Choose values that are appropriate to make a smooth transition. There are other ways to do this; for example, you could convert a succession of frames into a symbol and use the tweening function to change the transparency, but we would strongly suggest that you first spend time experimenting with the method described here to gain an appreciation of what can be accomplished on a frame-by-frame basis.

9. The secondary splash now stretches up, and the column of water becomes thinner as it, too, begins to feel the effects of gravity and wants to pull itself apart. The top portion blooms as water droplets begin to form (see Figure 8-14). Some of the water droplets from the initial splash are now forming small ripple waves. You can use the circle tool to draw these ovals and resize them progressively over frames with the Free Transform tool.

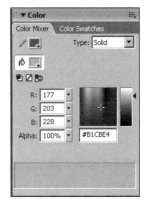

Figure 8-13. Alpha transparency control

Figure 8-14. The column of water becoming thinner as the top portion blooms

10. Next, we see the splash in its final stages as the water droplets begin to fall and the column of water has separated from the top portion (see Figure 8-15). Throughout the secondary splash, we were applying the Envelope tool to the main splash shape and to the body of water to create a subtle wavy motion to suggest the disturbance on the surface of the water. The main splash continues to become more transparent.

Figure 8-15. The column of water separates as the main splash become more transparent.

11. Finally, we're back to a calm sea with a last ripple wave emanating from the center of the event (see Figure 8-16).

Figure 8-16. The last water droplets dissipate as the ripple wave expands outward.

Fire

There are many different types of fire and flames and almost as many different approaches to animating them. We're going to focus on making a simple flame that can be used as a foundation for more complex types of fire.

1. Start by drawing a rough sketch of the flame shape similar to Figure 8-17. A rounded base and a couple squiggly lines that come to a point is all you need. Select the artwork, and press F8 to symbolize it. Then, double-click the symbol to edit it in place.

2. This flame is going to be an eight-frame cycle on twos, but to properly inbetween it, we'll need to copy frame 1 to frame 9. Extend the timeline to nine frames, and create a keyframe on frame 9.

3. Next, we need to draw the halfway point of the cycle. At frame 5, create a blank keyframe. Turn on onion skinning, and from the Onion Skin menu, click Onion 2 so that the onion skin shows the two frames before and after the current frame (see Figure 8-18). Sketch out another rough flame, but this time, the squiggled lines should be almost a mirror image of the first keyframe.

Figure 8-17. The rough sketch of the flame

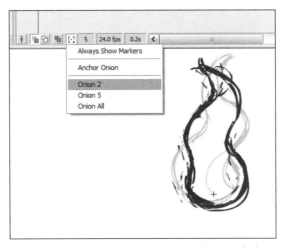

Figure 8-18. Use onion skinning to see the drawings before and after the current keyframe.

4. Now, there are just two inbetweens to make, and the rough flame cycle will be complete. Create blank keyframes on frames 3 and 7. Use onion skinning to see the drawings before and after. When you draw the inbetween frames, think of the peaks and valleys of the squiggle lines as rising. As you work on a section of the flame, you can draw little dashes to mark the peaks or valleys of the neighboring keyframes and draw the inbetween peaks and valleys halfway between them (see Figure 8-19).

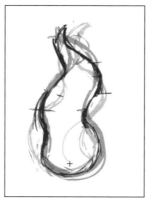

Figure 8-19. Drawing little dashes indicating the peaks and valleys of the curve can help you when drawing inbetweens.

5. From the Control menu, click Loop Playback (see Figure 8-20). Then, press Enter to play the timeline and see how well the flame loops. If you spot problem areas, make adjustments to your rough drawings.

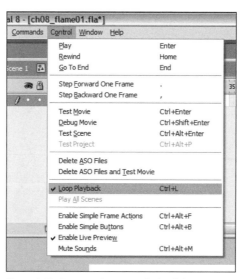

Figure 8-20. Turn on the Loop Playback feature to watch your animation loop.

6. You may notice a slight pause as the animation is looping, which is due to two things. First, we need to remove frame 9. It's a copy of the first frame, so it looks as though the first keyframe is three frames long instead of two. The other reason for the pause is that it takes Flash a second to rewind the timeline and start playing it again. Here's a way around this: First, exit the symbol; then, Right/Ctrl-click the symbol, and choose Edit in New Window(see Figure 8-21).

Center the flame in the new window by double-clicking the Hand tool icon in the toolbar. Turn on the Loop Playback feature again from the Control menu, and play the timeline. The animation should now loop smoothly.

Figure 8-21. Edit the symbol in a new window to loop the playback without any pauses.

7. Add a new layer, and lock the layer with the flame drawings. The new layer will be used to clean up the drawings. Using the Line or Pencil tool, trace a clean outline of the flame for each keyframe (see Figure 8-22). Hide the roughs, and play the animation to make sure the cleaned up drawings look right when animated.

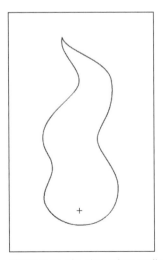

Figure 8-22. The cleaned up outline of the flame

8. The final step is to fill the cleaned up drawings and erase the out-lines. A radial gradient fill with a bright yellow center and orange edges makes for a good looking flame, but depending on the style you're using, a flat fill may look better. A quick way to get rid of the lines is to use the Eraser tool and use the Erase Lines option from the menu on the toolbar (see Figure 8-23). You can then turn on Edit Multiple Frames, zoom out to 10 percent, and erase all the lines with a single click.

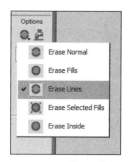

Figure 8-23. The Erase Lines option enables you to quickly erase the lines without erasing the fill.

That's all there is to a basic flame. You can use it as is, or use it as a building block for more complex flames. You can copy and paste the symbol several times, flipping it horizontally and altering its scale (see Figure 8-24). To see an example of this, open the file ch08_flame03.fla.

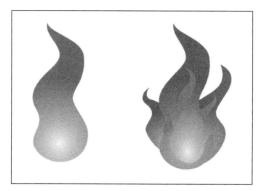

Figure 8-24. Scaling and flipping copies of the basic flame can create a more complex fire effect.

Smoke

As with fire, there are many types of smoke and many approaches to animating it. We're going to use a very simple method to make a large billowing plume of smoke similar to the type you might see coming from a smokestack or a steam engine.

1. Start by using the Brush tool to paint a grey puff of smoke (see Figure 8-25). Select the artwork, and press F8 to symbolize it. That's all you really need to start animating the smoke; if you want to add some more variation, you can create several more smoke symbols, but for now, one symbol will suffice.

Figure 8-25. A puff of smoke

2. Scale the symbol down, and move it to the bottom of the stage. The smoke needs time to rise, and 51 frames is a random number that just happens to be long enough for the smoke in this scene, so extend the timeline to 51 frames, and make a keyframe at frame 31. On frame 31, scale up the smoke symbol so that it's two or three times larger than the symbol on frame 1. Move the symbol to the top of the stage, and rotate it 180 degrees.

3. On frame 51, create another keyframe, and this time, slightly scale up the symbol, rotate it a few degrees, and move it off the stage. Add a motion tween, and watch the animation play.

4. It's not very impressive with one smoke symbol. Add a new layer and select all the frames of the smoke layer. While holding down the Alt key, drag and copy the frames from the smoke layer to the new layer. With the copied frames still selected, drag the frames horizontally across the timeline so that the new smoke animation starts on frame 5 (see Figure 8-26).

Figure 8-26. Drag and copy the frames from layer 1 into layer 2, and offset the starting frame.

5. If you play the animation now, you can see where this is going. It's starting to look better, but it still needs more layers of smoke. Make some more copies of the smoke layer, and progressively offset the starting keyframe by two to four frames. You can speed the process up by copying multiple layers at the same time.

6. Once you've gotten about eight layers of smoke, it's time to start adding some variation to the animation. For each layer, make small alterations to the animation. Some smoke symbols could start out smaller or larger. They can rotate at different speeds and in different directions, and they should end at different sizes and rotations.

7. For a really cool effect, you can use the blur and shadow filters introduced in Flash 8. Be warned, though, that this will dramatically affect the playback performance if you plan on delivering your files as SWFs. Before you can use the blur and shadow filters the symbols all need to be changed to movie clips. To convert the graphic symbols to movie clips, enable Edit Multiple Frames and drag the onion skin markers to encompass all the frames in the scene. Then press Ctrl/Cmd+A to select everything. From the Properties panel, click the menu on the far left, and change the symbols to Movie Clip (see figure 8-27).

Figure 8-27. Change the Graphic symbols to Movie Clip symbols so that filters can be used.

8. Leave Edit Multiple Frames turned on, and keep all the symbols selected. Open the Filters panel, and click the + button on the far left to add a filter. Add the Blur filter, and change the Blur X and Blur Y settings until you're satisfied with the amount of blur. We found that 24 was just enough that the edges looked really soft but the overall shape was still recognizable (see Figure 8-28).

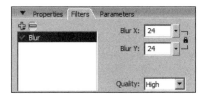

Figure 8-28. The settings used for the Blur filter

9. To complete the effect, add the Drop Shadow filter. This one has a few more options to deal with. Again, feel free to experiment with the settings until you're satisfied with the results; there's no exact science involved here, just play with the settings until it looks good. We used a Blur of 37, a Strength of 100%, Angle of 302, and a Distance of -32, and we picked a light grey (#999999) for the color. One setting you will certainly want to use is Inner Shadow. This will apply the shadow to the symbol itself rather than having the shadow fall on objects behind the symbol (see Figure 8-29).

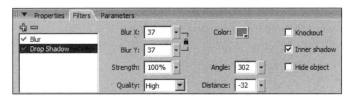

Figure 8-29. The settings used for the Drop Shadow filter

10. When you're done with the filters, you can turn off Edit Multiple Frames and watch as your computer struggles to play back the animation. Because these movie clips are only one frame, you can still export to video using this effect, so don't be too alarmed by the performance hit caused by using these filters.

This is a pretty short sequence. If you want, you can lengthen it by copying the frames from the eight layers into eight new layers and offsetting the starting keyframes (see Figure 8-30). You can also experiment with altering the color or alpha value as the smoke rises. As with the fire, if you layer in different colored and sized smoke symbols, you can get some more interesting styles of smoke. This technique can also be used for other effects such as missile contrails or billowing clouds. To see the final effect, open the file ch08_smoke02.fla.

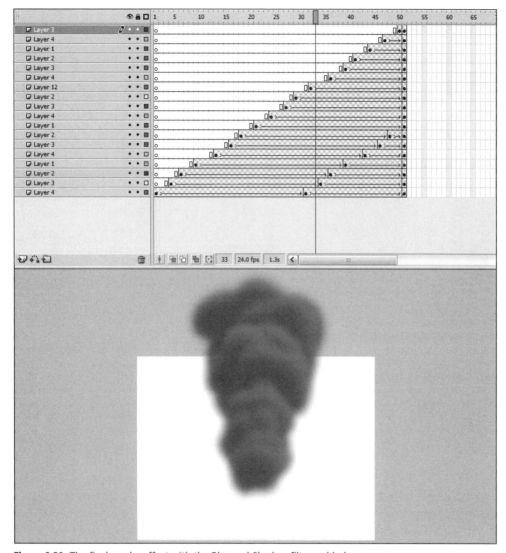

Figure 8-30. The final smoke effect with the Blur and Shadow filters added

Debris

Flying debris is a common effect that you'll probably find yourself doing at some point in your career. Whether it's breaking glass, a monster bursting through a wall, or an explosion, Flash enables you to get the job done quickly and easily!

1. Start by opening the file ch08_debris01.fla. This pile of rubble is going to fly up and bounce around as though something buried beneath it suddenly burst out (see Figure 8-31).

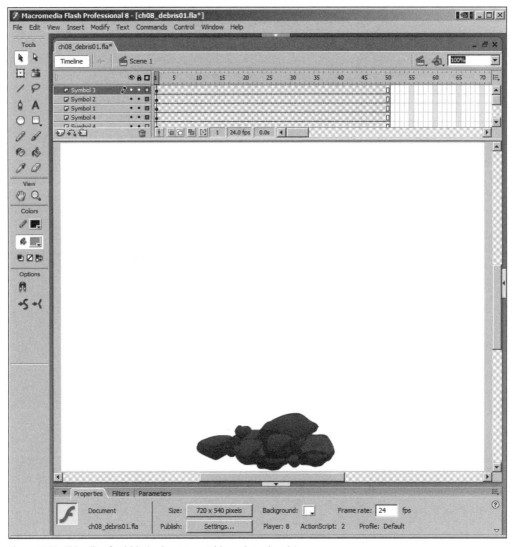

Figure 8-31. This pile of rubble is about to get blown into the air!

2. Select the first layer, and hide all the others so they don't distract you. First, we're going to block the path and timing of the symbol. For this one, let's use 14 frames for the first bounce, 10 frames for the second bounce, and 6 frames for the final bounce. The length of these bounces will be determined largely by how high the pieces fly and the force with which they are thrown into the air. As the energy used to move the debris is depleted and gravity takes its toll, the pieces will have shorter bounces requiring fewer frames. Make a keyframe at frame 8, and move the symbol up to about the middle of the stage, rotate it 90 degrees clockwise, and move it to the right a bit (see Figure 8-32).

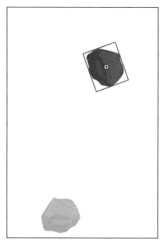

Figure 8-32. Move the symbol up and to the right for the peak of the first bounce.

3. Make a keyframe at frame 15, and move the symbol back down to the bottom of the stage; rotate it another 90 degrees clockwise, and move it farther to the right. The distance you move the symbol to the right should be the same as the distance between frames 1 and 8. You can turn on onion skinning to make it easier to see how much you need to move the symbol to the right (see Figure 8-33).

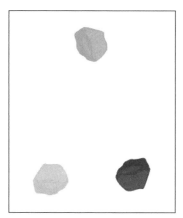

Figure 8-33. Use the onion skinning feature to help you determine the placement of the debris.

4. Make a keyframe at frame 20, and move the symbol up just about the height of the symbol itself. In the last two steps, the symbol was rotated a total of 180 degrees, turning it upside down. We want the symbol to land right side up, but the final bounce is too small for a complete rotation. So for this second bounce, we'll rotate it about 80 degrees clockwise, and move it to the right again.

5. Make a keyframe at frame 25, move the symbol back down to the bottom of the stage, rotate it another 80 degrees clockwise, and move it to the right.

6. For the final bounce, make a keyframe at frame 31, and just move the symbol to the right. In the previous two steps, we rotated the symbol a total of 160 degrees, so to have the symbol land right side up, we need to rotate it 20 degrees clockwise (see Figure 8-34).

Figure 8-34. The final blocking of the animation

The path right now is too linear; the debris needs to move in arcs. An easy way to accomplish this is to use guide layers. If you drag a normal layer onto a guide layer, Flash will attempt to use the guide layer as a motion guide for tweened animation. The guide layer needs to have a line to follow, and the keyframes of the tweened symbol need to line up to the guide line. Since the animation is already blocked, the extension DrawGuide (see Chapter 5) will speed up this process by blocking out the guide line for you.

7. Select all the keyframes in the first layer, and run the DrawGuide extension from the Commands menu. A new guide layer will be created with straight lines that follow the path of the symbol on the layer you previously selected (see Figure 8-35).

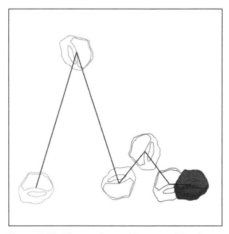

Figure 8-35. The motion guide created by the DrawGuide extension.

8. This path is still linear, so the lines need to be adjusted to follow nice, smooth arcs. The final straight line should be pulled into a small arc for the debris to settle (see Figure 8-36).

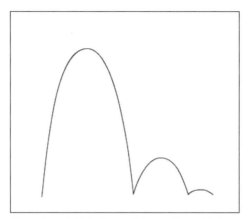

Figure 8-36. Pull the lines of the motion guide into arcs.

9. Add motion tweens to the debris, and drag the layer onto the guide layer (see Figure 8-37). The debris layer should become indented, indicating that it is now a guided layer. When you play the timeline, the debris should now follow the arcs in the guide layer.

Figure 8-37. An animation layer being guided by a guide layer

10. The path that the debris follows looks better now, but the motion looks too mechanical. The debris needs to slow in as it reaches the peak of the arc and slow out as it starts to fall back to the ground. For the first arc, eases of 75 and -75 should do the trick. For the second arc, use eases of 50 and -50, and for the final one, leave the ease at 0.

If you're using Flash 8 or higher, this is a good opportunity to make use of Custom Ease. The motion of the debris should have slow ins and slow outs, but the rotation should be either linear or slowing in to the final position, not slowing in and out at the peaks of the arcs.

11. Select frame 1 of the debris layer, and in the Properties panel, click the Edit button next to the Ease slider. Press Ctrl/Cmd+C to copy the curve. Next, uncheck the check box labeled Use one setting for all properties. Press Ctrl/Cmd+V to paste the curve, and click OK (see Figure 8-38). Follow this same process for the rest of the tweened frames.

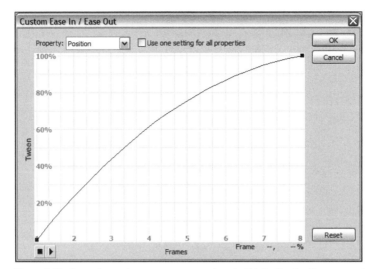

Figure 8-38. Copy the custom ease curve, and paste it into the Position property.

That takes care of one of the pieces of debris. Follow the same process to animate the rest of the pieces (see Figure 8-39). Be sure to add some variation to the timing of the bounces, the height of the arcs, and the horizontal distance the debris travels. The same concept used for debris can also be used for other effects, such as sparks or confetti. Motion guides are good for more than effects; they can also be used to animate the path of a fish or a space ship. To see how the final animation turned out, open the file ch08_debris02.fla.

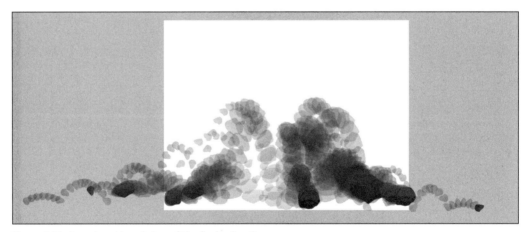

Figure 8-39. An onion skinned view of the final animation

Summary

In this chapter, we covered

- Creating highlights and shadow modeling for a character
- Creating a splash in a body of water and some of the characteristic properties of water
- Ways of creating effects for
  - Fire
  - Smoke
  - Debris

The methods in this chapter are by no means the only ways of achieving these effects. We hope, however, that they might inspire you to further explore the potential of the tools in Flash that you have at your disposal and also aid you in developing your own unique methods of working. It all comes back to work, patience, and practice. We hope that studying and applying some of these techniques to your animation will help you to achieve your desired results. The next chapter will cover using After Effects at various stages in your projects.

Chapter 9

WHY USE AFTER EFFECTS?

By Barry J. Kelly

Is it possible to make an entire animated piece in Flash and Flash alone? Yes. Is it a good idea? Probably not if your project is getting long—let's say, over 1 minute. The more content you add and the more symbols in the document, the bigger the file size, which can lead to disorganized libraries and a less efficient project resulting in big headaches. Flash is a great character animation tool, but for editing and compositing, there are better tools. In these cases, doing some of the work in a dedicated motion graphic tool is often better. I tend to use After Effects, although there are other options available, such as Shake or Combustion, or editing in software like Adobe Premiere, Vegas Video, or Final Cut Pro. For more on After Effects, Flash, and Motion Graphics, check out *From After Effects to Flash: Poetry in Motion Graphics* by Tom Green and Tiago Dias (friends of ED, 2006, ISBN: 1-59059-748-4).

In this chapter, we'll discuss the advantages and disadvantages of using After Effects in the following six situations. You might consider using After Effects instead of Flash to composite and edit your animation when

- Your animation runs longer than 1 minute
- You are animating your scenes into separate FLAs (whether by yourself or as a member of a team)
- You want to incorporate complex camera mechanics
- You want to incorporate non-Flash assets (such as Photoshop BGs, and video clips)

- Your delivery requirements indicate something other than a SWF

- Effects and tool sets are desired that are not available in Flash

At the end, we will also go through the disadvantages of using After Effects instead of Flash.

Animation running longer than 1 minute

While it is possible to composite your animation in Flash, projects that are more than about 1 minute in length become unwieldy. Working in a frame-based timeline can get somewhat difficult when you have thousands upon thousands of frames in one timeline. Using an editing timeline based on SMPTE (Society of Motion Picture and Television Engineers) time code will prove more efficient with longer projects (for more on time code, see the section called "SMPTE Time Code" later in this chapter).

File size can quickly grow to several hundred megabytes, and the RAM usage can grow so large that work becomes very slow and crashes are possible. After Effects proves very handy in this area: it does require RAM usage, but it won't affect playback as much. After Effects, like any editing program, can handle almost any project length, and its overwhelming amount of multiformat capabilities allow you to composite and edit your project with less hassle.

Factors that increase file size, length, and content

A lot of factors can increase the file size of an FLA, including creating the assets you're animating, adding more animation, or importing files into your FLA (every file you import into Flash is embedded into that FLA's library).

When you import a file (e.g., a QuickTime movie) into Flash, Flash will compress and format the file into a Flash video file (FLV) and place it into that FLA's library, which will increase that FLA's file size. When you import a QuickTime movie into After Effects, After Effects creates a reference link to that file on your hard drive, so you can use and view that movie clip without creating a duplicate movie in After Effects. It links to the specific location of the source files, and these links make up the After Effects Project (AEP) file (see Figures 9-1 and 9-2). Many video-editing programs use a file-oriented system like this one, which is very efficient when properly managed.

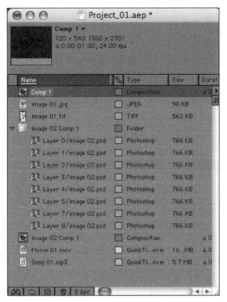

Figure 9-1. The Adobe After Effects project window shows the files that this project is using and referencing.

Figure 9-2. This screenshot displays the file path (located in the After Effects project window), which links to the file's actual location.

The use of reference files is the reason the AEP's file size is so small. It doesn't actually contain any content, just those links to the content and animation data (see Figure 9-3).

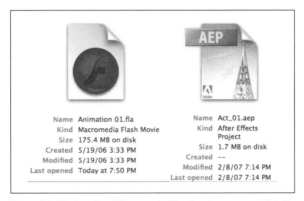

Figure 9-3. Notice the difference in file sizes between an FLA file and an AEP one.

207

An efficient way of working is to keep all your Flash and other source files in a centralized area on your hard drive specific to your project. That way, when you work with multiple applications, your files are already organized, making it easier to navigate, find files, and keep them organized in an application.

FLAs grow too large to handle

Large FLAs can impact your computer's performance. Merely opening an FLA that's over 100MB can slow your machine down for a few minutes before you ever see a frame on the stage. While the published SWF may be smaller than the FLA, you will still experience slowdown in playback if the SWF coming out of an oversized FLA. Also, sequences with frames numbering in the thousands become increasingly difficult to view and manage, and lengthy symbols set within even more lengthy symbols increase the chance of error. Moving and sliding keyframes and tweens could throw your animation off sync, from your symbolized acting or specific sounds and dialog. Having to resync your work can cause a lot of backtracking and navigating for the correct frame numbers in groups and symbols, which results in time lost you could have spent animating.

After Effects is a nondestructive program

Like most nonlinear editing programs, After Effects is a nondestructive program; the source files for all the clips you import, use, animate, and manipulate will not be affected in any way. This nondestructive nature is because of the reference link system; you are merely *using* the content, not changing it. For example, if you were to add a series of filters and split up a clip over different parts of your timeline, the original source clip used would remain exactly the way it was in its original location.

Animating in separate scenes

If you separately animate scenes in Flash into clips, you can bring them into an editing and compositing program to finish your project. Using individual scenes can also help you avoid creating large FLAs. You can use many programs, like Shake or Combustion, to composite, and you can edit in software like Adobe Premiere, Vegas Video, or Final Cut Pro. In this book, we will talk about using After Effects. After Effects is a strong composting and animation tool. It's also possible to edit in After Effects due to its use of time code within its timeline. If you've used editing software before, editing in After Effects can be a little different than in other applications, since you'll have to edit using layers rather than tracks, but using layers is totally doable.

The timeline in Flash is perfect for character animation, but for editing, the timeline needs to be more versatile and practical. You will need to be able to slide, cut, and trim your audio and video clips across a timeline to sync audio and video efficiently. In Flash, the timeline is based on frames, and your content is split between keyframes of animation, but Flash's ability to edit audio is very limited, and it's not practical for simply sliding or trimming clips. Editing in Flash involves a lot of copying, pasting, and moving groups of frames back and forth, whereas an editing tool enables you to easily change a clip's head and tail (terms referring to the beginning and ending of a clip) no matter if it is video, audio, or a still image.

Figure 9-4. A Flash animation within After Efftects

SMPTE time code

As mentioned earlier, Flash runs on frames, which is logical for animation. But for making an edited piece that spans minutes and that you possibly need to further alter in postproduction, SMPTE time code, or just time code for short, proves necessary and could be crucial to the project's output. The format of time code looks like this: 00:00:00:00. The numbers represent Hours: Minutes: Seconds: Frames (see Figure 9-5). SMPTE time code is a universal form in a timeline that would be necessary if your project was to be output for broadcast, feature film, or even web video.

Figure 9-5. Time code windows within After Effects

Time code also gives you the ability to create edit decision lists (EDLs) and log times for your project. An EDL is a text document containing a list of the names and time codes of your edit points. Though most often used in video, an EDL might be necessary in projects combining both video and animation or some big, high-end animation projects.

209

Avoid symbol naming conflicts

One problem that is easily avoided by animating into separate scenes is a symbol naming conflict. In Flash, symbol names can be a major problem if not handled properly (see Figure 9-6). Copying and pasting animation from one scene into another will take you to the Resolve Library Conflict dialog box, which prompts you to replace or not replace the existing symbol (see Figure 9-7). This prompt can be a very useful tool, but without organized symbol names, it can be destructive to your project. If you choose to replace symbols when different symbols share the same name, all those symbols will be overwritten, which could drastically change your entire piece for the worse. You can simply undo it, but you will have to spend the time renaming those symbols.

If you choose not to replace the existing symbols when prompted, those copied symbols simply aren't pasted over the existing ones; if you needed those copied symbols, that's another naming problem you'll have to remedy.

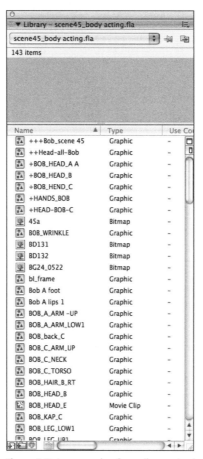

Figure 9-6. An example of a well organized, yet massive, character library

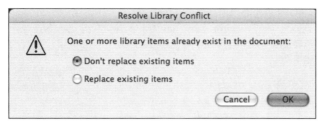

Figure 9-7. The options for replacing existing symbols

The ease of using separated scenes

Copying and pasting scenes together in Flash is burdensome. Copying and pasting scenes into one FLA may be a certain method of combining multiple scenes but is not always the best one. If you were to select all the frames within a layer (see Figure 9-8) and copy and paste them into a new scene (without needing to replace any symbols), the frames will appear exactly as you had them—but you may then need to spend time adjusting their sizes and placement (if you didn't follow the 100 Percent Rule from Chapter 4) or other registration issues that may arise. Also note that scenes that are in layers will need to be symbolized before you can copy and paste frames, because otherwise, the assets in those layers won't physically move as a whole. Every scene or element that has specific keyframes for animation across multiple layers will need also to be symbolized. When you make a group of layers into a symbol, they become one whole object, so when you copy and paste or drag and transform that symbol, it will change as a whole. Therefore, every clip needs to be its own symbol. But when you bring them into one timeline, you need to make sure each clip's symbols are organized so that existing symbols will not be mistakenly overwritten, possibly destroying your animation, causing you to undo lots of actions, and requiring unnecessary reorganization, all of which slow down your project. For more on library organization, see Chapter 2.

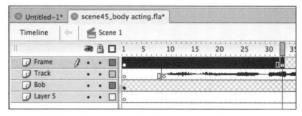

Figure 9-8. Selecting the first 31 frames in the Flash timeline

Using separate scenes is much easier to handle and edit with After Effects; each scene will be its own clip and layer within the After Effects timeline. There are no more symbol management or timing changes, because you are no longer in Flash; the animation will be used as if it were a flattened movie clip.

Imported scenes and files are easily updateable

Flash has the ability to update symbols within the library; this option is used when changes are made to existing animation or objects and those particular symbols may need to be updated wherever that symbol may also appear. After Effects has this same ability, as long as the original file is kept with the same name and in the same location, After Effects can update any file that is referenced within its project.

Let's say you import a SWF you made in Flash into After Effects, but there is something you needed to change. The clip is already in your timeline, and you don't want to have to redo the work you did in After Effects all over again on the new clip. Simply change what you needed back in Flash, and publish the SWF again, keeping the same name, thus overwriting the old version. When you go back into the AEP file, your file should be automatically updated. If it's not, go to the file in your project window, right-click it, and select Reload Footage (see Figure 9-9). Your footage is updated without changing your After Effects work.

Figure 9-9. The Reload Footage option updates the file in your project.

RAM usage and playback

In Flash, the more you add into your FLA, the more playback slows down, dependent on the amount of RAM you have. When animating characters, being able to see your character in full motion is crucial for timing and acting. Scrubbing through the timeline can only get you so far. When you have a great amount of highly detailed animation, design, and effects in your Flash file, SWFs and playback in the FLA will slow down and will appear to be dropping frames and skipping animation due to the amount of content and low amount of RAM available to display that content. Crashes may become common. Flash allows you to reduce the quality setting, which is extremely helpful, but an extremely large FLA will slow down on even the lowest setting.

Trimming

Trimming isn't too difficult in Flash; its just a matter of knowing your document and which keyframes are going to affect others when you move them. In theory, selecting your desired group of frames and dragging them where they belong is all you need to do. But if your desired frame is a symbol or grouped layer, the move could affect a lot of timing in lip sync and action if you don't pull over the correct start frame and end frame for that symbol.

Why is trimming easier in After Effects? When you bring in your SWF, image sequence, or document into After Effects, you're bringing in one clip. That's it. You have no elements to break down and worry about. You have the head of the clip, the tail of the clip, and the footage in between. You just slide the ends, which appear as grey handles (in After Effects 6.5) on both sides of a clip to meet your trimming needs (see Figure 9-10).

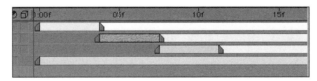

Figure 9-10. Notice the grey handles on the end of the clips for trimming.

In and out points

Simple navigation between clips is crucial for all editing. That's why most editing programs, including After Effects, have the ability to create and jump between in and out points, and Flash does not have this ability. In and out points are a way of selecting a section of frames/seconds within a clip or sequence. You can set in and out points (see Figures 9-11 and 9-12) if you need to watch or render only a certain section of your project. You can also use them as markers with which you can quickly jump from the beginning, the end, or a selection of a clip quickly and precisely.

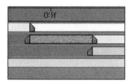

Figure 9-11. On a layer, the in and out points are the grey handles. Note that After Effects CS3 no longer has visible handles.

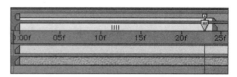

Figure 9-12. On the timeline itself, the in and out points of the work area are the grey handles on the white bar above the time ruler.

Animation incorporating complex camera mechanics

Even simple camera mechanics, like pans and zooms, are easier in After Effects than in Flash, but when you want to do something a little more complex, like a flying camera move, it is almost impossible in Flash. One reason is that Flash doesn't really have a "camera." You are limited to the stage and must move "the world."

Pans and zooms

In Flash, it is possible to rotate, skew, and resize your objects using motion tweening. However, using the motion tween adds a certain degree of unpredictability, because the transform options can't truly be keyframed individually. In After Effects, every element imported creates its own layer in the timeline, and every layer has these default Transform functions: Anchor Point, Position, Scale, Rotate, and Opacity (see Figure 9-13). Each function can be keyframed and altered individually for precise transform animation of any duration. After Effects also has an adjustable camera, which enables you to make multiplane camera moves and change the depth of field and lens sizes, making animation much smoother and more controllable than you would get in Flash alone (see Figure 9-14).

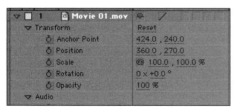

Figure 9-13. Transform options of an After Effects layer

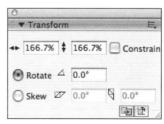

Figure 9-14. Transform window of a Flash object

Other complex camera movement

Flash works in layers to allow for multiplane movement. But again, many variables are thrown in when motion tweening complex camera movement. After Effects also works in layers, so you can do multiplane moves using its excellent transform functions. One major advantage of After Effects though, is Z space. The option to make a layer 3-D is another great asset of After Effects. If a shot requires that feeling of real depth, the ability to turn a layer into a 3-D layer and move in a simulated 3-D world can prove very valuable to a project.

Animation requiring non-Flash assets

You may want to incorporate non-Flash assets, such as Photoshop backgrounds or video clips, into your animation. If this is the case, After Effects offers many advantages over Flash. After Effects combines multiple formats including graphics, live action, 2-D animation, and 3-D animation (see Figure 9-15). And After Effects has an abundant amount of different acceptable formats, including JPEG, JPEG sequence, TIFF, PNG, PNG sequence, PSD MOV, AVI, WAV, AIFF, MP3, MP4, and SWF (see Figure 9-16). Also, as mentioned earlier, all of these assets are kept as linked references inside the After Effects project, rather than being imported directly into the project like they would be in Flash.

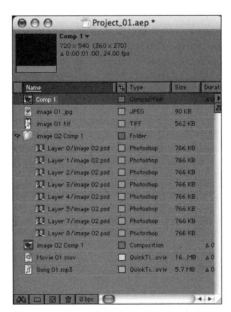

Figure 9-15. The After Effects project window

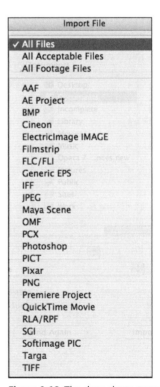

Figure 9-16. The drop-down menu of Import File formats

Frame rate control

One Flash document has one frame rate. But if you need to use bits of animation from previous projects that were created with different frame rates, you'll have to individually retime all those elements to the FLA you're pulling them into. If you use After Effects, you can bring different clips of various durations and frame rates and adjust them in the Interpret Footage window. You can adjust the frame rates of items with just a few clicks and changes, while maintaining your overall projects frame rate and duration (see Figure 9-17).

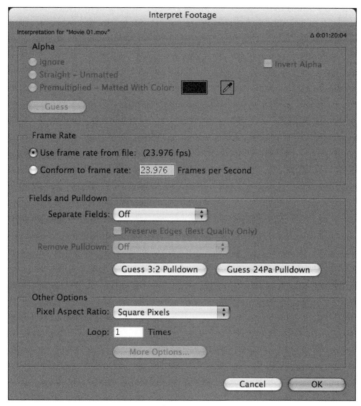

Figure 9-17. The Interpret Footage window

Animation requiring delivery of something other than a SWF

When you need to deliver something other than a SWF, After Effects gives you more control of your file output options. Flash can export SWFs, QuickTime movies (WAVs and AVIs on a PC), and various kinds of image sequences. After Effects can export a multitude of formats, which is why it's so valuable in a production pipeline to broadcast, web, and DVD. After Effects has access to many compressors and formats; for example, you can export a QuickTime movie using anything from H.264 compression to 10-bit uncompressed video or a choice of many other formats like images sequences, WAVs, AIFFs, MP3s, AVIs, EDLs (see Figures 9-18 and 9-19).

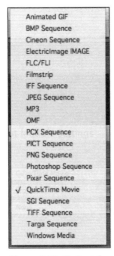

Figure 9-18. Output format selections found in the Render Queue

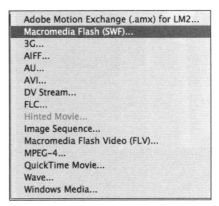

Figure 9-19. Output format selections found in the File ➤ Export menu

Export features

Another feature of After Effects is its ability to make render points in the timeline; the selection between these render points is considered the "work area" (see Figure 9-21) and are similar to in and out points but are used for exporting. When exporting, rendering the whole project isn't always necessary; you may need to see only a few seconds of animation. The render selection lets you render just a few frames, a few minutes, or whatever portion of your project you choose. These aren't set in stone, as the Render Settings dialog box shows (see Figure 9-20); you can set your start and end times for definite sections of a project.

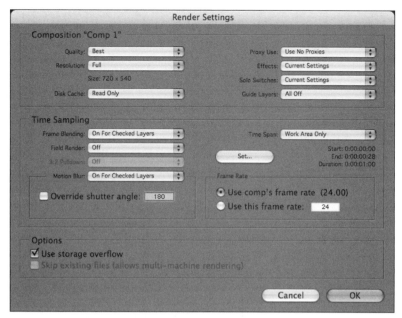

Figure 9-20. One of the Render Settings windows of an After Effects project

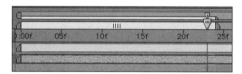

Figure 9-21. The in and out points of the work area can also be used as the render preview selection currently on this timeline.

Render queue

Let's say your project requires you to export multiple formats of your animation; for instance, you may need to make QuickTime movies of different sizes and codecs for final delivery. Well, you'd have to export one movie, wait for it to finish, set up and export the next one, wait for it to finish, and so on. After Effects has a render queue that makes it possible to set up a list of all the different outputs you want to export and, with the click of a button, render every listing in the queue. You can render multiple compositions, each with multiple formats, or even certain sections of one timeline, rendering only what's selected by your in and out points. The benefit of this is that if your project requires multiple formats to be exported, you could set up all the exports you need after you've finished your work, and with one click, export them all, one after the other going down the list in the queue.

Desired effects and tool sets are not available in Flash

After Effects opens up a whole world that is not available in Flash; an abundance of filters, camera techniques, audio manipulation, color keying, and rotoscoping are all available. It's not so much a simple visual effects tool as it is a multimedia compositor.

Transform options

Since every element gets its own layer with its own transform options in After Effects, animating multiple layers is easy with copy and paste. If you need to have multiple elements all growing in size and following one another from across the screen, all you have to do is animate one of those layers. Then copy and paste that layer's attributes into all the others. This makes animating multiple items much easier and faster than doing each layer separately in Flash. You can copy and paste any keyframed animation from one layer into any other with very little difficulty.

Transitions

It's definitely possible to do transitions in Flash, but there are a few kinks in achieving even commonly used transitions, such as the cross-dissolve. If you want to fade one clip into another in Flash, that clip needs to be its own symbol (so that you can adjust the alpha of the entire clip) and in its own layer. To create the dissolve, place the second clip in a layer beneath the first one, and then tween the alpha from 0 to 100 over a series of frames. This procedure can be used, but it has a big problem. Every element in that symbol fades individually, which just looks wrong—it's not only distracting but it looks like a mistake (see Figure 9-22). The clip needs to be a flattened image to give the appearance of a traditional fade. Because a clip in After Effects is flattened, those individual symbols aren't an issue. The clip fades naturally, and all you do is keyframe the opacity, from 100 percent to 0 percent, over a series of frames, with the next clip aligned beneath it.

Flash

After Effects

Figure 9-22. Compare the transparency issue as the image on the left fades in Flash (middle) and After Effects (right).

Sound editing

Flash is one of the most limited programs for audio usability. Getting an audio clip to begin where desired can be a headache, especially in a long animation sequence. The ability to choose between event sounds and stream sound can help. Stream audio is useful for lip sync and music, but Flash's tools are not very efficient for editing an audio clip's start points or for volume adjustment. After Effects brings in audio clips exactly like it does footage clips, with the same in and out point trimming options. It also provides a better volume adjustment function that you can alter and keyframe by the decibel, very much like a dedicated audio editing program (see Figure 9-23). After Effects also has an audio peak meter to give you a visual representation of the levels of audio in your project (see Figure 9-24).

Figure 9-23. The options of an audio layer in After Effects

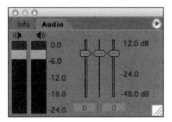

Figure 9-24. The audio peak meter window

Filters

With new versions of Flash, more filtering options have been added, but they noticeably increase your file size, and these new effects, like blurs, may not be viewable to those in your audience who haven't upgraded to the latest version of Flash. After Effects has an exceptional amount of filters. If you're familiar with Photoshop, most filters from Photoshop are available in After Effects, but they're suited for video rather than still images. Various filter types such as blurs, color corrections, and adjustments are available, as well as distortion options to liquefy your clips. Adding lens flares and rendering difference clouds, wipes, and transitions all fall into the After Effects package, giving you a great tool set to alter your animation. Figure 9-25 shows the drop-down menu of filter selections.

Figure 9-25. The default filter drop-down menu in After Effects

Masks, painting, and text tools

After Effects also comes with a number of mask options. The ability to add multiple masks to one object and add multiple points to those masks makes creating virtually any shape possible. Plus the ability to auto-trace the transparency of a layer to make its own mask can prove to be extremely helpful, if you need to trace an animated object's edges to capture the silhouette of a character or object. After Effects also comes with paint options for any touch ups, additional line work, or rotoscoping clean up. After Effects also has a very versatile text editor, with the ability to change the character mapping to various sizes and orientations. See Figure 9-26 to get a peek at the various tool palettes for masking, paint, and text.

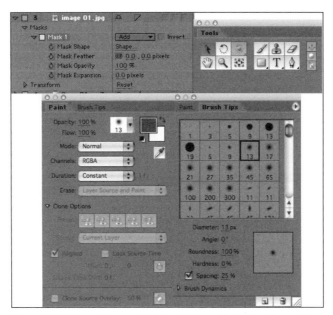

Figure 9-26. The masking and Paint windows with their various options

Disadvantages of using After Effects

Though there are disadvantages to using After Effects, they are general and would apply to any other compositing or editing program as well; they're mainly to do with removing your animation from its source in Flash. Since you're pulling your animation into another program, you're now working with the product of your original animation. For example, when using an image sequence from a 3-D program, you cannot manipulate that source animation in After Effects. If you need to go back into Flash and change your animation, you'll have to export it again so that the footage will be updated in your After Effects project file.

Loss of vector

Unfortunately, the vector information from a SWF does not carry over from Flash into After Effects, so the image is rasterized at its current state when imported into After Effects. If camera moves and size changes are necessary, you will need to increase the resolution (up-res) of your animation. Exporting a PNG or TARGA sequence at a higher resolution would do the trick; then, you could import the file as such and interpret it at the correct frame rate in After Effects.

You should anticipate this disadvantage in your project planning phase; visualizing your project in your storyboards or animatics gives you a rough idea of the changes in size and shape of camera angles, characters, and backgrounds from scene to scene.

SWF output

Nothing can create a SWF like Flash itself. After Effects can export SWFs, but an original SWF from a well-designed FLA can be efficiently small, which is what makes them extraordinarily useful for the Web.

Linking footage

Linking footage is both an advantage and disadvantage of using After Effects. The advantage is that After Effects uses reference links to its footage like I mentioned earlier, which makes an After Effects project file very small in size. The disadvantage is that without its linked footage, that AEP file is useless. When footage is moved or when an entire project has to be moved to a new location, be it a computer or external hard drive, the project file and all the footage it references need to go with it. The referenced footage must always be available for After Effects to link to, because the AEP file is just a data file that uses the source material; if there's no footage to link to, there is nothing to work with.

Summary

This chapter compared and contrasted Flash and After Effects. There are many advantages to using a compositing and editing program like After Effects. The execution of the final phase of production is crucial to your animation, just like any other phase in production. This chapter touched on some of the benefits to using After Effects—like its file reference system, its abilities in simulating camera work, exporting files, and animating effects—as well as some of the cons to removing your animation from Flash. The next chapter will take you step by step through using some in-depth techniques to maximize the potential of your Flash animation.

Chapter 10

AFTER EFFECTS AND CAMERA MECHANICS

By Barry J. Kelly

Chapter 9 compared Flash to After Effects. In this chapter, we will go through the process of importing Flash animation into After Effects and using the After Effects toolset to push the potential of your animation. We will hit on the following points:

- Exporting out of Flash
- Importing into After Effects
- Setting up your After Effects project
- Editing and compositing in After Effects
- Multiplane motion
- Moving the camera
  - Moving the camera using layers
  - Moving the camera using 3-D layers

An important thing to think about initially is how the camera will work in your project. Will there be a lot of dramatic and technical camera moves for your project? Or will the character animation be the driving force of your project and the camera just a static wide shot with maybe a few pans here or there? The answers to these questions should be determined before animation begins, as this affects the size of your background and the placement of your characters. As we dive farther into the chapter, it will become more evident whether your project was planned well enough.

I'm starting with the assumption that your project has been animated into separate scenes and individual FLAs, and we will be putting those scenes together in After Effects.

Exporting out of Flash

The two formats that are easiest for exporting out of Flash and into After Effects are: SWFs and image sequences. Which one you use depends on what is happening in the animation in your FLA. Is there a camera move in this particular scene? Are all your elements—backgrounds (BGs), characters, foreground, effects—in one FLA, or are they spread out into individual FLAs? Were your BGs created separately in Adobe Photoshop?

Exporting a SWF

If a scene has no camera moves, already has its background incorporated, and is pretty much complete, you should use a SWF, because the SWF will be a small file size, which will improve render time and RAM use in After Effects. Note that After Effects 6.5 and lower will only read a SWF correctly if it's exported with the correct publish settings.

The FLA that we will be using is made up of four parts: a trash can in the foreground; Crazy Jeff, our main character; a street scene in the background; and some sky in the distant background (see Figure 10-1).

Figure 10-1. Our Flash animation scene

Exporting for After Effects 7 and up

If you are using After Effects version 7.0 or a later version, you can simply publish as normal. Go to File ➤ Publish, or use the keyboard shortcut Ctrl+Enter or Cmd+Return.

Exporting for After Effects 6.5 and lower

If you're using something below version 7, you've got a bit more work to do. In earlier versions of After Effects, SWFs will only import correctly if published using the following settings:

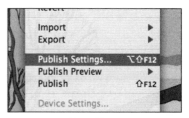

1. In Flash, go to File ➤ Publish Settings (see Figure 10-2).

2. Select the Flash tab at the top.

3. Check the Flash Player 6 box.

4. Make sure Compression is not checked. The only selection that should be selected in this entire window should be the Flash Player 6 (see Figure 10-3).

Figure 10-2. The Publish settings found under the File Menu

5. Finally, click Publish. You can also save these settings as a new profile if you wish.

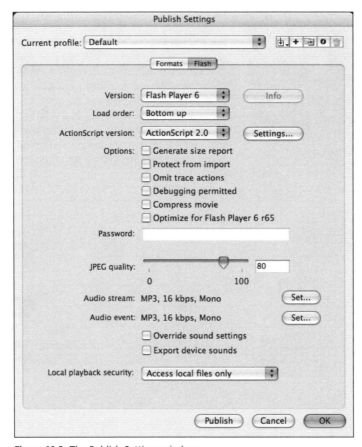

Figure 10-3. The Publish Settings window

Exporting an image sequence

If your scene needs a camera move, effects, or if some part of it needs to be separate from the rest of your animation, you should export it as an image sequence rather than a SWF. You can export from Flash in many different image formats, such as JPEG, PNG, and TARGA, but for this chapter, we will use PNGs (portable network graphics). Why PNGs? Unlike JPEGs, PNGs have an alpha channel available, which we'll need for the transparency in the character animation and elements.

You will also need to consider what kind of camera moves you will be making before you export your image sequence. Because the images will be bitmaps rather than vectors, you can't depend on them scaling smoothly. If you'll be zooming closer on your characters, you'll need the images to be larger so that they'll be of good quality both up close and far away. If you plan to pan from left to right or up to down around your image, you'll need to make sure that you export a large enough background image to enable you to pan across it. Since Flash is vector based, it has the ability to shrink or enlarge the scale of an image without losing quality, making possible high-resolution exports of backgrounds, characters, and elements.

Figure 10-4. All the elements that make up our shot: character, background, and foreground.

To create an image sequence, your elements should be either all in one FLA or separated into individual FLAs. To begin with, we'll be exporting an FLA that has all our elements placed within it (see Figure 10-4).

For this scene, our camera will be slowly moving in closer on our characters. So we'll need to export our elements into separate PNG sequences. If we look at the scene, we are going to separate them by *plane*. There are four main elements that make up the planes here (see Figures 10-5 through 10-8): the trash can in the foreground, our character, the background of the house on the street, and the sky (for more on why these should be separated, see the multiplane motion section later in this chapter).

Figure 10-5. Our foreground element, the trash can

Figure 10-6. Our character, Crazy Jeff is another element.

Figure 10-7. Our BG element, the house, and street

Figure 10-8. Our other BG element, the sky

All your elements should already be on different layers in your FLA; if not, separate them into different layers now. In general, the way to export is to turn off the layers you don't need, so the only one showing is the one you do need. Export that layer using the method described in the following steps, and repeat the process for all the layers you need. Alternatively, a plug-in made for exporting layers called LayerEx can be used. If you choose to do them manually, follow these steps:

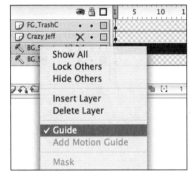

1. Right/Ctrl-click a layer you don't want to be seen, and select Guide (see Figure 10-9). Making the layer a guide layer will prevent it from exporting when you go to Publish or Export, thus turning it off. It also helps hide the layer after making it a guide.

Figure 10-9. Select Guide to make a guide layer.

2. Go through all the layers you don't want to export and turn them into guides by right/Ctrl-clicking and selecting Guide. Once that's completed, only the layer you want to export should be a regular layer. Figure 10-10 shows all layers as guide layers except Crazy Jeff.

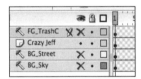

Figure 10-10. In this example. I will be exporting the Crazy Jeff layer.

3. Go to File ➤ Export ➤ Movie. Type a name, and choose the file path.

4. Under Format, select PNG Sequence, and click OK (see Figure 10-11).

5. The Export PNG window will now open. Since we will be zooming in on these characters, we'll need to export them bigger, or up-res them. We are going to double their height and width. The scene is 720×480, so we'll export at 1440×960 (see Figure 10-12).

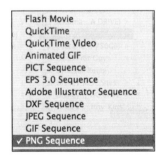

Figure 10-11. Select PNG from the format list.

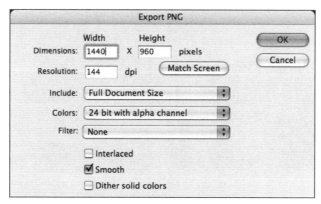

Figure 10-12. PNG export settings

6. Select 24 bit with Alpha Channel (for our transparency). Smooth can also be selected if you wish; Smooth applies anti-aliasing to an exported bitmap to produce a higher quality bitmap image and improve text display quality, which may be helpful for your animation.

7. Click OK. Now, when you look at where you saved your files, you'll see a series of PNG files, all named with a suffix number added at the end indicating the order in which they should play out.

8. Repeat steps 1–7 on all other layers that you need to export.

If your elements are in separate FLAs (for instance, your BG may be in one FLA and your character animation in another), repeat the same steps. Make guide layers of those you don't want to export, and keep what you do want to export.

Exporting is subjective

Exporting can be very subjective; every scene is different and has different needs. Whether a camera move is panning or tracking in, or in a static wide angle view, every scene can call for different elements to be exported separately to make a shot work.

Sometimes, exporting a whole sequence for each element may not be necessary. For instance, in our example, the background and foreground never actually change. Because of this, technically, you would need to create only a sequence of the character animation. The other elements could just be exported as still images. The advantage of this is that it not only saves disk space but renders a lot more quickly in After Effects. Obviously, if there had been a car driving by in the background, the whole thing would have to be exported as separate image sequences. Think about the needs of each part of the scene individually, and you can save yourself a lot of time and extra work.

Elements from other applications

Sometimes, a project might use elements from other programs, such as Photoshop, Illustrator, or a 3-D application. You should find that most image programs nowadays have the ability to export PNGs or PNG sequences. If your project used BGs created in Photoshop, for instance, you would need to go to File ➤ Save As, choose PNG for the Format with Alpha Channel set to 24 bit, and use it the same way.

Importing into After Effects

Importing is very easy. After Effects can take a number of formats, and there are a few ways to import.

1. Go to the File menu, and select Import (or use the keyboard shortcut Ctrl/Cmd+I).

2. Select File (or Multiple files).

3. Find what you need in the browser, and choose it.

4. If you are importing an image sequence, select all the images you are importing by holding Shift and dragging the mouse over all of them. Check the PNG sequence check box (see Figure 10-13).

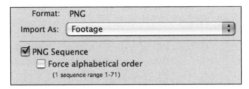

Figure 10-13. When importing a PNG sequence, make sure PNG sequence is checked.

Alternatively, you can drag files from your file browser directly into the After Effects project window. To drag an image sequence in order, you must have the sequence in its own folder on your disk drive. If not, the images will import separately.

Interpreting footage

When you import a SWF or video file into After Effects, the program will pick up its dimensions and what frame rate it was created in. Image sequences do not come with this information, so after you import an image sequence into After Effects, you will have to tell After Effects what its frame rate is. To do this, use the Interpret Footage option.

1. Right/Ctrl-click on the PNG sequence file in the project window, and select Interpret Footage ➤ Main (or use the keyboard shortcut Ctrl/Cmd+F).

2. In the Interpret Footage window, you can change the interpretation of Frame Rate, Fields, Channels, and Pixel Aspect Ratios of individual files in your project. Since our image sequence is at 30 frames per second, will have to change it to 24 in the frame rate text box (see Figure 10-14).

Figure 10-14. Setting the frame rate to 24 fps

It is especially important to check the frame rate, because the After Effects defaults may be set to anything, but our Flash movies may be running at 24 fps. Remember to always reinterpret footage that will need a change in frame rate, especially if you are using many clips of different frame rates. Make a habit of setting the rate every time you import a new image sequence.

Setting up your After Effects project

This section is a general overview of managing your animation in After Effects, an After Effects primer if you will. I'll give a brief rundown of keeping your source files organized for After Effects, using layers and the timeline, editing clips, and previewing your work.

Organizing your project files

The project file manager in After Effects is similar to using the library in Flash, where your assets are stored, except After Effects will be using the file reference link system to use your source material as was explained in Chapter 9. It's important to keep your source files close together on your hard drive, or wherever you place the files that you're going to use. Having them spread out all across your computer makes it harder to work on them in After Effects. If you keep all your files in the same area, it will be much easier to find and relink footage. This will also keep your project organized as a whole.

Using the Project File Manager

The Project File Manager works like any other file management system. You bring in files, delete them, organize them into folders, and view their information. I usually make a few folders for the basics: a folder for video, one for animation, one for BGs (see Figure 10-15) one for still Images, another for sound, and one folder for miscellaneous files or whatever I happen to bring in. Keeping them organized makes life easier for you and your project.

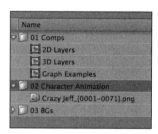

Figure 10-15. Here, we've created folders for our comps, character animation, and BGs.

There are four buttons along the bottom of the Project File Manager window that you will find useful as your project grows and demands greater organization (see Figure 10-16).

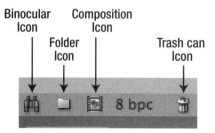

Figure 10-16. The four icon buttons found at the bottom of the project window

The binocular icon is a search option; click it to type keywords to look for a source file. The folder icon creates a new folder. The composition icon creates a composition of whatever file is selected in the project window; it will make the composition at the dimensions and frame rate of the currently selected fie. The trash can button deletes any selected files.

Starting a new composition

A composition in After Effects is the combination of elements and their actions within a timeline. We will make a composition using our image sequences of characters and BGs as the elements, and animate actions by transforming them by size and position across the seconds of the timeline.

At the beginning of this section, the Flash document we exported from was created at the dimensions 720×480, running at 24 fps. Our composition will also be created at those exact same settings.

1. Select Composition ➤ New Composition (or use the keyboard shortcut Ctrl/Cmd+N).

2. For Width enter 720, and for Height enter 480; set Frame Rate to 24 and Pixel Aspect Ratio to D1/DV NTSC (0.9), as shown in Figure 10-17.

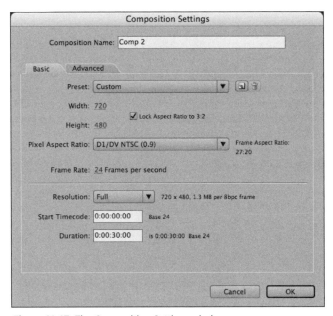

Figure 10-17. The Composition Settings window

3. The first of the three lower options is Resolution, which reflects the quality of our comp window preview. It can be set to Full, Half, Third, or Quarter. This does not affect the final quality of your animation; it just gives you the option to work at lower image quality, so that your system can work faster. The higher the quality (like Full), the longer it takes to preview your work; a lesser quality like Half takes less time to render, but you see a low-resolution preview in the composition window. In this example, we'll leave it at Full; if you have an old or slow machine, it might be a good idea to work on Half or a lower quality. You can change this at any time while you're working; a panel to set resolution is conveniently placed at the bottom of the composition window.

4. The Start Timecode field sets the time at which your timeline begins; the numbers represent Days:Hours:Minutes:Seconds. We can leave this set at 00:00:00:00.

5. The Duration needs to be set at least to the length of your animation. Our animation is only a few seconds; we'll set it on nice round number of 30 seconds.

233

Layers

Once a new composition is opened, you can drag footage to your timeline. Each piece of footage creates a layer in the timeline window. Each layer works like a movie clip; a layer may only be a still image, but it still works like a clip. What makes it like a clip is that it has a duration with adjustable in and out points: the in point is the where the clip starts, and the out point is where the clip ends, or cuts. These are adjustable; the clip will always have the same duration, but you can move the in and out points to determine what portion of the clip we actually see. For more on using in and out points, see the section of this chapter called "In and out points: Editing with layers."

The layer order in the timeline (see figure 10-18) determines what layers are visually on top of and below one another. Like Flash, the layer at the top of the layer order will appear on the top in the composition window.

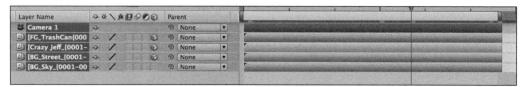

Figure 10-18. The layer order in the timeline—the layer at the top appears visually on the top of the layers below it in the composition window.

Figure 10-19. The arrow on the left side of the name to display the Transform option

Figure 10-20. The arrow to display the drop-down menu of Transform properties of a layer

Each layer has its own transform properties and its own drop-down menu in the timeline, which displays the properties: Anchor Point, Position, Scale, Rotation, and Opacity. To find these, click the arrow on the left side of the layer name (see Figure 10-19). You'll see the Transform option under it.

Click the drop-down arrow next to Transform to display your properties (see Figure 10-20).

These transform properties are adjustable by values, which are the numbers that sit on the right of the transform properties (see Figure 10-21).

Anchor Point and Position are represented by X and Y (X,Y) coordinates. Scale is represented by percent values in height and width. Rotation is marked by rotation number, which represents the number of complete 360 degree spins, and then in degrees, from 0–360, and Opacity is indicated by a percentage value from 0% to 100%, with 0% being completely transparent.

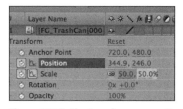

Figure 10-21. The transform properties

Not only can each of these properties be adjusted but each can be animated using keyframes.

In and out points: editing with layers

In and out points are the start and end points of a clip. In versions of After Effects before CS3, you will find two grey handles on each side of every clip (see Figure 10-22). In After Effects CS3, the handles are removed, but the edges still work like handles on both sides of the layer clip (see Figure 10-23). You can drag or pull these to any length the clip will allow; use them to trim your clips for editing.

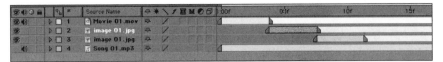

Figure 10-22. After Effects 6.5 handles

Figure 10-23. Handles in After Effects CS3

A clip of video, animation, or anything with an actual duration can't be extended beyond its duration, only trimmed down. If a movie is 25 frames long, you can't simply drag the out point to make it 30 frames; you can only trim the clip shorter. When you trim a clip shorter, sliding the in and out points inward on the clip, the excess footage is shown in the layer as a darker faded color of the layer (see Figure 10-24), and the brighter color is the actual portion of the clip that will be shown.

Figure 10-24. Notice the top layer in this screenshot. Its in and out points have been pulled in. The excess footage is shown in the darker areas on both of its sides.

A still image, however, isn't actually a movie; it has no duration information, so it is infinite. Still images can be extended to as long as the length of the timeline itself.

Each of these layer clips is also moveable. You can simply click the layer in the timeline window and drag it to where you want.

In the timeline, the blue handle on top of the time ruler is the current-time indicator, much like the playhead in Flash (see Figure 10-25). This marks the frame that is currently displayed in your composition window. You move this by grabbing its blue handle at the top of the timeline or using keyboard shortcuts. These shortcuts can send you to the out point of a clip or to the end or the beginning of the timeline.

Figure 10-25. The timeline marker cuts down the timeline, similar to the playhead in Flash.

Here are some navigational keyboard shortcuts:

- **I**: Jumps to the in point of the selected clip/layer.
- **O**: Jumps to the out point of the selected clip/layer.
- **Home**: Sends you to the beginning of the timeline.
- **End**: Sends you to the end of the timeline.

For editing, keyboard shortcuts always prove quicker than sliding clips. Here are some helpful editing keyboard shortcuts:

- **[**: Moves the selected clip's in point to the current position in the timeline; moves entire clip but does not change the duration
- **Alt+]**: Moves the selected clip's out point to the current position in the timeline; moves the entire clip but does not change the duration
- **Alt+[**: Sets the clip's in point to the current position in the timeline; does change the duration
- **Alt+]**: Sets the clip's out point to the current position in the timeline; does change the duration

Keyframes

Like in tweening in Flash, keyframes are what we use to animate in After Effects; it's the same concept. Keyframes are the markers for change in value.

For example, if we want to make a ball cross the screen from the left side to the right side over five frames, our starting frame, Keyframe 1 would show the ball on the left side. Our last frame, Keyframe 5, would show the ball on the right. We could set Flash to tween between these two keyframes. After Effects, though, will automatically create the motion. By default, After Effects will automatically animate the change in value between keyframes of a layer.

Create keyframes by clicking the stopwatch button next to the chosen transform property (see Figure 10-26).

Figure 10-26. Notice the stopwatch icons for each of the transform properties.

To create more keyframes, click the keyframe button to the left of the stopwatch (see Figure 10-27), or just change the value at a different point in the timeline (see Figure 10-28).

Figure 10-27. Notice the diamonds to the left; these are the keyframe buttons.

Figure 10-28. These are what keyframes look like in your timeline. They have different shapes; for more on what these shapes mean, see the section "Interpolation and editing graphs."

More keyframes will be automatically added by changing the values of that particular property. If we create a keyframe on the scale and position properties, move forward in the timeline five frames, and change the value of the scale and position on just that last frame, After Effects will recognize the change from the first keyframe and automatically create a keyframe where you are now making the change in the timeline.

Each keyframe's timing is variable. Each transform property has editable graphs for altering speed and changing values such as degrees for rotation or percentage for scale. These graphs visually display the change in value of your animation keyframes. You will use the graphs to add ease to your animation timing, smoothly easing in and out of motions. Adjusting points using a Bezier curve can make the timing of transform animation completely controllable. This is especially useful in making smooth, precise camera moves; see the section later in this chapter called "Interpolation and editing graphs."

Tool palette

The general tool palette sits next to the Composition Window in After Effects. We will not be using many of the tools in this book, as there isn't really a call for them in what we are doing here. Figure 10-29 shows the tool palette.

Figure 10-29. The general tool palette

From left to right, the icons on the tool palette are as follows:

- **Selection tool**: The default mouse arrow for general use.
- **Hand tool**: For dragging and panning what's in view in the composition window.
- **Magnifying glass tool**: For zooming in and out.
- **Rotation tool**: For rotating the selected layer.
- **Orbit camera tool**: For rotating around a point of interest (discussed later on in this chapter) when using 3-D layers and cameras.
- **Pan behind tool**: For moving a layer's anchor point without affecting its current position.
- **Mask tool**: For adding masks to the currently selected layer, which will now have a Mask option when opened up in the timeline where settings for the mask can be adjusted.
- **Pen tool**: For adding or altering points on Bezier curves for masks and vector lines.
- **Text tool**: For opening the After Effects text generator. Using text creates a new layer for the text with not only its own transform properties but character mapping options as well.
- **Brush tool**: For painting on the selected layer. This tool automatically adds the Paint filter when you touch the paint brush, which is adjusted by the paint and brush settings windows.
- **Eraser tool**: For erasing. This tool adds a Paint filter and works like a brush tool that deletes pieces of the image.
- **Clone stamp tool**: For copying pixels of a layer to a different part of that same layer.
- **Puppet tool**: This new feature in After Effects CS3 gives you the ability to create points on an image that are linked together. These points can then be animated to stretch, skew, and distort the layer, which gives an almost puppet-like control of a still image,

Effects

There are numerous available filters in After Effects. There is a selection in the top menu called Effects. Click it, and the drop-down menu displays the available effect filters. Or you can Right/Ctrl-click a layer in the timeline and select a filter from there.

Among the many filters, some useful filters are in the Blur and Distort menus. Found in the Blur menu, a Lens Blur or a Gaussian can be used to blur objects to simulate rack focus effects (see Figure 10-32), shifting planes of focus from one object to another. Or you can use the Motion Blur filter to make something appear to be moving fast.

Figure 10-30. The Lens Blur/Gaussian effect

In the Distort filters, you could use Corner Pin, which enables you to move the individual positions of the four corners of your layer to extremely skew objects, like skewing shadows to look like they run along a flat floor.

When an effect is selected, it becomes a part of the layer, listed in the same drop-down area as the layer's transform options. The filters can be adjusted there under the layer, or double-clicking that filter in the timeline window will open up the filter's options in their own layer with graphic controls.

Precompositions

A selection of layers can be precomposed into one layer, creating a new separate comp. Precomposing creates a new composition containing just those original selected layers and replaces them where they were in the timeline. Creating a precomposition can be compared to creating an animation in Flash and then converting that animation into a symbol to paste into another FLA, where we would select all the layers and frames we wanted and convert them into a symbol so that all those layers fit into one layer.

Precomposing layers is very helpful when your timeline has an abundant amount of them. Every composition in our project can be brought into another composition's timeline as a clip. To see the step by step process to precompose a selection of layers, see the section called "Creating a precomp" in this chapter.

RAM preview and rendering

A RAM preview is an on-the-spot render of what is currently in your timeline. It may not preview the entire timeline but only what your machine and settings allow, which is affected by many factors, such as how much RAM your machine has, what quality resolution you're currently previewing at (full, half, third, or quarter), and the intensity of the actions you're animating.

A machine with 2GB of RAM can render a larger portion of timeline than a machine with 512MB.

A RAM preview at one-third–quality resolution can render a much larger portion of the timeline that a full-quality one, because less quality means fewer pixels and details for the machine to render.

A RAM preview with less animation and fewer effects, which means less work that After Effects has to do, has less to render, so it'll be quicker. The more effects, transforming, 3-D layers, and action you create, the harder After Effects has to work, and the more RAM needs to be used, so you're able to render a smaller portion of your timeline.

Resolution also affects the RAM preview: a smaller 320×240 composition will render much faster than a 1920×1080 one, because the 320×240 composition has much less to render than the other.

By default, the RAM preview covers the entire timeline. Set in and out points for the RAM preview by pressing the B key for an in point and N for an out point (see Figure 10-31).

Figure 10-31. The RAM preview, work areas, and in and out points are located above the layers in the timeline window.

To watch a RAM preview of what's currently in between the in and out points of the work area, press 0 on the numerical key pad. This will render a preview of the selected area, complete with sound.

Multiplane motion

Camera moves are best achieved by using multiple planes to simulate depth. Quick, short, intensely blurred moves probably won't require a lot of multiplane separation. But to give a certain amount of depth to camera moves, separating your elements and animating them independently will really step up the quality and scale of your animation.

When animating motion depth, there are some speed and timing tips to follow, to make camera movements look natural in the animated world they exist in. If we were to start with three basic planes of a shot, we would have the foreground (FG), middle, and background (BG). Now, let's say there's an object in each plane. A general rule in motion perception is that the closer the object is to the viewer, the faster it will seem to move.

A real-life example would be when you're riding in a car. Buildings and trees that are close by seem to move swiftly past you, but the sun, sky, and mountains in the distance practically crawl by or may appear not to be moving at all.

Whether the shot is moving forward, backward, or from side to side, this rule still applies. If we are moving in closer on a shot, the object in the foreground will be moving toward the camera at a faster rate than the one in the middle ground, and the middle ground's objects will be moving closer to the camera at a faster rate than the background's. If you're moving from left to right, the foreground elements will rush right past the camera, the middle ground ones will pass much slower, and the background elements even slower than that.

Plane separation

In the previous section on exporting out of Flash, we exported the trash can in the foreground, our character Crazy Jeff in the middle ground, the neighborhood street in the background, and the sky in the distance. For a shot like this, this is a pretty basic separation. We have our foreground, middle ground, and background, but we also go the extra step to separate the sky. This is an incidence of an extreme background element, which is usually the sky, sun, or horizon. Sometimes, elements may be so extremely distant that they would move only a little or maybe not even at all, and these elements need to be on a separate plane. If that sky was part of the neighborhood street, when the BG plane moves closer to the camera, the sky would look like it was attached to a house on the street, which would look unnatural. Keeping the sky on its own plane really makes objects in front of it stand out.

Moving the camera

Once we've got all our elements in the timeline, we can proceed with the animation of our camera moves. We are trying to get the camera from point A to point B. There are two ways to go about making these multiplane camera moves efficiently. One way is by using layers in After Effects and changing transform options, and the other is using the 3-D layers option available in After Effects. Neither technique is superior to the other, so give both a go and see which you prefer. In this section, we will run through the process of creating the same moving camera shot, using both techniques.

Moving the camera using layers

This technique mainly involves transforming the scale and position of layers to simulate depth.

Your elements should be in the layer order that the viewer will see them in, so stack them with foreground on top and the background on the bottom.

The general idea is to set up the shot by framing it at the first position of the camera move and creating a keyframe. Then you can frame the shot at the second position of the camera move creating another keyframe, so that After Effects will animate the motion between the two keyframes.

Remember that we exported the image sequence out of Flash at twice the original document size, so the clip of the image sequence will be a little big when we bring it in.

To set up the beginning of our shot, point A (see Figure 10-32), we'll have to frame the shot while fitting all our elements in the shot.

Figure 10-32. Point A

Under the layer Transform properties, change the Scale anywhere from 0% to 100% by typing in the field.

We'll scale this to what frames up well, so let's make all our elements 50% scale (see Figure 10-33). You can also change scale by eye, by grabbing the handles in the comp window and sizing the selected image with the mouse.

Figure 10-33. Scale all animated layers at 50%.

In the next few steps, we'll animate a camera move that starts from a wide angle of Crazy Jeff on the street, that pushes into a close up on his face. We'll start the new move by framing up Crazy Jeff at point A where he will be at the beginning of the camera move. We'll also have to change the position of elements like our trashcan and street BG, to frame the shot.

To change the position, you can use the layer Position property in the timeline. Double-clicking the X and Y value fields enables you to type in a value.

The exact Position values in this example, shown in Figure 10-34, are as follows (all layers start with a Scale of 50%):

- **Trash can**: 344.9, 246
- **Crazy Jeff**: 355, 248
- **Street**: 360, 247

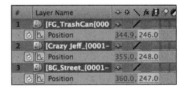

Figure 10-34. Position values at point A

You can also scroll over the X,Y values of the Position. When the cursor changes to a hand, hold the mouse button, and drag to the right to increase the number, or drag to the left to decrease it.

Another way to change the position is by clicking the selected layer in the Composition window, clicking and holding down the mouse button, and dragging the layer.

Once you have your elements in place, you're ready start using keyframes.

Animating the camera move

Keyframes are the groundwork for our animation. In general, you set keyframes where specific events need to occur, and After Effects animates what's between those keyframes to lead up to those events.

You can set keyframes for every transform option. Scale, position, and rotation are individually keyframed to combine into the motions you wish to make. We can keyframe the scale of a layer to grow from 100 percent to 200 percent, while keyframing the position of that same layer to move from the top of the screen to the bottom of the screen and rotating the entire path the layer follows using keyframes on the rotation option.

Using keyframes is what will actually make your camera move. Again, similar to motion tweening in Flash, you set your keyframes, and After Effects automatically creates the animation between them. However, with keyframes for each property, you can be more specific about the type of animation you want and really make After Effects do everything you need it to.

Add a keyframe manually at the frame where you want the camera move to begin by clicking the stop watch icon next to the transform properties (see Figure 10-35). Then add more keyframes by clicking the diamond check box that appears to the left of the stop watch button. Clicking the diamond will add a keyframe on the frame where the timeline marker currently sits. To erase all the keyframes, click the stopwatch again.

Figure 10-35. Notice the stop watch and keyframe buttons on the left.

Keyframing the scale Now, we'll begin creating the keyframes to animate the camera move:

1. Select all the layers that need to be changed. Here, it would be everything except the sky (see Figure 10-36).

2. Starting at the keyframe where the camera move begins, in this case the first frame in the timeline, we should have already adjusted the scale and position to what we need. On the first frame of the timeline, click the stopwatch button on Scale to create your first keyframe.

Figure 10-36. Selecting all the layers we are going to animate

3. Then, we'll set our Scale property at point B. Our end keyframe should be at about 01:13 (01 second, 13 frames) at a value of 80% on *all* our layers.

4. Since Crazy Jeff is the focus of this shot, we'll make him 90% on the end keyframe in his layer (see Figure 10-37).

Keyframing position Now, we'll keyframe the positions of our elements. We should select all the layers that we adjusted the scale for and drop position keyframes on the first frame in the timeline for *all* the layers. You can choose to frame the shots by eye, or use these exact values:

Figure 10-37. Scale values at point B

1. For the trash can, we'll start on a Position keyframe of 344.9, 246.

2. Since the trash is on the closest plane and thus needs to move faster, we'll set its end keyframe sooner than the others, at 01:02. Then, we'll set its end Position keyframe at 33.8, 251.0, which should take it out of frame.

3. Now, we'll set Crazy Jeff's position. He'll start at a Position keyframe of 355, 248 and end at a keyframe at 01:13 at the Position 75.0, 238.0.

4. Next, we'll set the house BG at a starting keyframe Position of 360, 247 and an ending keyframe at 01:13 with Position set to 111.0, 255.0 (see Figure 10-38). Our shot should almost be framed up (see Figure 10-39).

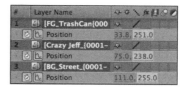

Figure 10-38. The position values for point B

5. The sky would move very little, realistically, so we'll leave it alone for now.

6. Do a RAM preview. Set your in an out points on the timeline using the B key for in and the N key for out, and press 0 on the numerical keypad to begin the preview (refer to Figure 10-21).

Figure 10-39. The result at point B

The preview may look smooth, but it might also look slightly unnatural. Why? Because every element is moving at the same speed, with all the same timing. As I mentioned earlier, though, closer objects should move faster than distant objects.

We could move the position of keyframes earlier in the timeline to make them happen faster, or we could change the interpolation and use the graphs editor while keeping our keyframes where they are.

Interpolation and editing graphs

Interpolation is the process of filling in the unknown data between two keyframes or values. Interpolation generates that data; in other words, it's the tweening between keyframes. There are a few settings for interpolation—Linear, Bezier, Auto Bezier, and Hold Interpolation—and you have the ability to edit the speeds of your animation with these settings, using the velocity graphs and the Graph Editor.

Our interpolation is represented using a 2-D graph that is completely editable and enables us to precisely change the timing of our animation.

There are two kinds of interpolation: spatial and temporal. When using temporal interpolation, you edit the interpolation using the graphs; for spatial interpolation, you use the element's motion paths in the comp window. In this chapter, we will use temporal interpolation, as it is more precise for using exact values.

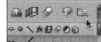

To find the velocity graphs, click the view graphs icon located at the top of the timeline (see Figure 10-40). When you have a layer selected, the graph icon appears next to each transform option (e.g., Scale).

Figure 10-40. The view graphs icon

Reading graphs

Once the graph is open, we can see the X axis (see Figure 10-41) of the graph is our composition time-line, the amount of time passing between our keyframes. The Y axis (see Figure 10-42) is the amount of change in speed or percentage/degree value. A speed graph would be useful associated with Position to show the speed of an object moving from one place to another. A value graph would be more useful with something like Scale or Opacity, where percentages are involved.

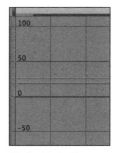

Figure 10-41. The timeline, the horizontal data of a graph

Figure 10-42. The rate of change, in units of percentage or pixels, on the vertical axis of a graph

There will be a line graph for each transform property. For instance, scale would have its own line graph, as would Position and the other transform options. You are able to identify which graph is associated with which property by color: the color of the line graph matches the color behind the value of a property. Or you can double-click a property, and it will be highlighted in the graph editor.

Reading the vertical part of the graph, which is the rate of change, and the horizontal, which displays time, we can see how much and how fast a layer is changing over a period of time. The more drastic a drop or increase in a curve the more drastic the change. A long upward progressing curve will have a smoother progressive rate of change, and a curve with sharp, short drops will have quicker rates of change.

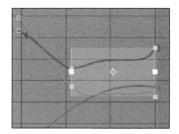

Figure 10-43. The multiple small squares along the graph are the keyframe points, which adjust the interpolation.

Your keyframes appear at the same time as they did in layers but are now represented by square points (see Figure 10-43) that make up the lines of the graph—those lines are the interpolation.

As I stated earlier, there are different settings for interpolation:

- **Linear** is usually the default for interpolation (see Figure 10-44); between keyframes, it moves at a constant speed and usually looks solid and mechanical.

Figure 10-44. A graph with linear Interpolation

- **Bezier** is more precise to the user's controls, to make smooth motions between keyframes, because those keyframes can be adjusted independently (see Figure 10-45).
- **Auto Bezier** automatically creates a smooth transition between keyframes, dependent on the current values of added keyframes (see Figure 10-45).
- **Continuous Bezier** creates a smooth rate of change, but manually. It's continuous, because it will change the keyframes that come before and after it (see Figure 10-45).

Figure 10-45. A graph of what any of the three Bezier selections would look like; all of them have smooth curves.

- **Hold** holds the value of a keyframe and doesn't change until it reaches the next keyframe; there's no inbetweening (see Figure 10-46).

To change the interpolation, right/Ctrl-click on a keyframe, and choose Keyframe Interpolation.

Keyframes in a graph have direction handles attached to one or both sides (a graph would have a handle on both sides if it had keyframes on both sides of it).

Editing the Graphs At default, the graphs will most likely appear to be a straight line, linear interpolation. In order to adjust the keyframes, we should change them to Bezier; the Crazy Jeff layer will be used for these examples.

1. Right/Ctrl-click Bezier handle, and select Keyframe Interpolation (see Figure 10-47).

2. Select Temporal Interpolation, and select Bezier from the drop-down menu (see Figure 10-48).

Figure 10-46. A graph of hold interpolation, holding the same value until the next keyframe

Figure 10-47. After right-clicking a keyframe, select Keyframe Interpolation.

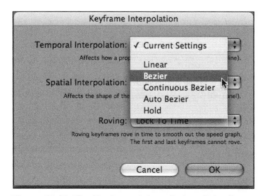

Figure 10-48. The Keyframe Interpolation dialog box

The square points that are our keyframes now have adjustable Bezier points on their handles, which control the points/keyframes in the Bezier curves (see Figure 10-49). The length of these handles determines the influence of the interpolation, easing in or out of a keyframe—the longer the handle, the more influence.

Figure 10-49. The keyframe's Bezier handle coming out from the left, controls influence

245

On the speed graph, the rate of change is measured by pixels per second (px/sec), and the value graphs are measured in degrees or percentages.

As I mentioned earlier, there are speed graphs, and there are value graphs. We use both. Speed is more useful in position, whereas value is more useful when editing something like scale, but both types of graphs come in handy for all properties.

To change between the two

1. Click the Graph Type/Options button on the bottom of the Graph Editor.

2. Choose Edit Value Graph.

If Position is the selected graph, notice that two line graphs were added; this is because there are two values for position, X and Y (see Figure 10-50). Scale would have two line graphs for value as well, one for height and one for width. Rotation would have one line for degree values, and Opacity would have one for percentage between 0 and 100 percent.

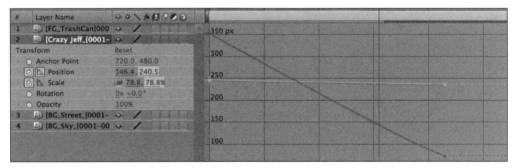

Figure 10-50. Notice in this value graph, that there are two values for Position, the darker line represents the X value, and the lighter represents the Y value. Scale looks the same, except with height and width values.

3. Go back to the Graph Type/Options menu, and choose Edit Speed Graph.

Notice Position is now a one-line graph, strictly for speed, the rate at which it would be moving (see Figure 10-51). In the speed graph view, the Y axis is now speed. The higher up on the graph you move, the faster the animation. Another example would be Scale in the speed graph view; the one line graph represents the speed of its increasing or decreasing size, and all of the properties are one line graph, the speed graph view, that represents the speed at which a property's value changes.

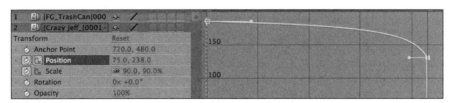

Figure 10-51. The speed graph of Position is now just one graph, for speed alone.

This concept is easier to understand with hands-on experience, observing the graphs' behavior while adjusting them. Take some time to mess around with the properties and different types of graphs to really get an understanding of how to adjust them to get the precise timing you want.

A keyframe has a different shape for each kind of interpolation (see Figure 10-52). If we were to switch back to look at our timeline, our keyframes would have changed from diamonds that represent linear interpolations to arrows that represent Bezier interpolation or circles to represent the Auto Bezier selection.

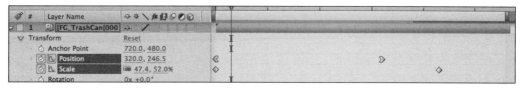

Figure 10-52. The keyframes here are of different shapes. The Position property keyframes use arrows indicating ease in and out because they are Bezier. The Scale property is linear animation, so the keyframes are the shape of diamonds. Hold interpolation keyframes take the shape of squares.

Editing graphs for the Crazy Jeff camera move Now, for the closest objects, which in this case would be the trash can, the rate of change will be faster, and the distant objects, like Jeff and the house, will be a bit slower. For most of these animations and camera moves, it might be more helpful to adjust and frame everything by eye, but for learning purposes, the exact data used in this camera move follows.

For the closest layer, the curve will be made to curve upward, increasing in speed over time.

1. For the trash can layer, we are starting on a keyframe at a Position of 344.9, 246 and a Scale of 50%.

2. Our end keyframe will be at a position of 33.8, 251 at a Scale of 80%.

3. Looking at this in the Graph Editor, set the graph type to Speed Graph (since we've already keyframed our positions earlier, we only need to adjust speed).

4. The graph appears to be a straight line (see Figure 10-53). As we approach the end keyframe, the trash can needs to move increasingly faster, so we will need to convert that last keyframe to Bezier interpolation.

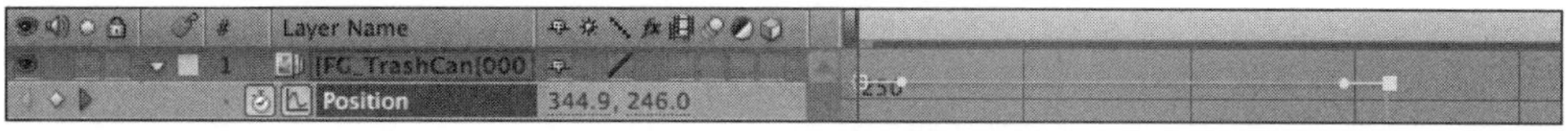

Figure 10-53. The trash can's graph is straight, because it is still linear.

5. Right/Ctrl-click the keyframe, and select Keyframe Interpolation.

6. Set Temporal Interpolation to Bezier.

7. Now, grab the end keyframe, and drag it up to 280.48 px/sec (see Figure 10-54).

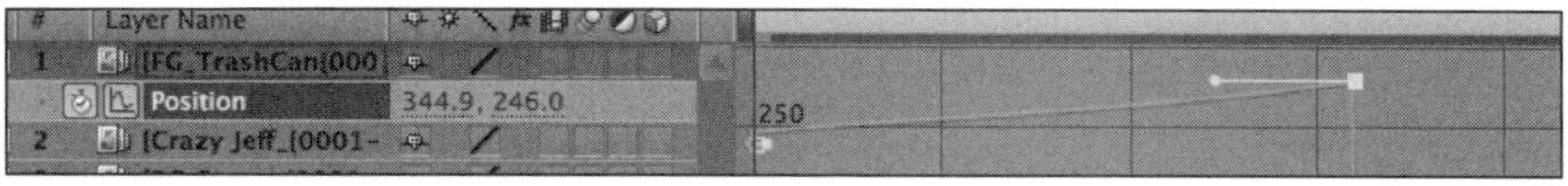

Figure 10-54. The trashcan's graph now at Bezier, curving upward to increase speed

8. Since this animation increases 30 percent in scale in such a short amount of frames, it seems to look fine as is.

9. Now, the trash can should increase in speed and size, as a closer plane should.

For Crazy Jeff and the street, we will need a more progressive curve downward. Our Crazy Jeff element starts at 50 percent and grows to our ending keyframe of 90 percent.

Our street BG element starts at 50 percent and grows to our ending keyframe of 80 percent.

Scale should be taken care of, but our timing on the Position animation will need some tweaking:

1. On the Position property, Crazy Jeff starts at 355, 248 and ends at 75, 238.

2. The house BG starts at a Position of 360, 247 and ends at 111, 255.

3. Select Position for Both Layers.

4. Change the Graph type to Speed Graph.

5. Now, these layers should move fairly similarly, but Jeff should move slightly faster. At the first keyframe, we should set Crazy Jeff to about 186 px/sec, pulling the influence to about 40 percent.

6. The end keyframe for Crazy Jeff should slow down to about 130 px/sec with about 16 percent influence. The graph should look like Figure 10-55.

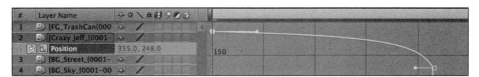

Figure 10-55. Crazy Jeff's graph brought downward to slow and ease to a stop

7. The Street BG should move similarly but slightly slower, start at about 136 px/sec and pull the handle to about 40 percent influence (see Figure 10-56).

8. Then, the end keyframe should be dragged down a little, to about 125 px/sec, and the influence should be pulled in to about 15 percent.

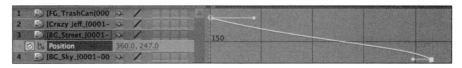

Figure 10-56. The street BG's graph, brought downward to slow and ease to a stop

9. At this point, we should start seeing the type of movement that we want,

By the end of these first adjustments, your graphs should look something like Figure 10-57.

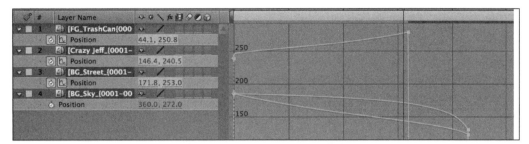

Figure 10-57. At the end of adjusting, the graph should look something like this.

We need to keep both the house's and Crazy Jeff's timing pretty similar. If Crazy Jeff moves too fast or too slow, he'll be sliding across the BG. One of the most crucial points during camera moves is registration of your characters to their BG.

Registration and Sliding Registration refers to an object's placement in its environment. This is mainly concerning characters and backgrounds. The characters should remain grounded, or registered, within the background, the world that they live in. In this instance, Crazy Jeff should remain fairly solid in relationship to the street.

A big problem that can happen in camera moves is a registration issue like sliding. Characters may be walking or still during a camera move. If an element's timing is off, characters or BGs will appear to be moving with no force or reason. This just looks odd, unnatural, and very amateur. It separates the character too much from the world you've created. Sometimes it may be unavoidable, but keep registration as clean as possible.

As long as we keep Crazy Jeff's feet fairly solid with the ground, this camera move should remain fairly clean and simple as far as registration goes.

After the initial adjustment, do a RAM preview of this particular move to preview your work.

If it doesn't look perfect at first run, we may need to go back and adjust some of the curves in the graphs, even change certain values of Position or Scale or any of other transform properties to get the desired result. The basics are the same: frame your shot, add your keyframes, and the rest is just tweaking and making adjustments here and there till you get what you want.

Blurs and focus effects can also be added to the animation to improve it even more. We will get more into effects and tips in the last chapter of this book. But first, we'll redo this camera move using the 3-D Layer technique to make a multi plane camera move.

Moving the camera using 3-D layers

An advantage to using After Effects is the 3-D capabilities. In this section, we will re-create the camera move we did in the previous section using 3-D layers. The 3-D layer option allows the ability to orient your layers in 3-D space, animate in 3-D space, and use 3-D cameras and lights in 3-D space.

When using regular layers, we simulated a camera move by increasing the size of our elements and moving them over a series of keyframes for every individual layer element.

249

In 3-D, it may sound simpler: we position our elements and keyframe a 3-D camera to move throughout our elements to animate the camera move. The element of 3-D, though, is a veritable task, the same as regular layers. Why? Because of that extra element that makes 3-D three-dimensional—
Z space.

Z space

Z space is the factor of depth. Instead of just aligning our elements to horizontal and vertical, X and Y, coordinates, the factor of depth, Z, is added (see Figure 10-58). Increasing this value moves an element farther away; decreasing this value brings it closer.

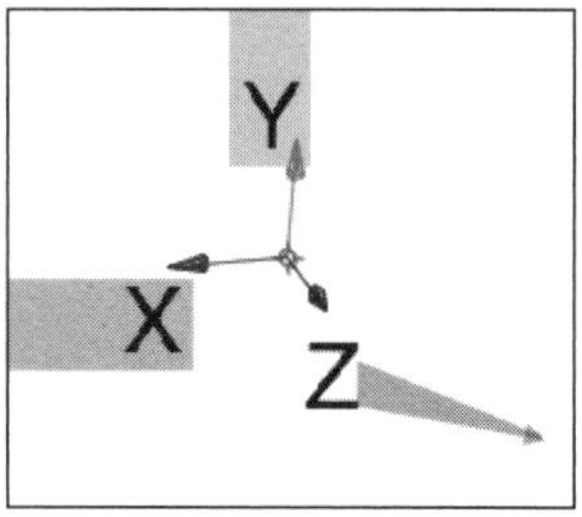

Placing your elements in 3-D

In 3-D animation, the big difference from using regular layers is that there is less animating of the layers and more animating of the camera. So placement of your layers in 3-D space is very important.

Figure 10-58. X goes horizontally; Y goes vertically; and Z goes into the distance.

Let's bring in our Crazy Jeff and BG elements into the timeline and set up the shot at the start of the move, point A. We'll set it up exactly like we set up point A using regular layers (see Figure 10-59). Here are the exact numbers for Position and Scale (all the other transform properties were left at the default values):

1. We'll set the Scale for all our layers (except the sky) at 50%, so that they all fit.

2. For the trash can, we'll start on a Position keyframe of 344.9, 246.

3. Next, we'll set Crazy Jeff. He'll start at a Position keyframe of 355, 248.

4. Now, we'll set the house BG at a starting keyframe 360, 247.

Figure 10-59. The original framing of Point A

After our elements are set up the way we want them, let's convert them to 3-D layers. Now again, we probably don't need movement in the sky, so convert all others to 3-D, leaving the sky.

Do one of the following:

- Click the 3-D layer box for that layer in the timeline (see Figure 10-60).
- Or select the layer, and go to Layer ➤ 3D Layer (see Figure 10-61).

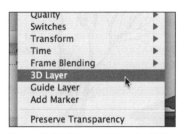

Figure 10-60. The cube icon represents the 3-D layer option check box.

Figure 10-61. You can also select 3D Layer from the Layer drop-down menu.

After you have converted the layers to 3-D, click the Transform option for one of your layers.

Notice the addition of Z space values in your options. Our elements are still in exactly the same positions but now have additional transform properties that make 3-D movement and positioning possible. Anchor Point, Position, and Scale have an added Z value, and there are new properties: Orientation, X Rotation, Y Rotation, and Z Rotation (see Figure 10-62).

▽ Transform	Reset
⬥ Anchor Point	720.0, 480.0, 0.0
⬥ Position	338.0, 223.0, 17.0
⬥ Scale	⊞ 50.0, 50.0, 100.0%
⬥ Orientation	0.0°, 0.0°, 0.0°
⬥ X Rotation	0x +0.0°
⬥ Y Rotation	0x +0.0°
⬥ Z Rotation	0x +0.0°
⬥ Opacity	100%

Figure 10-62. The new properties of a 3-D layer

These new properties are all rotation based; in other words, they all turn around the Anchor Point, using a degree value. The major difference is that Orientation can be keyframed on all axes at the same time, and the others, the X Rotation, Y Rotation, and Z Rotation properties, are keyframed by their own individual axis.

Also notice, in the composition window, there is an axes handle for the selected layer(s) (see Figure 10-63). Red controls the X axis. Green controls the Y axis. Blue controls the Z axis. Grab these handles to manually move the layers.

When you scroll over an axis handle, the mouse icon will change to display which handle you are adjusting. An X will appear over the X handle, a Y when you scroll over the Y, and of course, Z will appear over the Z handle.

Figure 10-63. Notice the handles for the 3-D axes.

251

Working with 3-D space really needs some hands-on practice; experiment transforming in 3-D space with all the transform properties to get a feel for the 3-D mechanics.

Transforming elements under 3-D views

Moving elements in 3-D space is hard from just one camera view, but luckily, you can view the composition from different angles. Along the bottom of the composition window is a 3-D view pop-up menu selection. Select and choose the view that helps you most. You can also go to View ➤ Switch 3D view and choose from there. Or you can choose from the drop-down menus located at the bottom of the composition (see Figures 10-64 and 10-65).

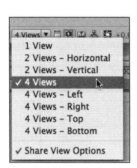
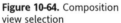

Figure 10-64. Composition view selection

Figure 10-65. Camera selection

Our default view is what is called Active Camera. You can also look at multiple views at the same time by selecting two or four composition views in the comp window workspace, by choosing Window ➤ Workspace ➤ Two Comp or Four Comp views (see Figure 10-66).

Figure 10-66. Notice the multiple angles in this Four Comp view.

Now that we've got our views set up, we can start to work with the shot.

For the elements in this shot, depth is the only real factor we'll need to adjust. Each plane will need to be separated by a distance in Z space to simulate depth. We'll set up this shot starting at the beginning of our camera move.

1. We have our trash can in the foreground, so let's decrease our Z value, bringing the can closer to us. We'll bring our Z value to 137.

As elements come closer, they may start to drift off frame (see Figure 10-67). As something gets closer to the camera, almost passing it, it starts to go beyond the camera's field of vision. In this case, the trash can will be close enough to almost pass by the camera as it drifts toward the left side of the frame.

Figure 10-67. The trash can is now slightly off frame to the left.

2. We'll need to force the trash can into frame, putting it back into the camera's view. So, we'll need to adjust the X and Y values to bring our trash can back into frame a little more (see Figure 10-68). The exact Position numbers for this composition are 406, 240, 137.

Figure 10-68. The trash can is now more accurately placed in the frame.

3. Next, we'll adjust Crazy Jeff, though he's actually in a pretty good spot. To give him more distance from the trash can, let's increase the Z space value but by only 17, and adjust X and Y values accordingly to nudge him into decent framing. Our final Position values for him are 338, 223, 17.

4. Next, we can push the street BG back further, giving each element a little distance between them (see Figure 10-69). Repeating what we did in the previous adjustments by increasing the Z value, in this example, the Z is pushed back to 156. Adjusting the framing of the shot using X and Y, in this example, the Position of the house BG is 382, 240, 156.

Figure 10-69. Notice the distance of the objects.

Note that the street BG should be relatively close to our character to prevent them from sliding. Also watch out for the edges of elements layers, and make sure no cracks show; by cracks, I mean places where we see the edges of a BG or any element that shouldn't be visible (see Figure 10-70). In this example, the trash can isn't a completely drawn trash can, only part of one. We need to make sure we don't see those unfinished edges and that the elements in the image cover the screen as desired.

Figure 10-70. Notice the arrows on the bottom and the left, pointing out the unwanted edges or cracks of our house BG.

As I said before, when moving in 3-D space, it's likely that more animation will involve the camera than the elements themselves, so let's look at that now.

The 3-D camera

After Effects allows you to create and control cameras in 3-D space. This camera is a customized object that can be animated along X, Y, and Z axes and has its own specific properties like focal length, apertures, focal distance, depth of field, and so on. It may be the most important and useful tool for using 3-D layers.

If you're unfamiliar with 3-D cameras, to explain it simply, we would set our elements in our environment and use a camera to move around them, instead of moving the elements themselves. It's like building a set, placing your characters on that set, and taking a camera to shoot them and develop the cinematic angles and camera moves. You're placing the elements and then actually animating a virtual camera to perform your camera moves and shoot.

To create a camera, go to Layer ➤ Select New ➤ Camera (see Figure 10-71).

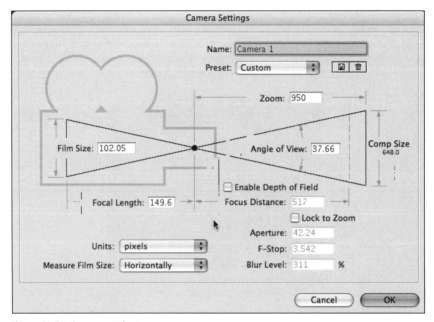

Figure 10-71. Camera settings

When we create a camera, it is set to our current view by default, which is helpful to us, since we already set up our shot. A camera's transform options operate like any other 3-D layer, but one major difference is the addition of a point of interest (see Figure 10-72).

> *The point of interest is the location of the subject of the camera. It's what the camera is looking at. When you move the camera's position along the X, Y, and Z axes, the camera will always look at the point of interest. The point of interest is also like any other 3-D layer property; its values can be changed, keyframed, and animated.*

You can turn the Point of Interest property off, and the camera will face whichever Position it's currently set to. Point of Interest is useful if you want to have the camera move specifically in one direction while looking in another. It is possible to do this without Point of interest, using only Position, but Point of Interest gives you the ability to keyframe itself and Position individually.

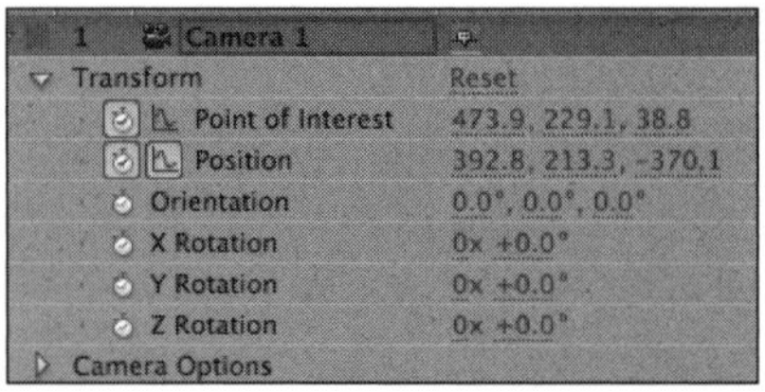

Figure 10-72. The additional properties that come with a Camera: Point of Interest at the top and Camera Options on the bottom.

There is also another property the camera adds; Camera Options. Camera Options contains properties for Zoom and Depth of Field, which entails Focus Distance, Aperture, and Blur Level (see Figure 10-73).

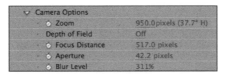

Figure 10-73. The Camera Options menu shows that, in this chapter's example, we have turned Depth of Field off.

Zoom is a keyframeable property that controls zooming in; we will not use this since zooming in loses the multiplane effect, as it does in real life. We are trucking in, that is, physically moving to get the effect of depth. Depth of Field is used for controlling our focus properties; in this exercise, this option is turned off to disable those features. In this exercise, we will not use these options, but for more on these features, check in the "Blur effects" section of the tips and tricks chapter at the end of this book.

For the examples in this book, we will use the Point of Interest property. Make sure to remember the camera will always be looking at the point of interest, regardless of where you're positioning the camera (see Figures 10-74 and 10-75).

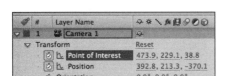

Figure 10-74. Point of Interest has adjustable X, Y, and Z coordinates.

Figure 10-75. Notice the arrow pointing to the point of interest.

Moving the 3-D camera

We will animate the camera like we would any other element, by using keyframes. The camera position and the point of interest will be the two changing values in our keyframes:

1. Select View ➤ Custom View 2 (Top view).

2. Recall that, when we created our camera, it defaulted to our composition's active camera, so our shot was already set up. Under the camera's Position and Point Of Interest, where the camera move begins, click the stopwatch buttons to add a keyframe to each layer (see Figure 10-76). This will be point A.

Figure 10-76. Point A's Point of Interest and Position

3. Move farther down the timeline, and drop a keyframe at point B, where the camera move will end (see Figure 10-77).

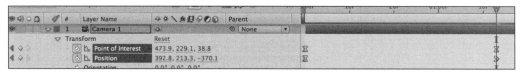

Figure 10-77. Add keyframes for points A and B.

4. At point B, under Camera 1's Position, increase the Z value. Notice the camera position changes in the composition view. Position the camera so that the trash can is almost past and almost out of frame.

5. Return to Camera 1 view. Our camera has been moved in, but our framing is now off, because we haven't adjusted Point of Interest yet (see Figures 10-78 and 10-79).

Figure 10-78. Notice where the point of interest is postioned.

Figure 10-79. The camera is offset from Crazy Jeff.

6. Adjust the values of Point of Interest so that the camera looks at Crazy Jeff (see Figure 10-80).

Figure 10-80. Now the point of interest is on Crazy Jeff.

7. Adjusting the point of interest may make your characters appear to tilt or twist (see Figure 10-81). We will have to adjust the point of interest and position until our image does not look skewed at all.

Figure 10-81. Watch out for odd perspectives when adjusting your camera's position and point of interest.

Changing the position may offset your original framing; to restore that framing, you'll need to adjust the point of interest. Changing the point of interest may make unwanted edges of objects visible; to fix that, you may have to change the position so that your elements are framed as you want them. In short, every time we adjust the point of interest, we will have to compensate for the change with adjusting the position for the new point of interest, or vice versa.

8. We want to get our characters framed similar to the way that we had them set up at the end of the camera move in our earlier example using regular layers. To do that, we are going to have to move the camera in closer to Jeff, making the shot a close up of his torso and head with the house behind him. Proceed to move the camera close using the Z Position property, increasing the value to bring the camera closer to Jeff. In this example, we bring the camera to −370.1.

9. If we lose our framing again, adjust the Position X and Y values accordingly, as well as the Point of Interest value, if necessary, to keep Crazy Jeff in frame (see Figure 10-82). In this example, our final settings for point B on the camera were a Point of Interest of 473.9, 229.1, 38.8 and a Position of 392.8, 213.3, -370.1 (see Figure 10-83).

Figure 10-82. The framing of point B, relatively close to the versions done with layers

Figure 10-83. Point B's Point of Interest and Position values

10. Do a RAM preview of the animation. The multiplane effect becomes present, though the camera movement is a little stiff. Let's adjust the graph curve to make the move come to a nice smooth stop.

11. Select the Camera layer.

12. Open the Graph Editor, and look at the Position property. It's most likely a straight line,

13. We want the camera to come to a smooth clean stop, so grab the handle of the end keyframe. Bring it down a little, and bring the influence to the left to create a small progressive Bezier curve. The numbers in this example were 46.3 px/sec with an Influence of about 30 percent (see Figure 10-84).

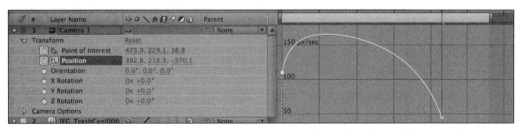

Figure 10-84. The selected Position property's speed graph. After we bring down the end keyframe, these curves slow the camera move to a smooth stop.

15. Do a RAM preview now. The move should come to smoother, more subtle stop.

Complex camera moves

Many different projects could require many different camera moves. This chapter goes over very basic camera movements between point A and point B. Your project may require going to points C, D, and E— apply these same steps to reach those points.

The basic technique is as follows:

1. Frame the shot (point A), which involves all your adjustments in scale, position, rotation, and so forth; drop your keyframes where they're necessary.

2. Frame point B, and adjust the timing in the shot using the velocity graphs.

3. When the shot involves more than points A and B, add the other keyframes, and adjust the positions to whatever the shot requires.

Some cases may have such complex camera moves that it may prove best to do the move frame by frame, which would mean dropping a keyframe on every single frame between A and B. Some detail-intensive shots may just call for that kind of care; it isn't uncommon.

Creating a precomp

After you've made all your adjustments and finished your camera move, you may have a section of layers all sitting on top of each other (see Figure 10-85). To keep your space organized, you can combine all these layers into one precomp to save space in your timeline window. As mentioned earlier, the way to do this is as follows:

1. Select the layers you want to include (see Figure 10-85).

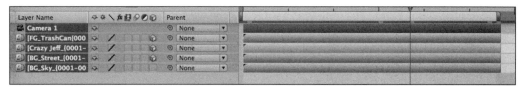

Figure 10-85. Select your stacked layers to precompose them into one layer.

2. Go to Compositions ➤ Pre-compose (see Figure 10-86), or use the keyboard shortcut Ctrl/Cmd+Shift+C.

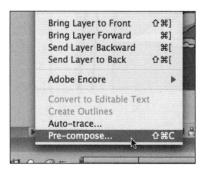

Figure 10-86. Select the Pre-compose option from the Compositions menu

3. A dialog box with a few options will appear (see Figure 10-87). The first lets you name your new precomp.

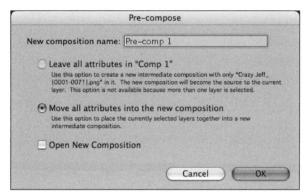

Figure 10-87. The Pre-compose dialog box

4. The next option is Leave All Attributes in "Comp 1" (or whatever the name of the current composition is); this will bring your current selected layer into the new comp but leave all your transform keyframes, effects, masks, and so forth. This is only available when you have one layer selected; you're unable to choose this with multiple layers.

5. The second option is Move all attributes into the new composition; if you are selecting multiple layers, you have to choose this.

6. Next comes Open New Composition; select this if you want the new precomp to open the moment you click OK. Choose depending on your projects' needs. Figure 10-88 shows the layers precomposited into one layer.

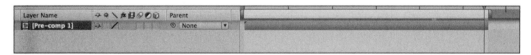

Figure 10-88. Your layers are precomposited into one layer.

7. If you need to adjust those layers, right-click the layer, and select Open Composition, and the layers appear just as they were but in a new separate composition.

After you've got your composition made, move on to finish the rest of your projects using After Effect's toolset.

Summary

The camera is an important tool. There are a multitude of ways to push the potential of your animation and move beyond the limits of Flash. In this chapter, I went over some of those ways: using regular layers, introducing the 3-D element to your project, adding depth that will ultimately add more quality to your animation. After Effects is a powerful asset to animation; there are even more techniques to add to your creative arsenal, such as adding effects like blurs to simulate focus pulls of a camera lens, or lens flares to simulate a reaction to light in the world of your animation (see Chapter 12). The camera is what makes viewing your animation possible, traditionally and digitally—always keep its actions in your mind.

Chapter 11

MAKING FLASH NOT LOOK LIKE FLASH

By Dave Wolfe and Allan Rosson

This chapter will cover a number of techniques to help you refine your work and give it a more polished and professional look. It has taken a number of years for Flash to rise above the stigma of being thought of as used only for "crude Internet animation." Flash is finally taking its rightful place as an industry tool capable of producing wonderfully detailed and fluid animation. Creating this kind of work depends largely on the skill and experience of the artists involved and, to a certain degree, the budgetary constraints of any given project. We will examine line styles, traditional animation techniques, color choices, and using some of the tools in Flash to create subtle distortions for your animated characters that will enhance the illusion of life.

Varied line styles

One dead giveaway that Flash was used in a production is the constant-thickness lines with round endcaps. Using different line styles makes the drawings look more interesting and sets your work apart from all the other Flash animation out there. Some styles are subtle; others are not so subtle. We're going to take a look at three different line styles you can use to make your work stand out.

Ragged lines

Flash has a few different styles you can apply to the standard stroke to give a different look to the line. The first style is the easiest to apply to your drawings; the ragged style gives the appearance that the lines were drawn with a shaky hand rather than the perfect lines and curves usually found in computer animation.

1. Open the file ch11_01.fla. Double-click the nose symbol to edit it in place (see Figure 11-1).

Figure 11-1. Edit the nose symbol to change the line style.

2. Select the outline, and click Custom in the Properties panel to open the Stroke Style window.

3. Change the Type to Ragged (see Figure 11-2).

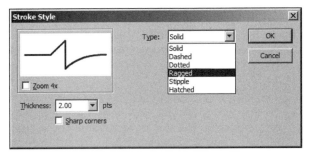

Figure 11-2. Change the stroke's Type to Ragged.

4. Three options appear (see Figure 11-3). Leave the Pattern as Simple. Change the Wave Height to Wild, and change the Wave Length to Medium. Click OK.

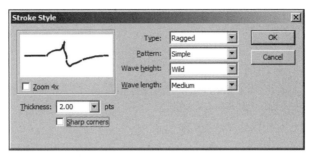

Figure 11-3. Changing the Type to Ragged reveals more options to experiment with.

5. If you aren't happy with the look of the line, you can experiment with the options some more. When you're satisfied with the results, exit the symbol, and double-click the ear to edit it in place. Using the Ink Bottle tool, click the outlines to apply the Ragged style to the lines. Continue this process for the entire head (see Figure 11-4).

Figure 11-4. The head after all symbols have the Ragged stroke style applied.

And that's all there is to it. If you use one of Flash's custom line styles on your own project, you may find it distracting to create the artwork using the custom style. It's usually easier to create the artwork using the standard line style first and then apply a custom style when the artwork is complete.

267

Varied line thickness

The next line style we're going to use is one that has a varied thickness. There are several ways to accomplish this in Flash. The technique shown here offers a great deal of precision and consistency in the line weight:

1. Open the file ch11_02.fla. Double-click the nose symbol to edit it in place.

2. Select the outline, and cut it. Create a new layer, and paste the outline using the Paste in Place command in the Edit menu (see Figure 11-5).

Figure 11-5. Separate the outline and fill on different layers.

3. From the Modify menu, click Shape; then click Convert Lines to Fills.

> *Converting a line into a fill isn't easily reversed if at some point in the future you want to edit the outline. To make it easier, create a new layer and change it to a guide layer. Using the* Paste in Place *command, paste another copy of the outlines into the guide layer; then hide it. If you need to edit the outline or you want to create a variant of this symbol later on, you can copy the lines out of the guide layer rather than redrawing them.*

4. Select the layer with the lines that have been converted to fills, and zoom in close to the end-cap of the line at the top of the nose. The endcap is made up of five points. Using the Subselection tool, delete the two points on either side of the center point of the endcap (see Figure 11-6). Pull the center point further along the path of the line to give it a tapered look. You may need to adjust the position of the two remaining points on either side of the center point and adjust the Bezier handles as well. Repeat the process on the endcap of the nostril.

5. Select the points at the tip of the nose, and thicken the line a little by moving the points on the left side a little further to the left and the points on the right side a little further to the right (see Figure 11-7).

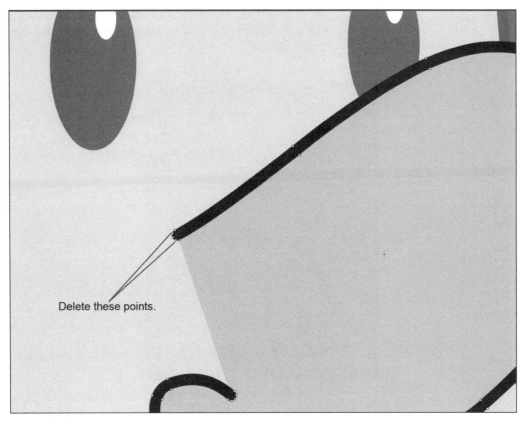

Figure 11-6. Reshape the endcap to taper the line.

Figure 11-7. The final thick to thin line

6. As before, when you finish adjusting these lines, repeat the process on the rest of the lines in the head. This technique is a little more tedious and time consuming than the previous one, but you end up with a nice-looking line with tapered ends that you can easily edit if you need to.

Figure 11-8. The finished head with varied line thickness

Using Illustrator brush styles

The final technique we're going to use involves Adobe Illustrator. Illustrator comes with several brush styles you can apply to lines, and you can create your own custom brushes:

1. Open the file ch11_03.fla. Double-click the ear symbol to edit it in place.

2. As in the previous example, separate the lines from the fill by putting them on a different layer. Keep a copy of the lines in a guide layer in case you need to edit them later.

3. If you're using Flash MX 2004 or earlier, simply select the outlines, copy them, and paste them into a new document in Illustrator. If you're using Flash 8 or CS3, there is a bug that causes curves to become straight lines when pasted from Flash into Illustrator (pasting art from Illustrator into Flash works correctly). This is also true of artwork created in Flash 8 or CS3 that is opened in Flash MX 2004. To get around this, you'll have to go to the File menu, click Export, then click Export Image. Before you do this, change the fill layer to a guide so it won't export; all we want is the outline. Save the image as EPS 3.0; then open the EPS file in Illustrator.

4. The artwork in Illustrator is grouped. Ungroup the artwork by selecting it and clicking Ungroup from the Object menu.

5. If you saved your work as an EPS file, the lines are also saved as a compound path. Select the artwork, and from the Object menu, select Compound Path; then click Release (see Figure 11-9).

Figure 11-9. The Layers palette after the artwork has been ungrouped and the compound path has been released

6. Open the Brushes palette by clicking Brushes in the Window menu.

7. Select all the artwork, and click the Charcoal - Thin brush in the Brushes palette to apply that brush to the artwork (see Figure 11-10).

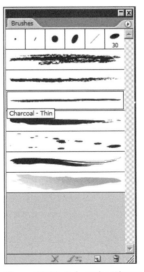

Figure 11-10. Select the Charcoal-Thin brush to apply it to the line.

271

8. The line now has the charcoal brush applied to it, but the inner ear lines are incorrect. There should be one long curve with a smaller curve coming out on the bottom left. Illustrator has broken this into three lines. To fix this, deselect the artwork and then select the smaller curve to the left of the large curve. When it's selected, a colored square will appear next to it on the far right side of the Layers palette. Hide that layer by clicking the eye icon (see Figure 11-11).

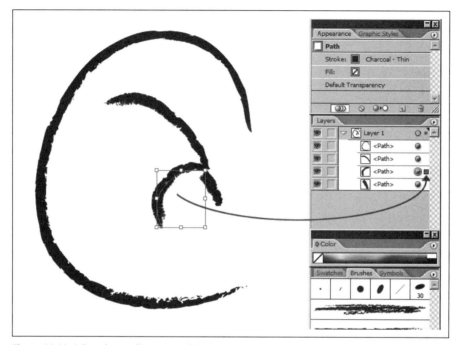

Figure 11-11. Select the smaller curve of the inner ear, and hide that layer.

9. Use the Direct Selection tool to select the point shared by the remaining two curves of the inner ear. Right/Ctrl-click the document, and click Join from the context menu (see Figure 11-12).

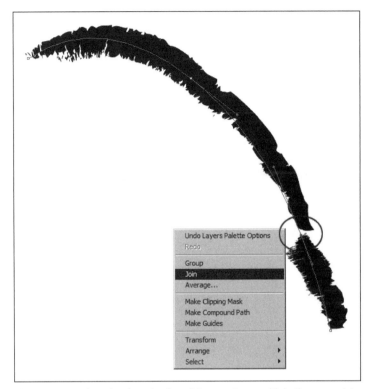

Figure 11-12. Select the shared point of the two lines and join the curves into one line.

10. The Join panel will open. Click Smooth; then click OK. The large curve of the inner ear should now be one continuous line. Unhide the smaller curve, and the ear should look like the one in Figure 11-13.

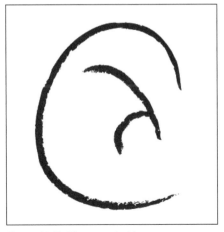

Figure 11-13. The corrected inner ear curves

11. Select all the artwork, copy it, and paste it into Flash. You'll have to use the Paste in Center command to paste the Illustrator artwork into Flash; Paste in Place won't paste the artwork. Move the pasted artwork into the correct position, and change the guided fill layer back to Normal.

12. Exit the symbol, and continue this process for the rest of the symbols in the head. After all the Flash lines have been replaced with Illustrator lines, the head should look like the one in Figure 11-14.

Figure 11-14. The final head with the charcoal outline

Using Illustrator brushes gives you an unlimited variety of line styles to use. In addition to the brushes that come with Illustrator, you can easily create new brushes by dragging artwork into the Brushes palette.

Traditional animation

The cut-out style of animation usually done in Flash is very economical, but some people prefer the look of traditional animation. Although there is software available that is better suited to a traditional animation pipeline, Flash can be used as a low budget ink and paint tool. You can also save a lot of time and money by drawing directly in Flash rather than scanning drawings done on paper.

The process of doing traditional animation in Flash is pretty straightforward. Make some thumbnail poses on one layer that can then be used as a guide for the keys and breakdowns. Lock the Thumbnail layer, and draw the rough keys and breakdowns. Once the roughs are finished, and you're satisfied with the timing, lock the Roughs layer and add a new layer to do the cleanup. Next comes the fun task of inbetweening. Just as with the keys and breakdowns, use separate layers for rough and clean inbetweens. Make sure all the lines are closed so you can fill them with the paint bucket. Figure 11-15 shows a rough drawing next to the cleaned-up version.

Figure 11-15. The rough key and cleaned drawing

When drawing in Flash, some prefer the Pencil tool and others prefer the Brush tool. Whichever tool you choose, a Wacom tablet, Tablet PC, or Cintiq is a must. You'll have far more control than with a mouse, and the stylus has a more natural feel to it. When using the Brush tool, you'll want to enable pressure sensitivity and, if your tablet supports it, tilt sensitivity. These options are found on the toolbar when the Brush tool is selected, below the Brush Shape option (see Figure 11-16). The Pressure and Tilt options will only be available if a tablet is detected.

Figure 11-16. The Pressure and Tilt options are found at the bottom of the Toolbar.

The Brush and Pencil tools also have other options that may come in handy. The Pencil tool has three different drawing modes: Straighten, Smooth, and Ink. Straighten will straighten your strokes, which is useful when you're trying to draw a straight line. If you have Shape Recognition enabled in the Preferences panel, it will also recognize when you're trying to draw an oval, triangle, or rectangle. The Preferences panel also has options for how strictly Flash will attempt to straighten or smooth your strokes. The Smooth drawing mode will attempt to smooth the curves you draw, but it will still leave sharp corners. The Ink drawing mode does not modify the stroke you draw. The options are available on the toolbar when the Pencil tool is selected.

Figure 11-17. The Brush tool has several different painting modes to choose from.

The Brush tool also has several different modes available on the toolbar (see Figure 11-17). Paint Normal will paint over lines and fills on the same layer; Drawing Objects, Groups, and Symbols are always above raw vector shapes. Paint Fills will paint over fills and empty areas, but below lines. Paint Behind will paint only empty areas on the layer. Paint Selected will only paint over the currently selected fill. Paint Inside will only paint over the fill where the brush stroke began and in empty areas on the layer. The Paint Normal mode will probably be used most often, but the other modes can be useful for tasks such as quickly painting some highlights without having to worry about painting outside the lines.

The Brush tool also has ten sizes to choose from. Keep in mind, however, that the brush size is relative to the screen and not an absolute size. If you're drawing with the zoom level at 100 percent and then zoom in to 200 percent to draw some details, the brush strokes will be half the size even though you didn't change the brush size (see Figure 11-18). This can be frustrating sometimes, but it also enables you to paint with very large strokes by zooming out from the image and paint with very fine strokes by zooming in very close to the image.

The Brush tool also has nine brush shapes to choose from, including circles, ovals, rectangles, and diagonal lines. Finally, you can change the smoothness of the brush strokes by expanding the Properties panel and adjusting the Smoothing slider.

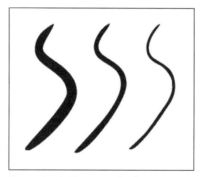

Figure 11-18. The same size brush painted at different zoom levels

Color choices

The choice of colors can have a dramatic impact on your production. Choosing an arrangement of colors that are pleasing to the eye will make your work look more professional. A lot of animation these days, especially web animation, uses bright, oversaturated colors. Instead of picking colors from the default color palette, consider mixing your own colors. This is especially important for coloring your backgrounds. You want the characters to stand out from the background, not get lost in it. Using contrasting colors and less saturation in the background will help make the characters stand out. Although you often want the characters to have bolder colors, they should still be less saturated than the colors in Flash's default color palette. If you want to make a character's shirt blue, for example, instead of using the RGB value of 0, 0, 255, try using something like 60, 60, 200. This is also a good excuse to sit down and watch some classic cartoons like Bugs Bunny or Woody Woodpecker. Woody's colors are blue, red, and orange; they're bright enough to stand out from the backgrounds and props without being overpoweringly saturated. You may want to visit http://kukler.adobe.com to create and download color themes for Adobe Creative Suite.

Figure 11-19. Consider using less saturated colors in your production.

Another option is to use bitmap fills instead of the solid flat colors typically used in Flash animation. You can use patterns for things such as plaid shirts or a polka dot dress, or you can use subtle textures to the solid fills. The important thing to remember is that the bitmap should be a tiling image, meaning it has no visible seams as the pattern is repeated. An easy way to check the seams on an image is to use the Offset filter in Photoshop. It's found in the Filter menu, in the Other submenu. The Horizontal and Vertical sliders should be set to half of the image's width and height, so for an image that is 500×500 pixels, the Horizontal and Vertical sliders should both be at 250 (see Figure 11-20). The Undefined Areas radio button should be set to Wrap Around. If you don't see any seams in the image after applying the Offset filter, then you can tile the image with no worries. If you do see seams, you can attempt to correct them in Photoshop by using the Healing Brush on the areas of the image that don't line up seamlessly, or you can buy a program like Seamless Texture Generator (available at http://seamlesstexturegenerator.com for $24.95) to automatically make seamless textures from photographs. You can also try searching for images that already tile seamlessly.

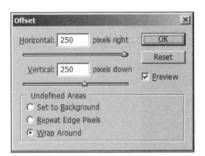

Figure 11-20. Use Photoshop's Offset filter to check for seams.

You can also use Photoshop to make your bitmap fills. One nice thing about many of Photoshop's filters is that, if the image dimensions are square, then the filter will tile without any seams. A good way to get some subtle texture in your colors is to use the cloud filter, which is found in the Filters menu under the Render submenu. Make the foreground color the color you want the fill to be, and make the background color slightly darker or lighter; then run the clouds filter.

277

To use a bitmap as a fill in Flash, open the Color Mixer from the Window menu. Make sure Fill Color is selected, and from the Type menu, choose Bitmap. You're then prompted to load a bitmap from disk. After loading the bitmap, you can use the Paint Bucket tool to apply the bitmap fill. To adjust the scale or rotation of the fill, use the Fill Transform tool, and click the fill. A transformation handle will appear enabling you to make the desired changes. Figure 11-21 shows how bitmap fills can be used to add a pattern to a character's costume.

Figure 11-21. Plaid Speedos are all the rage on the beaches of southern France.

Creating distortion for animation

The use of distortion is one of the fundamental principles in traditional animation for achieving a believable illusion of movement. It is particularly useful in Flash to help alleviate any feeling of stiffness, especially when animating with symbols. Distortion, or drag as it is sometimes called, happens when part of a character or an object moves through space at such a rate of speed that it causes a visible change to the shape of the character or object. This distortion is most often in direct proportion to the speed with which the object travels. In Figure 11-22, the Lounger has produced a red rose in the middle of his song, tossed it in the air, and upon catching it, drawn it closer to him in the final frame.

The second to the last frame shows the rose in its most distorted form. Obviously, this example does not display the entire sequence but only those poses necessary for discussion. This kind of effect helps the eye to follow an object through the fastest part of an action. If you try to move a character or an object through space at too great a speed without any distortion, it becomes more difficult for the brain to make sense of what the eyes are trying to capture. Distortion effectively fills in the gaps while preserving the speed of an action.

Figure 11-22. Shows the amount of distortion to the rose at its fastest moment in the action

Distorting symbols

You can add some very simple but effective distortion, or drag, to your symbols by using a combination of the Free Transform tool and the Rotate and Skew tool. First, select the symbol you wish to distort, and then select the Free Transform tool just under the arrow on the top left side of your toolbar. This will activate the options underneath the main toolbar. Next, select the Rotate and Skew tool just underneath the Snap To Objects tool (or the red magnet). This will highlight handles on the activated symbol, so you can pull these handles to the right or to the left or up or down depending on the direction of movement your animation is taking. It is very important to have this distortion go in the same direction as your action. Continuing with the rose example, in Figure 11-23, we can see that the rose is moving in a horizontal direction, so the handles of the symbol are moved also in a horizontal direction.

Recall that the amount of distortion is equal to the speed that the object is moving. Don't worry too much about what this distortion might do to a symbol when viewed as a still image. After all, it is meant to be viewed only in motion and to help create a more believable feeling of movement, rather than a graphic representation of the object itself (see Figure 11-24). This kind of distortion might take place on as few as one or two frames or it might occur on numerous frames within an action. It all depends upon what is required for that action.

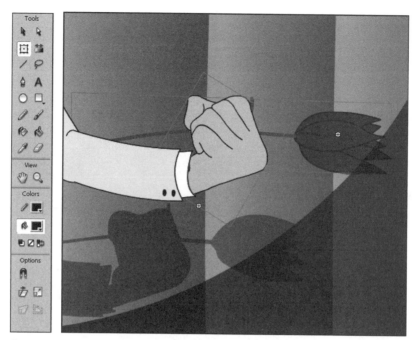

Figure 11-23. Symbols selected for distortion

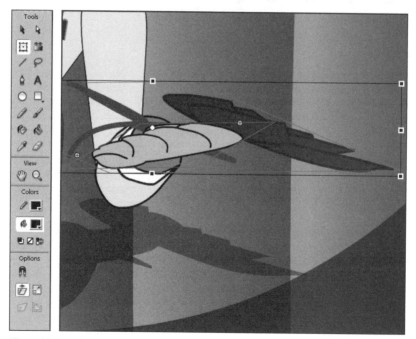

Figure 11-24. Using the skewing tool to distort symbols during a fast action

Creating traditional distortion

Distorting symbols with resizing or skewing is a kind of shortcut and can be accomplished rather quickly as you animate. If your project is for the Internet, creating distortion or drag in this way can help you to save on file size, because you are only manipulating symbols with these tools and not generating any new artwork. You can take advantage of another wonderful tool in Flash to create a more organic and traditional form or distortion and drag if your project is not limited by file size. For this method, we will be using the Envelope tool. First, select the symbols you wish to distort, and break them apart by pressing Ctrl/Cmd+B (see Figure 11-25).

Figure 11-25. Breaking the symbols down to vectors

> This method will also work if you are simply drawing shapes that have not yet been symbolized. For more information on symbolizing, please refer to Chapter 6.

Next, using your lasso or marquee tool, select the area or object you wish to distort. Then, make sure the Free Transform tool is selected, and select the Envelope tool. You will then see your selection surrounded by a series of handles (see Figure11-26). By clicking and dragging any one of these handles, you can distort your selected shape. Some experimentation will be required here, as this tool is very sensitive (see Figure 11-27). Be sure to apply this same kind of distortion to other symbols or parts of a character that would be affected by this type of movement (see Figures 11-28 and 11-29).

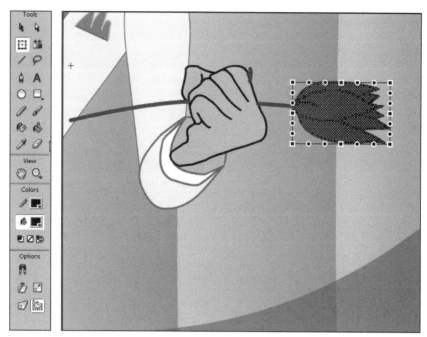

Figure 11-26. Isolating the rose for distortion

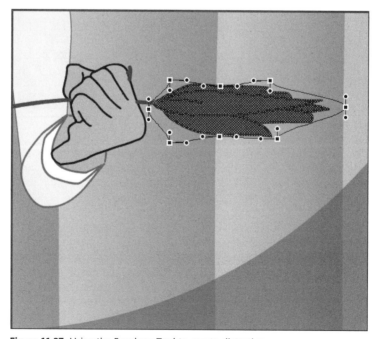

Figure 11-27. Using the Envelope Tool to create distortion

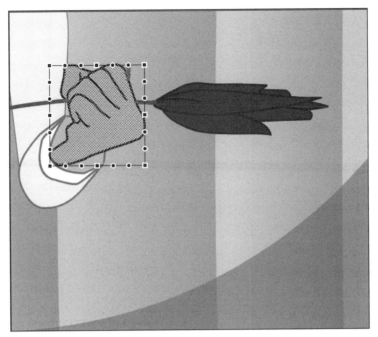

Figure 11-28. Isolating the hand for distortion

With some practice, you will find that you can easily distort a shape in a very fluid way to suit the needs of your animation. This can significantly cut down on the amount of time you would otherwise need to draw this kind of distortion effectively on a frame by frame basis. This method also helps to eliminate a lot of guesswork, because you can distort shapes over a succession of frames at any speed you wish and maintain a consistency of volume to the shape.

> *Something to keep in mind while using the* Envelope *tool is that if you choose to undo (Ctrl/Cmd+Z) a distortion you have made to a shape, you will lose the control handles of the envelope. You will need to reselect the* Envelope *tool after each time you choose to undo.*

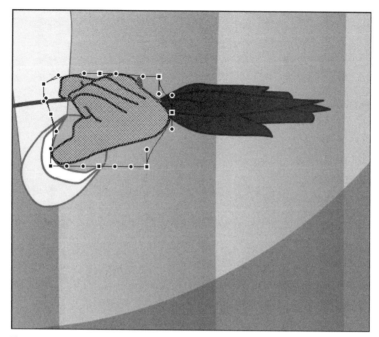

Figure 11-29. Creating distortion for the hand

Summary

In this chapter, we have covered quite a bit of territory concerning how to make your Flash animation not look like Flash animation. We have explored a variety of line styles and how these styles can have an impact on not only the overall look of a show but on the personalities of the characters themselves. You have seen various techniques and the tools that can be used to help you achieve a unique and polished quality to your own line work.

We've discussed traditional animation techniques and how they relate to the use of Flash and its wide array of tools. We've seen how those tools and techniques can help you to dovetail your animation skills and artistic visions with the needs of most any project you choose to undertake.

We examined the choices of color, color harmonies, and the tools to make fine adjustments to how your characters will stand out, or read, against a background. Other techniques such as bitmap fills were also explored.

Techniques for creating distortion or drag effects in your animation were presented to help give a more believable feel to the animation that you create. All of the techniques in this chapter have been and continue to be used with great success by us, the authors of this book. In the next chapter, we will go over some tips and tricks you can use to make your work a little easier. We hope that they will be of help to you too in all of your future Flash animation projects. Good luck!

Chapter 12

TIPS AND TRICKS

By Tim Jones, Barry Kelly, Allan S. Rosson, and Dave Wolfe

No book on Flash animation can ever detail every technique possible, and this certainly was not our goal as we set out to write this book. There are so many things you can do with Flash—and so many ways to do them—that it would be almost impossible to catalog them in a single book. In the previous chapters, we have outlined a character animation pipeline that has worked well for us and given you (we hope) some insight into methods and techniques that will help you in your own animation. In this chapter, we offer up those tips and tricks that did not fit neatly within the confines of the previous chapters but that you may find interesting and beneficial.

Animated Illustrator brushes

Adobe Illustrator has a cool feature that makes it easy to animate a complex design as though it were a simple line. By dragging artwork into the Brushes palette you create a new type of brush stroke that can be applied to a line. For example, you can animate a tail-wagging cycle by simply animating one line in Flash, exporting the lines as EPS files, and applying the tail brush stroke to the lines. You can then export the lines as a SWF and import the SWF into Flash. You can also use Illustrator's Blend tool to create inbetweens.

1. Open the file ch12_01.fla. This striped tail with a pointed tip might be found on a dragon, a demon, or some other nasty critter. It would also be a real pain to animate using only Flash. From the File menu, click Export and then Export Image. Export the image as EPS 3.0. Using EPS instead of Illustrator's native AI format will leave the colors as RGB rather than CMYK. If the colors are converted to CMYK, they become altered and tend to have a washed out appearance. If you're using Flash MX 2004 or earlier, you don't even need to export an EPS file; you can simply copy the symbol from Flash and paste it into a new RGB Illustrator document (a bug in Flash 8 and CS3 causes curves to become straight lines when copied from Flash and pasted into Illustrator, so it is necessary to export these files as EPS).

2. Open the EPS file in Illustrator. From the Window menu, open the Brushes palette. Select all the artwork, and drag it into the Brushes palette. This will open the New Brush dialog box. Select New Art Brush, and click OK (see Figure 12-1).

Figure 12-1. Create a new Art Brush.

3. The Art Brush Options dialog box will open. Type a name for the brush, and make sure the Direction is the arrow pointing down, Stroke From Top to Bottom. Colorization should be set to None; we don't want the color of the line to alter the color of the tail. Leave the Size at 100%, and leave the Proportional box and both of the Flip boxes unchecked (see Figure 12-2).

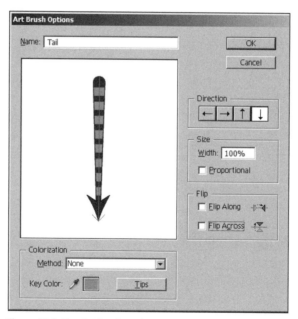

Figure 12-2. The Art Brush options

4. Select the tail artwork, and delete it. Use the Line Segment tool to draw a vertical line; holding the Shift key while you draw the line will keep the line straight. Make sure the line has a stroke color, so you can see it. The stroke will be changed to a brush later, but for now, a 1-point black stroke will do.

5. Select the line with the Selection tool, and copy the line. Move the line to the left, and then paste a copy of the line in place using the Paste in Front command from the Edit menu or by pressing Ctrl/Cmd+F. You should now have two vertical lines side by side (see Figure 12-3).

Figure 12-3. You should have two lines side by side in your Illustrator document.

6. To make this tail wag, we're going to need to make one of the lines a curve. Click and hold the Pen tool in the toolbar, and a menu with related tools will appear. Click the last one, the Convert Anchor Point tool (see Figure 12-4).

7. Click and drag the mouse on the bottom point of the right line. This will create a Bezier handle enabling you to adjust the curve. Use the Direct Selection tool (the white arrow) to select the bottom point and move it up and to the right. Adjust the Bezier handles until the curve looks something like the one shown in Figure 12-5.

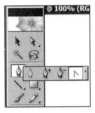

Figure 12-4. Use the Convert Anchor Point tool to convert the straight line into a curve.

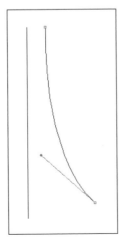

Figure 12-5. Adjust the curve using the Direct Selection tool.

8. That takes care of the curve we'll be using for the tail swinging to the right. Now for the other side—use the Selection tool to select the right curve and copy it. From the Object menu, click Transform and then click Scale. This will open the Scale dialog box. Click the radio button for Non-Uniform, change the Horizontal value to –100%, and click OK (see Figure 12-6). This will flip the curve.

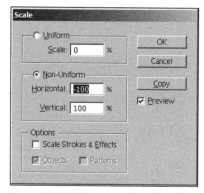

Figure 12-6. Flip the curve by scaling it –100%.

9. Move the flipped curve to the left of the straight line. Use the Paste in Front command from the Edit menu to paste the original curve in place. You should now have three lines arranged as shown in Figure 12-7.

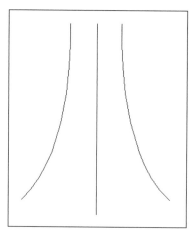

Figure 12-7. The final arrangement of the three lines

10. Select all three curves using the Selection tool; then click the tail brush in the Brushes palette to apply the tail symbol as a brush stroke (see Figure 12-8). If the tails look too fat or skinny, you may need to scale your lines using the Free Transform tool.

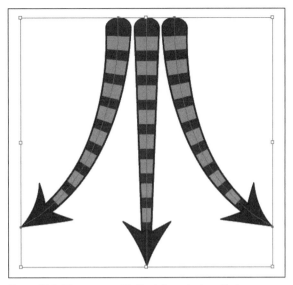

Figure 12-8. The curves with the tail symbol applied as a brush stroke

11. Now that we have the three keys for the animation, it's time to make some inbetweens. For that, we use the Blend tool. But first, move the curved tails on the sides closer to the straight tail in the center (see Figure 12-9). The top points should be on top of each other, so when the artwork is brought back into Flash, all the tails will line up with each other.

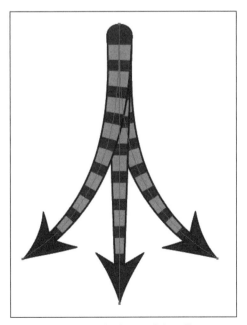

Figure 12-9. Line up the bases of the tails.

12. Select all three tails, and from the Object menu, click Blend and then Make. You should end up with two more tails between the curved tails and the straight tail, as shown in Figure 12-10.

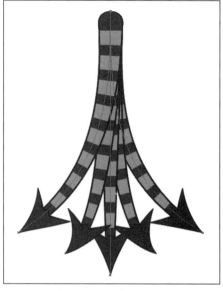

Figure 12-10. The tails with the Blend effect applied

13. Those two inbetweens aren't going to be enough for a smooth animation, so let's add a few more. Go back to the Object menu, click Blend, and then click Blend Options. Change the Spacing to Specified Steps, and make the value 5 (see Figure 12-11). You can increase the number of steps if you want the animation to be slower. Click OK.

Figure 12-11. Increase the number of steps if you want more inbetweens.

14. Now, to bring the animated tail into Flash, click File, and then click Export. Export the file as a SWF, and click Save. This will open the SWF format options dialog box. From the Export As menu, choose AI Layers to SWF Frames. If you're using Illustrator CS2, uncheck the Generate HTML box. Check the box for Animate Blends, select the In Sequence radio button, and click OK. If you're using Illustrator CS3, click the Advanced button, check the box for Animate Blends, and select the In Sequence radio button. See Figure 12-12 for the export options available in Illustrator CS2 and CS3.

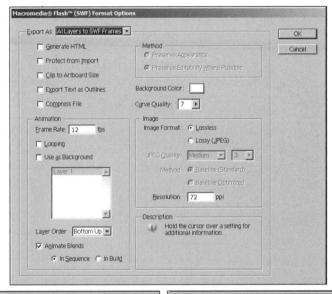

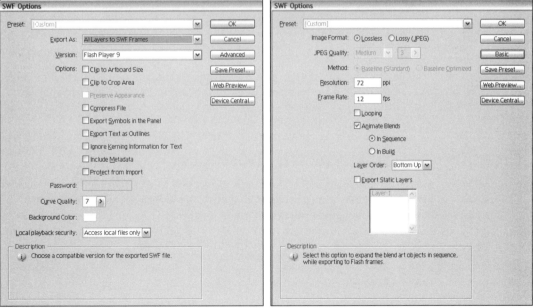

Figure 12-12. The SWF export options for Illustrator CS2 and the Basic and Advanced export options for Illustrator CS3

293

15. Switch back to Flash, and create a new layer. From the File menu, click Import and Import to Stage. Select the SWF you exported from Illustrator, and click Open. The blended tails are imported as a sequence of frames. If you play the animation, you'll see that the tail moves a bit oddly and kind of dips down into the straight tail position. This is because the blends are linear. To fix this, you'll have to stretch the tails on the inbetween frames so that the tips follow a smooth arc (see Figure 12-13).

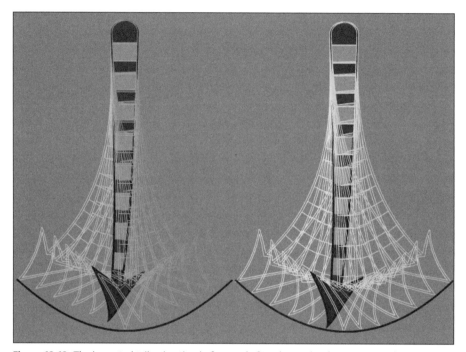

Figure 12-13. The imported tail animation before and after the arc has been corrected

This technique can be used for pony tails, ropes, rubber hose limbs, and much, much more. If you need more control over your inbetweens than the Blend tool allows, you can animate your lines in Flash and apply the brush strokes in Illustrator. To see the final animation, open the file ch12_02.fla.

Creating custom keyboard shortcuts

Creating your own set of custom keyboard shortcuts is a great way to speed up your animation workflow. Many of the default shortcuts in Flash are of little use to the animator, and you'll definitely want to add some shortcuts for some of the extensions you've installed.

From the Edit menu, click Keyboard Shortcuts. The default set of shortcuts you're presented with will be either Adobe Standard or Macromedia Standard, depending on your version of Flash. This default set of shortcuts can't be altered, so you must first duplicate the set. Click the Duplicate Set button, type a name for the new set of keyboard shortcuts, and then click OK (see Figure 12-14).

Now you can edit the keyboard shortcuts. The list of commands is structured like the menu in Flash. For example, say you wanted to change the F6 shortcut from Convert to Keyframes to Insert Keyframe (which is much more useful for animators). Scroll to the Insert list of commands; if the list is collapsed, double-click Insert to expand the list or click the plus symbol (+) to the left of Insert. Expand the Timeline command list, and select Keyframe. Below the Description, click the + button next to Shortcuts. Press the F6 key on the keyboard, and click the Change button. A window will pop up warning you that F6 is already assigned to the Convert to Keyframes command. Click the Reassign button, and now F6 will insert a keyframe at the current frame instead of converting the selected frames to keyframes. When you have finished assigning your custom keyboard shortcuts, click the OK button to apply the changes.

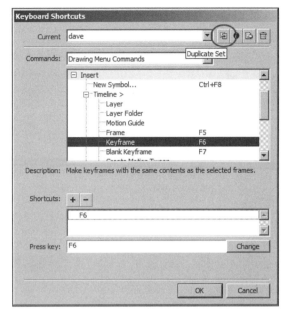

Figure 12-14. Creating custom keyboard shortcuts is an easy way to speed up your animation workflow.

Fixing broken shortcuts

When you add or remove a custom command, oftentimes the hotkeys will have all been shifted up or down. To quickly fix this, simply open the Edit Keyboard Shortcuts window, and click OK. You don't need to change anything. This trick also works when your custom keyboard shortcuts randomly stop responding. Simply opening the Edit Keyboard Shortcuts window and clicking OK will make the shortcuts work again.

Super zoom!

Flash has a zoom limit of 2,000 percent. There are times when this just isn't enough. Oftentimes, the problem is caused by creating the artwork too small; it's usually best to create your characters quite a bit larger than may seem necessary to avoid the issue of not being able to zoom in close enough to a character. However, there is a workaround: you can scale the artwork much larger than 2,000 percent. By scaling up the symbol rather than trying to zoom into it, you can get the same effect as zooming in closer than 2,000 percent. When you're done editing the symbol, you can scale it back down to its original size. There is a limit to Flash's precision though, so this trick will only work up to a point. It's best to avoid this problem altogether by creating your artwork at a large scale from the start.

Fade in and fade out

This tip seems almost so obvious that it goes without saying, but I've seen this simple effect made very complicated so many times that it deserves a place in this chapter. Fade ins and fade outs are perhaps the most common form of transition used in visual storytelling, and if you are animating in Flash, chances are you have had to do this many times. Believe it or not, I've seen beginning animators who have not set their scenes up inside clips try to fade out each individual element on the stage to achieve this effect. If, however, you are somewhat familiar with Flash and are working inside clips, there are a couple of methods that are widely used.

The first, and most problematic, is to set your document background color to black (or whatever color you are fading into and/or out of) and use the alpha properties of the clip to achieve the effect. For instance, let's assume we want to add a fade in at the beginning of "King Klaus" using this method.

1. On frame 1 of layer Animation01, click the instance of ++shot_01 on the stage, and then in the Properties panel, set Color to Alpha and Alpha Amount to 0% as shown in Figure 12-15.

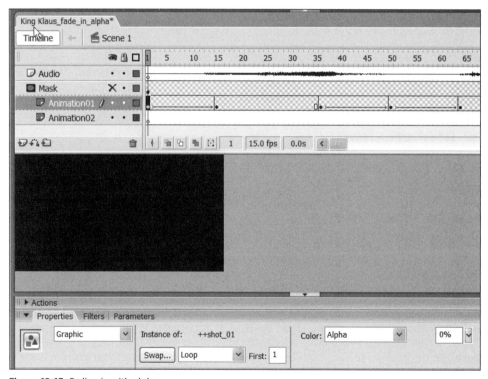

Figure 12-15. Fading in with alpha

2. Then on frame 15 (assuming you want a 1-second fade in), set another key frame, and set Alpha Amount to 100%.

3. Go back to frame 1, and create a motion tween.

You have now created a fade in, but—as we discussed earlier in the book—it may not be the effect you were hoping for. Since Flash applies the alpha value to each library item separately, we start to see through some elements on the stage that we don't want to see through. Notice in Figure 12-16 that we can see through the mantle to the curtain.

The second widely used technique is almost the same, but instead of using alpha, we use brightness. This effect works reasonably well when fading in or out from white and black, because brightness can be modified from −100% (black) to 100% (white). At 0%, there is no brightness applied, and the clip appears in its normal state. The one proviso with this technique, however, is that it adds more file size and is slightly harder for the CPU to render than the simple technique I will describe next. Chances are, if you are doing fade ins and fade outs in Flash (as opposed to After Effects or some other compositing program), you are delivering your animation as a SWF, and file size and playback issues are important. Therefore, consider this simple technique instead:

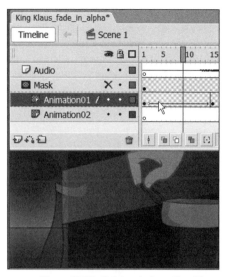

Figure 12-16. Unintended results with an alpha fade

1. Create a color card equal to the size of your stage.
2. Symbolize it.
3. Place it in the layer above your animation.
4. Use an alpha fade on the color card.

This simple technique allows you to create the same fade-in and fade-out effects, allows you to use any color you want (not just white and black), is lower in file size, and is easier for the CPU to render because the calculation is on a simple, nonanimating color card, instead of all the elements within your animation clip. While it is harder to quantify the CPU burden of each effect, the simple size report shown in Figure 12-17 easily illustrates the advantage of this last approach.

King Klaus_fade_in_alpha.swf Movie Report				King Klaus_fade_in_brightness.swf Movie Report				King Klaus_fade_in_color card.swf Movie Report			
Frame #	Frame Bytes	Total Bytes	Scene	Frame #	Frame Bytes	Total Bytes	Scene	Frame #	Frame Bytes	Total Bytes	Scene
1	10286	10286	Scene 1 (AS 2.0	1	10300	10300	Scene 1 (AS 2.0 Class	1	10328	10328	Scene 1 (AS 2.0 Classe
2	715	11001		2	706	11006		2	147	10475	
3	529	11530		3	506	11512		3	212	10687	
4	1747	13277		4	1716	13228		4	1411	12098	
5	552	13829		5	528	13756		5	214	12312	
6	616	14445		6	592	14348		6	279	12591	
7	552	14997		7	528	14876		7	214	12805	
8	618	15615		8	592	15468		8	279	13084	
9	553	16168		9	527	15995		9	213	13297	
10	617	16785		10	591	16586		10	278	13575	
11	553	17338		11	527	17113		11	213	13788	
12	616	17954		12	590	17703		12	277	14065	
13	616	18570		13	590	18293		13	277	14342	
14	552	19122		14	525	18818		14	212	14554	
15	775	19897		15	760	19578		15	277	14831	

Figure 12-17. Side-by-side size comparisons of the three techniques

As you can see in Figure 12-17, the alpha, brightness, and color card technique reports (from left to right) show how much size is added to your file on a frame-by-frame basis. The first column of each report lists the frame number; the second column lists how much file size has been added for that frame; and the third column indicates the cumulative size of the file. Notice how the alpha and brightness examples add approximately 500 to 700 bytes per frame, while color card adds 200 bytes per frame as shown in Figure 12-18. When the fade in is complete at frame 15, compare the cumulative file size of each technique. Notice that alpha is 19,897, brightness is 19,578, and color card is 14,831. If file size matters to you, the roughly 5,000 bytes you save with the color card method are worth noting.

King Klaus.swf Movie Report			King Klaus_fade_in_color card.s		
Frame #	Frame Bytes	Total	Frame #	Frame Bytes	Total
1	10277	10277	1	10328	10328
2	138	10415	2	147	10475
3	203	10618	3	212	10687
4	1410	12028	4	1411	12098
5	205	12233	5	214	12312
6	270	12503	6	279	12591
7	205	12708	7	214	12805
8	270	12978	8	279	13084
9	204	13182	9	213	13297
10	269	13451	10	278	13575
11	204	13655	11	213	13788
12	268	13923	12	277	14065
13	268	14191	13	277	14342
14	203	14394	14	212	14554
15	268	14662	15	277	14831

Figure 12-18. The color card option adds less than 200 bytes.

Reversing frames

Creating animation can be a very tedious process. Even simple actions require a lot of thought and planning to be effective. Reversing frames can sometimes help you to build your animated sequences more quickly. One thing to keep in mind, however, is that the timing for an action playing in the forward direction may not always be correct once you try to use those same frames in a reverse direction. Did you ever notice the camera trick used in some old films when an object flies into frame past an actor and must land in a perfectly placed location? Many times the actor's movements, if not carefully controlled, appear odd because the film is displayed in reverse to accomplish the effect. This is what I mean by the timing of the action. Let's look at a few examples of reversing frames to help build a sequence. In Figure 12-19, the character is looking screen left and then turns to look screen right.

Figure 12-19. The character is turning from screen left to right.

Our character here, known as Dare Devil Dog, has just crashed through a mountainside after doing a stunt and has accidentally discovered a diamond mine. After striking a match, he looks screen left, then right (see Figure 12-20), and after a short pause, he will look back to screen left again, returning to his original position. Instead of having to create the movements frame by frame for him to once again look back to screen left, I simply used what I'd already made and reversed those frames. Here is how you can do it for your animation:

1. Select the frames you wish to reverse (see Figure 12-21).

2. Hold down the Alt key, and slide the frames along the timeline to the location where you want them to play.

3. In your Modify drop-down menu, select Timeline/Reverse Frames.

As you scroll back and forth along the timeline, check to see that playing the frames in reverse won't cause a strange-looking effect as described in the introduction of this tip. If you do see a strange effect that gives the feeling that the character is simply moving in reverse, you can remedy this by adjusting the position of a symbol to help support the direction of the action or the spacing of movement between frames so that the timing or speed of the actions are more natural for a forward movement (see Figure 12-22). Please refer to Chapter 6 for additional information on timing and speed of actions.

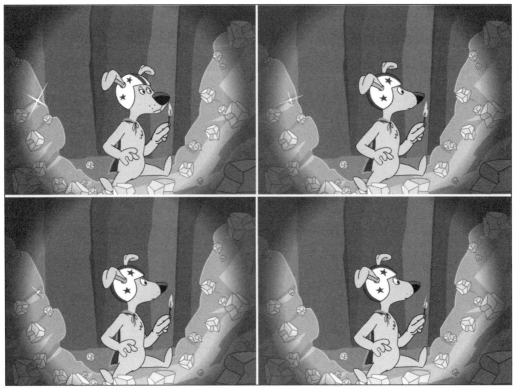

Figure 12-20. Character continues to turn to screen right.

Figure 12-21. Selecting frames to reverse

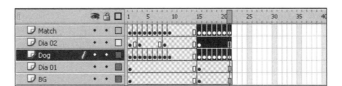

Figure 12-22. Frames reversed with a pause in between

This procedure may seem elementary, but it can significantly speed up your work when applied effectively. Reversing frames can be used for a wide variety of actions. It can be very effective when characters are engaged in conversation and their arm and hand gestures need to be carefully planned. When reversing a character's hand and or arm gesture, be careful about the position of the hand as the action is reversed. In Figure 12-23, the arm positions on frames 6 through 10 have been reversed. The hands have been adjusted to suit the action. If the hands were not adjusted and the arm action simply reversed, it would produce the strange effect previously discussed and betray the fact that the frames were reversed. By adjusting the hand positions, we get the correct follow-through motion as the arm swings forward.

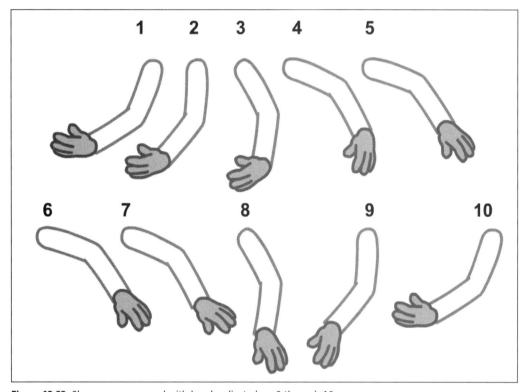

Figure 12-23. Shows arms reversed with hands adjusted on 6 through 10

Another use for reversing frames might be when a character is bending or reaching down to pick up a small or light object. Once the character reaches down to the extreme pose or position, the frames can be reversed to return the character to the starting position. A character reaching down to pick up a heavy object, however, would require a different approach to the timing of the action due to the object's weight and its effect on the character's balance. In Figure 12-24, the basic action of the man reaching down to pick up Rocket Robin was reversed after position 3. The only changes made on positions 4 though 6 were to his hands and arms. Most often, reversing frames will not accomplish 100 percent of the task, but it can put you well on the way. This will save you time that is better spent on the polish and subtle embellishments to your animation.

Figure 12-24. Reversal of basic body action with adjustments to arms and hands

As you work on your animation, you will be amazed at the number of different situations you will find where the reversing of frames can work really well. Try to plan your poses and actions so that you can get the most out of all of your frames.

Blurs in After Effects

Blurs are very useful filters of After Effects. The blurs in After Effects are much more controllable and dynamic and are of a better quality than the blurs in Flash. The human eye naturally perceives fast motion to be very blurry, and the eye naturally focuses on objects and planes of your attention, leaving everything else in a blurred, out-of-focus state.

Figure 12-25. Notice the Motion Blur icon to which the mouse arrow is pointing.

One way to create this blurred effect is to click the Motion Blur icon located in the timeline panel, along with the layer option icons (see Figure 12-25).

The Motion Blur icon adds some blur to the selected layer, but it has no control settings and is a general purpose blur. If you need specific directions, animation, and changes added to the blur, you can use After Effects's many Blur effects.

With the Directional Blur filter, you can make your objects appear to be moving at blur-inducing speeds. By using the Gaussian Blur or Focus Blur, you can simulate shifts in focus like a camera or the human eye itself.

Creating motion blur using the Directional Blur effect

Directional Blur can be used to help give moving objects or camera moves a greater sense of speed. If we take an object, say, a ball flying across the screen, the ball is moving fairly quickly. To emphasize the speed and to simulate what the human eye would see, we'll add a motion blur to it.

Directional Blur works on two properties, Direction and Blur Length. Direction is the angle that you set the blur to follow, and Blur Length is exactly how it sounds, the length of the blur you add to the layer.

Once you have imported your animation into After Effects, put it in a composition. In this example, we'll use a PNG of a ball (see Figure 12-26) flying across the screen.

Figure 12-26. This ball is flying from the right to the left, and it could use a little blur.

1. Once you have added the animation layer into the timeline, duplicate the layer to which you wish to add the blur effect.

2. Go to Effects, or Right/Ctrl-click the layer to which you wish to add the blur, and select Effects.

3. Select Blur & Sharpen, and then select Directional Blur.

4. The Directional Blur effects drop-down menu appears in your layer under the timeline, click the arrow to the right of the effect to open up the Directional Blur properties (see Figure 12-27).

5. Since the ball is moving horizontally, we'll pick an angle of 90 degrees.

6. Then increase the Blur Length to add the blur to the layer.

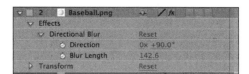

Figure 12-27. The effect properties for Directional Blur

7. Keep the blurred layer underneath the regular layer, and slightly move the blurred layer to trail the regular one (see Figure 12-28).

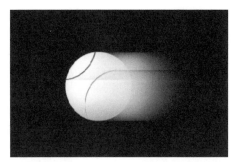

Figure 12-28. The blur is applied to the ball.

Effects can be keyframed like any other After Effects layer. For instance, we can have the ball increase blurriness the farther it travels.

1. Create a keyframe in the timeline on the Blur Length property. Place it at the beginning of the ball passing (see Figure 12-29).

Figure 12-29. The marker here is on the first keyframe made.

2. Set the Blur Length to a low number like 10.0.

3. Then, create another keyframe closer to the end of the ball passing and increase the Blur Length number to something like 300.0 (see Figure 12-30).

Figure 12-30. Now, the marker is on the end keyframe.

4. Do a RAM preview, and observe the growing blur trail on the ball (see Figure 12-31).

You could apply this effect to loads of things, from a character running, to a superhero or jet flying by the screen, to cars or anything that needs to appear to be traveling at high speeds.

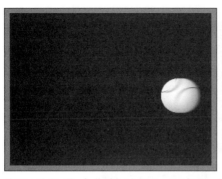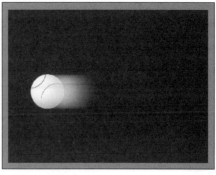

Figure 12-31. The ball's blur increases as it travels across the screen.

Creating a quick focus blur using the Gaussian Blur effect

A way to enhance your animation would be to use blurs to make objects appear out of focus and give depth to the planes used in your animation. Classic traditional animation was shot using optical cameras in the early years of animation, so now, using digital software and digital cameras, we can attempt to re-create the effects that worked so well in modern digital animation.

To start, we need our objects separated into layers, so that we can control the blur effects on the layers independently. In this example, we have our character already separated from the background; for information on exporting our elements onto separate planes, see Chapter 10.

1. Create a new composition, and put our separated elements into the timeline. Frame your elements to your needs. In this example, our character named Crazy Jeff is standing out in front of his house; the composition is a close up of his face with the house behind (see Figure 12-32), and it's set up at 720×480 pixels and running at 30 fps.

Figure 12-32. This is the composition of the example, with the character and BG separated.

2. For starters, we'll just make the background out of focus and keep Crazy Jeff in the foreground in focus. Since the character and background are on two separate layers, we'll need to adjust only the background layer BG_Street. Right/Ctrl-click the BG_Street layer, and select Effects, or go up to the top menu and select Effects and then Blur & Sharpen. Then select Gaussian Blur.

3. Gaussian Blur is an effect that blurs in horizontal and vertical directions. Click the Effects dropdown menu in the Effects tab of the BG_Street layer in timeline. Here, you can select Blur Dimensions and change whether it blurs Horizontal and Vertical, only Horizontal or only Vertical (see Figure 12-33). For this effect, we'll need both, so keep it selected at Horizontal and Vertical. The other property Blur Length is self explanatory; increase this figure to make the layer more blurry.

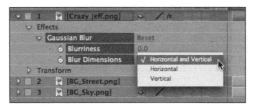

Figure 12-33. The dimension options

4. Set the Blurriness property value to 15, and observe the results (see Figure 12-34). Notice that the background appears out of focus and Crazy Jeff in focus, thus simulating the depth of field behavior of an optical camera.

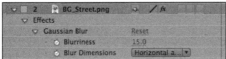

Figure 12-34. When we increase the Blur Length to 15, the frame goes blurry.

Next, we'll animate a rack focus technique. A rack focus is the adjustment of a camera lens to focus on the subject of your project. Like any other layer or effect, we can animate properties, like the amount of Blur Length, using keyframes.

1. Set up our scene yet again. Add the Gaussian Blur effect to both the character and background layers, by right/Ctrl-clicking the layer and selecting Effects, then Blur & Sharpen, then Gaussian Blur.

2. Set the Blur Dimensions on the BG_Street layer to a value of 15. Leave the Crazy Jeff layer as is for now (see Figure 12-35).

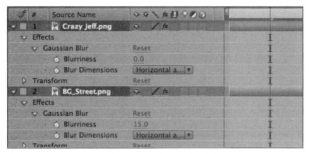

Figure 12-35. We added Gaussian Blur to both layers.

3. Let's create a keyframe at frame 10 on both layers. Select both layers at the same time; move the marker to the tenth frame in the timeline, and click the stopwatch icon next to one of the layers. A keyframe should drop on that frame in both layers, since we had them both selected (see Figure 12-36).

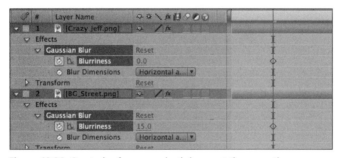

Figure 12-36. Create keyframes on both layers at the same time.

4. Move 20 frames down the timeline. We should now be at 1 second in the timeline. On our Crazy Jeff layer, in the Gaussian Blur properties, increase the Blur Length to 15, and a keyframe should be automatically added (see Figure 12-37).

Figure 12-37. 20 frames down the timeline, a new keyframe is added after increasing the Blur Length to 15.

5. On our BG_Street layer, in the Gaussian Blur properties, decrease the Blur Length to 0 (see Figure 12-38).

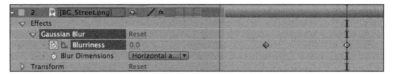

Figure 12-38. Setting the Blur Length on the background to 0

6. Do a RAM preview, and observe the rack focus effect shown in Figure 12-39.

Figure 12-39. The last keyframe should look like this in the example.

This is a very quick way to produce this effect; adjust settings in Blur Length and timing to fit your project.

Transitions in After Effects

Numerous transitions can be created in After Effects. After Effects is, after all, a motion graphics tool as well, so the possibilities are pretty much endless. Here are three transitions that are quick, common, and useful.

Dissolves

A dissolve is the decreasing of the opacity of an image to reveal another beneath it. It's probably the most commonly used transition in editing, and it's mainly used to express that a long period of time has passed over a matter of frames or a second.

To create a dissolve transition, we need two images, or the last few frames of one clip and the first few frames of another clip. In this example, we will dissolve between two still images, but the same steps can be used to dissolve into any layer in After Effects.

1. Simply place two layers into a composition, so that at some point in the timeline, the layers are one on top of the other (see Figure 12-40). Usually, it's the beginning and end frames of a clip.

Figure 12-40. The setup for this comp should have the head and tail of two clips overlapping.

2. Open the Transform properties of the top layer (see Figure 12-41).

3. On the top layer, create a keyframe in the Opacity property somewhere early in the timeline. If it's not already, set the Opacity at 100% as shown in Figure 12-42.

Figure 12-41. We'll be adjusting the opacity property.

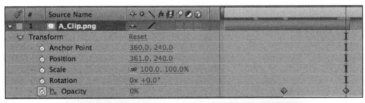

Figure 12-42. The opacity where the marker sits is currently 100%.

4. Next, move down the time 10–15 frames, and set another keyframe. This time change the Opacity to 0%. The clips should appear to be dissolving from one to the next (see Figure 12-43).

Figure 12-43. The top layer should be 0% on the the second keyframe. The ghost image is the dissolve effect we should be achieving.

Observe the dissolving effect. This was simple and easy to do, and it's a way to create traditional editing techniques in After Effects.

Blur wipes

The blur wipe is a smooth, quick transition that works well in animation; use it to simulate a super quick camera move to take you to a different angle or location.

1. Select the two clips you want to have transition from one to the other. Duplicate them by pressing Ctrl/Cmd+D (see Figure 12-44).

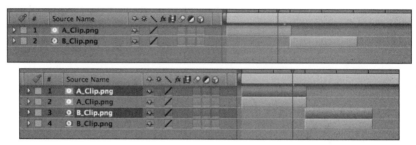

Figure 12-44. The clips should be set up end to end and then duplicated, as shown.

2. While you have those two clips selected, go to Layer, and select Pre-Compose. Name the comp Blur Trans 01, and select Move All attributes into the new composition (see Figure 12-45). Then open that composition.

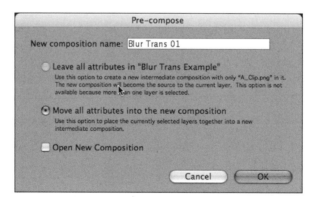

Figure 12-45. The Pre-compose dialog box

3. Slide the in point of the first clip until the last five frames are all that remain in the clip. Then, slide the out point of the second clip so all that remains are the first five frames of the second clip. Set the layers atop one another, and move them to beginning of the composition, so the clips start and end at the same time (see Figure 12-46).

Figure 12-46. Move the clips to the beginning of the pre-composition.

4. Go to Composition, and select Composition Settings. Double the width of the Blur Trans 01 composition, and make the comp length 5 seconds to match the length of our clips (see Figure 12-47).

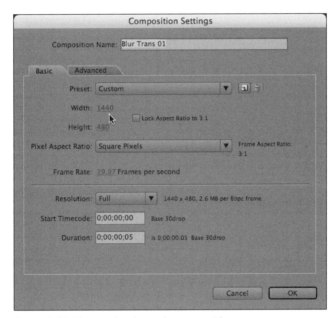

Figure 12-47. Observe the change in comp settings.

5. Next, position the two layers so that they are side by side in the composition, as shown in Figure 12-48.

Figure 12-48. Now that the comp has been doubled in width, position the clips so they are side by side.

311

6. Return to the main composition, and set the Blur Trans 01 composition where you want the transition to take place in the timeline (see Figure 12-49).

7. Now position the Blur Trans 01 layer so that the first clip is in frame.

8. Set a keyframe in the Position property for the first and second frames of the transition. Then move to the end of the Blur Trans 01 layer, frame 5, and set keyframes on the last two frames, making a total of four keyframes as shown in Figure 12-50.

Figure 12-49. In the original composition, slide the clip to where the transition will take place; in this example, it is over the heads and tails of the two clips.

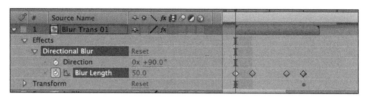

Figure 12-50. Our four keyframes are set over a period of the five-frame-long clip.

9. On the end keyframe, position the layer so the second clip now fills the shot. It should now quickly slide from one shot to the next.

10. Now it's time to add the blur. Right/Ctrl-click the Blur Trans 01 layer, and select Effects, then Blur & Sharpen, and then choose Directional Blur.

11. Now, in the Blur Trans 01 layer, open the Effects property, change the Direction to 90.0 degrees (see Figure 12-51).

12. Under Blur Length, create a keyframe in the first frame of the Blur Trans 01 comp, and set the Blur Length to 50%. Move down one frame, and set another keyframe. Change the Blur Length to 200%.

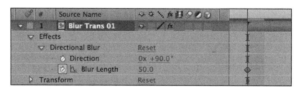

Figure 12-51. After the directional blur was added, a keyframe was created in frame 01 for the Blur Length property.

13. Next, move down two frames, keyframe, and set the Blur Length to 200%. Then move to the end of the Blur Trans 01 layer, and on the last frame, set another key frame to 50%, leaving a total of four keyframes (see Figure 12-52).

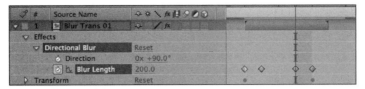

Figure 12-52. We should have four keyframes, two at the beginning and two at the end of the clip.

14. Do a RAM preview, and watch the blur transition (shown in Figure 12-53). If the transition appears too quick, add a few frames, and spread the keyframes accordingly.

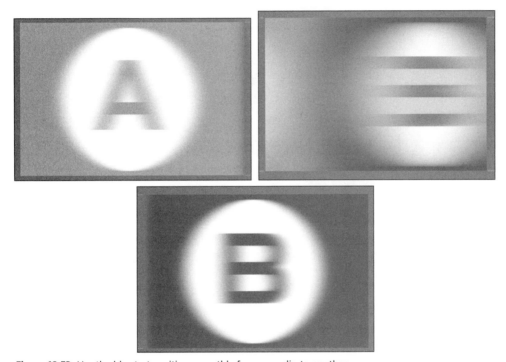

Figure 12-53. Use the blur to transition smoothly from one clip to another.

Photo flashes

Now, this is an easy and effective trick if you need to cut to a photographic-style image into your project. Or if you need to end on a photograph or still image, this is a good transition to add to the still captured effect.

313

1. Create a new white solid that is the size of your comp. Go to Layer ➤ New, and select Solid, and the Solid Settings menu will pop up (see Figure 12-54).

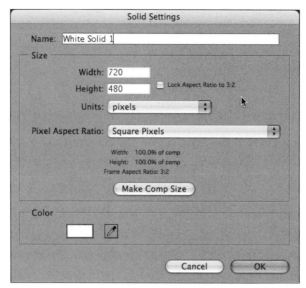

Figure 12-54. The Solid Settings dialog box that appears when you make a new Solid

2. Set the solid's in point where you want the flash to start, probably best at where the clips cut (see Figure 12-55).

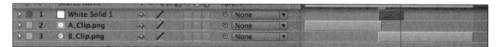

Figure 12-55. The white solid layer's in point is where the clips cut.

3. Two frames into the white solid layer, create a keyframe in the Opacity property.

4. Now, move 5–10 frames down the timeline, and set a new keyframe under Opacity decreasing it to 0%.

Do a RAM preview, and observe the flash and dissolve of a photo flash.

Glow effects in After Effects

Glow effects can come in handy fairly often. They can amp up effects animation like lightning, blasts, or explosions. In this example, we'll use some lightning animation. This animation is a PNG sequence with alpha to give it transparency. The lighting will be solid and visible, but the rest is transparent.

The best use of this technique is on effects animation that is a solid color. The lightning in this example has been made a solid light blue color. This color will become the color of the glow itself, and the shape and forms of the animation will serve as the white-hot center of the effect.

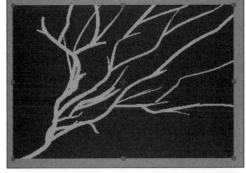

Figure 12-56. The initial setup requires the animated effect, solid in the color of the glow we want. Here, it will be light blue.

1. Take your effects animation, the lightning effect in this example (see Figure 12-56), and place it into a new composition.

2. Duplicate the lightning layer (see Figure 12-57).

3. Right/Ctrl-click the top layer, and go to Effects, then Blur & Sharpen, then Gaussian Blur.

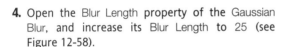

Figure 12-57. The lightning layer is duplicated. The original remains on the bottom.

4. Open the Blur Length property of the Gaussian Blur, and increase its Blur Length to 25 (see Figure 12-58).

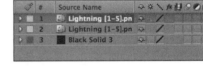

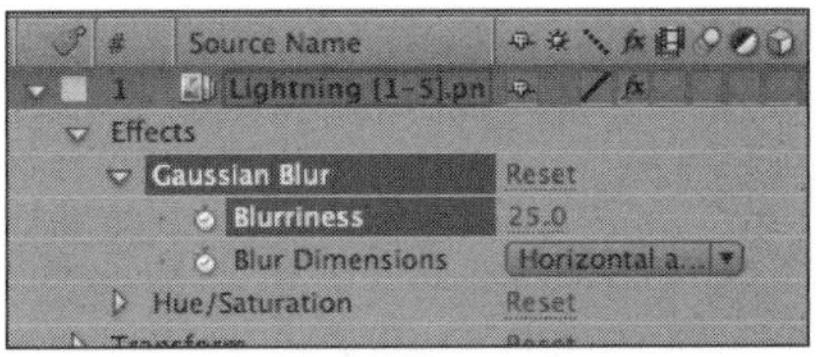

Figure 12-58. The Blur Length is set to 25.

5. Right/Ctrl-click the top layer, and select Blending Mode; then select Add. Now observe the effect (see Figure 12-59).

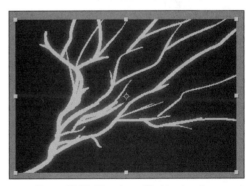

Figure 12-59. The glow effect is already present at this point.

315

6. For added effect, on the original layer (the bottom one), add a Hue/Saturation effect. Go to Effects ➤ Color Correction ➤ Hue/Saturation. And turn the Lightness to 100% (see Figure 12-60).

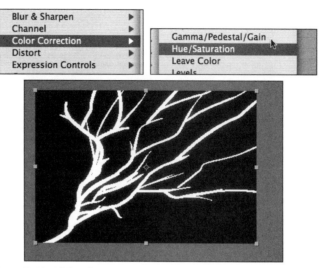

Figure 12-60. Adding the Hue/Saturation effect to the original (bottom) layer. After the lightness has been increased to 100, the white-hot effect is really achieved.

7. Observe the glow effect on the lightning; it gives that white-hot electric effect. Adjust the Blur Length and Opacity to your desire; experimenting with the other blending options can produce many effects, so try them all out to find effects you never thought about before.

Earthquake effects in After Effects

The earthquake effect is exactly as it sounds; it simulates the feeling of earthquake-like shakiness. There are two ways to do this: manually keyframing the position of a layer frame by frame or using the Motion Sketch feature. Keyframing is a bit more exact than using the Motion Sketch tool, so first we'll go over keyframing the position. Then, we'll touch on the Motion Sketch feature.

Creating an earthquake effect using Position keyframes

To do this, select the clip to which you wish to apply the affect. Make sure that your image is big enough to position the clip without exposing any edges (see Figure 12-61).

Figure 12-61. Here is the setup for our comp. As you can see by the guide line box surrounding it, the image is bigger than the comp's resolution, so we have room to shake the image.

1. Create a keyframe in the Position property where you want the shaking to begin.

2. Move over to the next frame, and position the image slightly off center, only a few pixels. In my opinion, a quick and easy way to remember shake motion, is to make a "W" or "M" pattern with our Position keyframes. Move down one more frame and begin to make that "W" pattern (see Figure 12-62) with every keyframe you make—the more extreme the move, the more jarring the shaking will appear to be.

Figure 12-62. The keyframes are set apart only by a few pixels and in a "W" pattern.

3. If your clip is long, and the shake needs to last a while, an easy way to get this done is to use the copy and paste tool. After around ten keyframes of position changes (see Figure 12-63), copy those first ten frames and paste them over and over again, for as long as you need the shaking to continue.

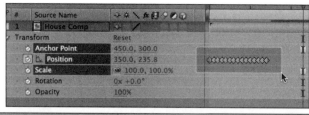

Figure 12-63. After selecting all the keyframes we already made, we can copy and paste them over and over again.

4. To have the shaking settle down to a stop, make the last 5–10 keyframes in Position settle down by making each shake more subtle by the time they come to an end. Each keyframed position will be closer to the position before it, getting them closer and closer as they come to a stop (see Figure 12-64).

5. Next, duplicate the layer you just applied the shake effect to. Slide this clip to start one frame after the original clip started shaking (see Figure 12-65).

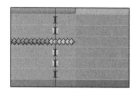

Figure 12-64. The last 5–10 keyframes (selected here) can be used to bring the shaking to a stop.

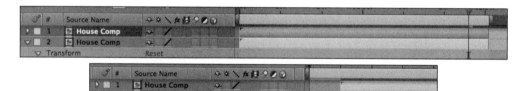

Figure 12-65. We've duplicated the layer we've "shaken" and offset it to start one frame after the original layer.

6. Turn the Opacity on this layer to around 30% to 40% to create a ghost image effect to enhance the shaking feeling (see Figure 12-66).

7. After previewing the effect, adjust to your liking by making the keyframed shakes more extreme or more subtle to fit the needs of your project.

Figure 12-66. And with the ghost image, the earthquake effect is achieved.

Creating an earthquake shake using the Motion Sketch tool

You can also use the Motion Sketch tool to simulate the earthquake shake effect. The Motion Sketch tool works like a recorder: once you start it, it records the movement of a layer for a period of time and inputs the movement into keyframes. Basically, you could set it to record and capture the actions you perform to a layer in real time.

Start with our house background already in a composition, and select the layer. Then go to Window, and select Motion Sketch (see Figure 12-67). A Motion Sketch tab will appear in an After Effects property dialog box (see Figure 12-68).

Figure 12-67. Selecting the Motion Sketch option from the Window menu

Then, set the work area in the timeline to the amount of time you would like the shake to last. Click Start Capture. Next, click and drag to shake the layer as you would like the shake to be performed. The Motion Sketch tool should capture your movements.

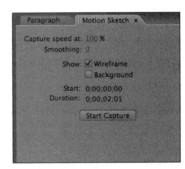

Do a RAM preview and play back the animation. If the shake effect is not to your liking, repeat the steps, or adjust the keyframes individually to your needs. After you have the desired shake effect, repeat steps 5 and 6 in the previous section to achieve a stylized camera shake.

Figure 12-68. The Motion Sketch tab

Summary

In this chapter, we presented a few extra tips for Flash and a few extras for After Effects. In this book, we stepped through a number a techniques and processes used in professional Flash character animation. You learned how to build a character and organize its Library and how to animate that character in two processes, the frame-by-frame method and the motion tween method. Then, we discussed how to composite your character animation into its background and create camera moves and effects, thus finishing the final stages to complete a scene of animation.

The more knowledge you have about the process, the better you can plan your production, which means your production pipeline will run more smoothly and efficiently. This book presents only the tip of the iceberg and includes just a handful of techniques; we couldn't possibly fit everything into one book. There are many different approaches with many different results. These applications are merely tools, just another pencil or brush, which can be used in many different ways to create your masterpiece. Use this information to push the potential of your skills and the potential of your ideas and creations.

Now, take this information, and go make an animated short, comedy, sci-fi action, or something no one has seen before. Help another project pull through, team up with other animators and start a project together, contributing to one of the world's greatest entertainment art forms. Now get animating!

INDEX

X

X axis
  3-D camera, 255, 256
  reading graphs, 243, 244
X Rotation property, After Effects
  placing elements in 3-D, 251

Y

Y axis
  3-D camera, 255, 256
  reading graphs, 243, 244
Y Rotation property, After Effects
  placing elements in 3-D, 251

Z

Z axis
  3-D camera, 255, 256
Z order, 145
  changing, 163
Z Rotation property, After Effects
  placing elements in 3-D, 251
Z space
  3-D layers, 250
  complex camera mechanics in animation, 214
  placing elements in 3-D, 251
  transforming elements under 3-D views, 253
Zoom property, After Effects, 257
zooms
  complex camera mechanics in animation, 213
  super zoom, 295

XML for Flash
Sas Jacobs
1-59059-543-2 $39.99 [US]

Actionscript Animation
Keith Peters
1-59059-518-1 $39.99 [US]

Flash 8
Sham Bhangal and Kristian Besley
1-59059-542-4 $36.99 [US]

ASP.NET 2.0 for Flash
Ryan Moore
1-59059-517-3 $39.99 [US]

Flash 8 Video
Tom Green Jordan Chilcott
1-59059-651-X $44.99 [US]

EXPERIENCE THE DESIGNER TO DESIGNER™ DIFFERENCE

Flash Applications for Mobile Devices
Richard Leggett, Weyert de Boer, Scott Janousek
1-59059-558-0 $49.99 [US]

New Masters of Flash Volume 3
1-59059-314-6 $59.99 [US]

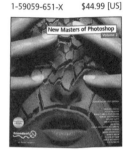
New Masters of Photoshop Volume 2
1-59059-315-4 $59.99 [US]

Object-Oriented ActionScript for Flash 8
Peter Elst with Todd Yard
1-59059-619-6 $44.99 [US]

Extending Flash MX 2004
Complete Guide and Reference to JavaScript Flash
Keith Peters and Todd Yard
1-59059-304-9 $49.99 [US]

Apache Essentials
Install, Configure, Maintain
Garrett Hart Lewallen
1-59059-355-3 $24.99 [US]

Dreamweaver MX 2004 Design, Projects
Rachel Andrew, Craig Grannell, Allan Kent, Christopher Schmitt
1-59059-409-6 $39.99 [US]

Tom Green & Tiago Dias
From After Effects to Flash
Poetry in Motion Graphics
1-59059-748-6 $49.99 [US]

AdvancED
ActionScript Components
Mastering the Flash Component Architecture
1-59059-593-9 $49.99 [US]

AdvancED
Flash Interface Design
1-59059-555-6 $44.99 [US]

DOM Scripting
Web Design with JavaScript and the Document Object Model
Jeremy Keith
1-59059-533-5 $34.99 [US]

Web Accessibility
Web Standards and Regulatory Compliance
1-59059-638-2 $49.99 [US]

HTML Mastery
Semantics, Standards, and Styling
Paul Haine
1-59059-765-6 $34.99 [US]

Blog Design Solutions
1-59059-581-5 $39.99 [US]

CSS Mastery
Advanced Web Standards Solutions
Andy Budd
1-59059-614-5 $34.99 [US]

Flash Application Design Solutions
The Flash Usability Handbook
Ka Wai Cheung and Craig Bryant
1-59059-594-7 $39.99 [US]

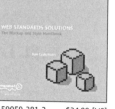
WEB STANDARDS SOLUTIONS
The Markup and Style Handbook
Dan Cederholm
1-59059-381-2 $34.99 [US]

PODCAST SOLUTIONS
The Complete Guide to Podcasting
by Michael W. Geoghegan and Dan Klass
1-59059-554-8 $24.99 [US]